Intercultural Conversation

Pragmatics & Beyond New Series

Volume 118

Intercultural Conversation
by Winnie Cheng

Intercultural Conversation

Winnie Cheng
The Hong Kong Polytechnic University

John Benjamins Publishing Company
Amsterdam / Philadelphia

∞ TM The paper used in this publication meets the minimum requirements of American National Standard for Information Sciences – Permanence of Paper for Printed Library Materials, ANSI Z39.48-1984.

Library of Congress Cataloging-in-Publication Data

Cheng, Winnie
Intercultural Conversation / Winnie Cheng.
p. cm. (Pragmatics & Beyond, New Series, ISSN 0922-842X ; v. 118)
Includes bibliographical references and index.
1. Intercultural communication--China--Hong Kong. I. Title: Study of Hong Kong Chinese. II. Title. III. Series.

HM1211.C45 2003
303.48'2-dc22 2003062996
ISBN 90 272 5360 9 (Eur.) / 1 58811 465 1 (US) (Hb; alk. paper)

John Benjamins Publishing Co. · P.O. Box 36224 · 1020 ME Amsterdam · The Netherlands
John Benjamins North America · P.O. Box 27519 · Philadelphia PA 19118-0519 · USA

Contents

List of figures and tables

Figures

Tables

Acknowledgements

I am greatly indebted to Professor Amy B. M. Tsui of the University of Hong Kong whose critical and insightful comments have been invaluable throughout the writing of this study. I am also grateful to those friends and colleagues who helped me to collect data for the study. Last but not least, I thank my family whose love, support and patience have given me the motivation necessary to complete such a long and demanding study.

Transcription notation

The transcription notation used in this book is mainly based on Jefferson's system for transcribing talk to written form, which is more extensively explained in Atkinson and heritage (1984).

Symbol	Meaning
...	Intervening utterances which have been omitted.
[	Simultaneous or overlapping utterances
(.)	A short, untimed pause or a gap of silence (a micro-pause), equal to a one-syllable-length pause.
((laugh))	Non-linguistic features: vocalizations and non-verbal aspects of the speech situation.
(inaudible)	Indecipherable utterances.
7A:	Speakers are identified by letters, and each line is
8B:	numbered for ease of identification in the discussion.

Chapter 1

Communication across cultures

Introduction to the study

This is a research study of intercultural communication. The genre of communication examined is conversation. Conversation between culturally different speakers is the quintessence of the cultural phenomena of interpersonal communication and human relationships. The present study examines conversation between Hong Kong Chinese and their friends or colleagues who are native speakers of English in order to investigate the ways in which the culturally divergent participants manage the organizational and interpersonal aspects of the unfolding conversation, and focuses on five conversational features, which tend to be culturally laden, namely preference organization, compliments and compliment responses, simultaneous talk, discourse topic management and discourse information structure.

To begin with, a distinction needs to be made between cross-cultural and intercultural communication, though both refer to communication across cultures. Cross-cultural communication compares native discourse across cultures (for example, management meetings of Japanese and those of Americans), while intercultural communication compares the discourse of people of different cultural and linguistic backgrounds interacting either in a lingua franca or in one of the participants' native language (Bargiela-Chiappini and Harris 1997; Lustig and Koester 1999). Between the two, intercultural communication is a less developed and investigated approach to communication across cultures (Clyne 1994).

Culture is "a learned set of shared interpretations about beliefs, values, and norms, which affect the behaviours of a relatively large group of people" (Lustig and Koester 1999: 30). It is an ensemble of social experiences, thought structures, expectations, and behavioural practices identifiable through norms and beliefs that are historically transmitted and shared by a people (Collier and Thomas 1988). Communication and culture are inextricably linked (Brislin 2000). Language is an evolved cultural pattern (Bandura 1986). This is because culture can influence the communicative behaviour and style of an individual either directly, through the socialization of the individual within the culture, or indirectly, as the individual learns the language of the culture. Through socialization processes, cultural members acquire distinct beliefs, values and perceptions of meaning, which are conveyed through communication processes (Krippendorff 1993).

Language is an inherently social phenomenon. Language is for communication, and meaning is jointly constructed by conversational participants. The purposes for an individual to produce language to make and construct meanings are very often influenced by his or her cultural disposition. Sociological approaches to studying discourse, such as ethnography of speaking (see, for example, Gumperz and Hymes 1972; Hymes 1972; Turner 1974; Psathas 1979; Sacks 1972; Saville-Troike 1982; Schegloff 1972; Gumperz 1982), which is concerned with understanding the use of language in the social contexts of everyday life, have pointed out that "communities differ significantly in ways of speaking, in patterns of repertoire and switching, in the roles and meanings of speech. They indicate differences with regard to beliefs, values, reference groups, norms and the like, as these enter into the ongoing system of language use" (Hymes 1972: 42). As Goffman (1955: 226) states, "In any society, whenever the physical possibility of spoken interaction arises, it seems that a system of practices, conventions, and procedural rules comes into play which functions as a means of guiding and organizing the flow of messages."

In the present research, conversational participants who came from different linguistic and cultural backgrounds interacted in one of the participants' native language, and that is, English. As culture can influence a speaker's actions toward others and his or her expectations regarding their actions toward him or her (Weiss with Stripp 1998), intercultural conversation often contains assumptions that are cultural and involves behaviours that are culturally determined. Intercultural conversation invokes cultural identities, as well as cultural knowledge, attitudes and values that are unique to the cultural affiliations of the individual participants. The individual conversationalists are therefore likely to differ in the way they perceive the communicative goals of conversation; the rules, procedures and strategies that govern the conduct, organization and management of conversation; as well as what constitutes appropriate conversational behaviour. Consequently, intercultural conversation, compared to conversation between native speakers, depends much more heavily on the shared responsibility and collaboration of the culturally divergent speakers in "converging" (Giles and Coupland 1991) their communicative behaviour to that of the interlocutor in order to negotiate "common, shared ground" (Mey 2001: 274).

This study begins by making a priori assumptions concerning cultural differences between Hong Kong Chinese and native English speakers in the ways they manage the interpersonal and organizational aspects of conversation. However, the study goes well beyond simply confirming or refuting assumptions relating to purported cultural differences in communication between the two groups of conversationalists. It also conducts thorough analyses of the actual forms of discourse, that is, intercultural conversations, with a view to revealing and understanding the conversational process and behaviour of the individual participants.

Discourse is conceived by Sherzer (1987: 306) as both "an embodiment, a filter, a creator and recreator, and a transmitter of culture" and "an embodiment of language". In other words, discourse is not only a vehicle by means of which culture and language are represented and reflected, but also actualization of "a creative process" towards which "language, culture, society, and the individual" contribute (Sherzer 1987: 306). Informed by this view about discourse, the study, through examining each of the five conversational features in the discourse, investigates how far these features are "an embodiment" of presumed cultural dispositions, as well as how individual conversationalists contribute to recreating, focusing, modifying, and transmitting culture and language and the intersection between culture and language (Sherzer 1987: 295). To achieve this aim, the study begins by putting forward hypotheses about conversational processes and behaviours that are purported to be characteristic of Hong Kong Chinese and native English speakers, and then tests the hypotheses by examining the intercultural discourses in a quantitative way. Following this, the intercultural discourses are qualitatively analyzed to look at what really goes on in the discourses in order to reveal the ways in which conversational interaction is performed, reconstructed and negotiated by the individual participants. The quantitative and qualitative analyses of the intercultural conversations provide complementary and corroborative information that facilitate the achievement of the study's aim.

The nature of discourse is one of the most important considerations in any communicative study. The study aims to examine intercultural conversational behaviour found in discourse that relates to "a situating of language in natural contexts of use" (Sherzer 1987: 296). Sherzer (1987: 296) defines context as both "the social and cultural backdrop, the grounds rules and assumptions of language usage" and "the immediate, ongoing, and emerging actualities of speech events". In a similar vein, Mey (2001: 279) remarks that in conversation any particular act of speaking is "highly dependent, as to its interpretation, on the cultural context in which it is performed or 'uttered'", and that any act of speaking needs "a proper context of utterance to be validly performed" and "doesn't properly make sense unless it is *situated*, as to both its linguistic and its cultural context … it is the context of culture and language which 'sets up' the language user to deal with a particular act of speaking (or non-speaking, as the case may be)". This study takes naturally occurring spoken discourse, in the form of intercultural conversations, between Hong Kong Chinese and native English speakers as the starting point, and analyzes what individual participants with cultural differences actually do in real-life encounters and how conversational acts are contextually actualized.

Chinese and Western cultures

Any study that tries to relate cultural phenomena to linguistic realizations has to consider both theoretical frameworks by means of which language and culture are conceived and properties that are specific to particular cultures and languages (Grundy 1998). Possible differences that exist in the cultural background and dispositions between Hong Kong Chinese and mainland Chinese, or the Chinese in other Southeast Asian countries has been discussed (Becker 1996). Nevertheless, as Becker points out, Hong Kong, as the gateway to China and China's "window to the West", witnesses the coexistence of traditional Chinese beliefs and customs and Western technologies, values and beliefs (Becker 1996: 2–3). A feature of Asian cultures is its long, rich and diverse cultural histories. In fact, contemporary Chinese social organization is typically traced back to Chinese historical events and traditional beliefs. Thus the recent, extremely rapid economic development of Southeast Asian societies with predominantly Chinese populations, such as Hong Kong, is held by many researchers to be based on Confucian values established 2,500 years ago (Kahn 1989).

The notion that the East and the West differ in values, beliefs and behavioural patterns has been widely discussed (see, for example, Asante and Gudykunst 1989; Gudykunst and Ting-Toomey 1988; Kim and Gudykunst 1988). In their conceptual taxonomies of cultural patterns (see, for example, Hall 1976, 1977; Hofstede 1980, 1983, 1991; Bond 1986), China and Hong Kong have been compared with other countries and regions in terms of various dimensions of cultural patterns. The following summarizes these important taxonomies that describe variations in cultural patterns, with an emphasis on the comparison between China/ Hong Kong and Western countries, particularly Britain, U.S.A. and Australia, since the native speakers of English who participated in the present study came from these countries. These taxonomies are Hall's (1976, 1977) high-context and low-context cultures, and Hofstede's (1980, 1983, 1991) cultural differences in work-related value orientations.

Hall (1977) classifies cultures broadly into high-context and low-context cultures. High- and low-context cultural patterns are based on cultural preferences for high-context or low-context messages. He has identified such cultures as China, Japan, Malaysia and Mexico as high-context cultures, and England, Germany and Sweden as low-context cultures. High-context messages are covert, implicit and internalized with much nonverbal coding and reserved reactions, while low-context messages are overt, explicit, plain, precise and concise with verbalized details and explicit and readily observable reactions. According to Hall (1977), such differences can be explained by the purposes in communicating. In high-context cultures, communication is for promoting and sustaining harmony among the interactants;

while in low-context cultures, communication is for conveying exact meanings. Hall's (1977) high- and low-context cultural patterns are extended to other variations in cultural patterns, one of which is the importance of ingroups and outgroups. Characteristics of high-context cultures, of which the Chinese are an example, include distinct ingroup and outgroup relationships, strong interpersonal bonds, and high commitment. In contrast, low-context cultures, of which the English are an example, are characterized by flexible ingroups and outgroups, fragile interpersonal bonds, and low commitment (see also Lustig and Koester 1999).

Hofstede's (1980, 1983, 1984, 1991, 1994) groundbreaking study of cultural differences in work-related value orientations, conducted in the late 1960's and early 1970's, surveyed approximately 100,000 IBM employees in over 50 countries. The study covered a worldwide scope. The results showed the ways the cultures of these countries resemble and differ from each other. By providing four dimensions of culture, namely individualism-collectivism, power distance, uncertainty avoidance and masculinity-femininity, as well as numerical scores, Hofstede has provided both a theory for differences between national cultures and a way to cross-check those differences. The individualism-collectivism dimension, indicating how far a society focuses on self-reliance instead of group support, most distinctly differentiates Western cultures from Eastern cultures, and has been a focus in many East-West cross-cultural or intercultural studies (see, for example, Yang and Bond 1990; Triandis et al. 1993). The power distance dimension is about the culture's belief regarding equal distribution of institutional power. Hofstede's (1991) ratings of 50 countries show that Hong Kong prefers medium power distance and medium collectivism, while U.S.A., Australia and Great Britain prefer a low power distance and individualism. The uncertainty avoidance dimension describes the relative cultural preference for and tolerance of ambiguity and change. Hofstede's study found that Hong Kong is much more tolerant of ambiguity and willing to accept change, dissent and deviance, compared to Australia and U.S.A., Great Britain is, however, not widely different from Hong Kong in uncertainty avoidance (Hofstede 1991). Finally, the masculinity-femininity dimension is about the degree to which a culture values such behaviours as assertiveness and the acquisition of wealth, or caring for others and the quality of life. All except the fourth dimension (i.e., masculinity-femininity) are relevant to the present study.

Face and politeness in Western and Chinese cultures

The notions of face and self-image are considered universal characteristics, and yet they are conceptualized differently from one culture to another, depending on the underlying cultural values and beliefs. The ways in which face-work manifests itself linguistically in communication also vary from one culture to another. However, it is apparent that face-work is always at work. The concept of "face" (*mianzi* in Mandarin and *minji* in Cantonese) is not new to Asians. It was first introduced by the Chinese anthropologist Hu in 1944 though the term "face" had been in use in English a few centuries before that (Scollon and Scollon 1995). Underpinning the notion of face is "self" (Scollon and Scollon 1995: 36), which refers to the "real" person underneath the face that is presented in communication. What makes the notion "self" so fascinating and dynamic, especially in intercultural communication, is that the assumptions and beliefs about the "self" that are involved in communication may differ significantly across cultures.

Asian and Western cultures differ in terms of the notion of "self" and how it is conceived. The Western "self" in communication is highly individualistic, self-motivated and open to ongoing negotiation and emphasizes independence (Scollon and Scollon 1995). The Asian "self" is a more collectivistic one, which is connected to membership in basic groups such as the family, the social circle and the workplace. The Asian "self" is part of a larger social group and is more conscious of the consequences of their actions on the addressee (Scollon and Scollon 1995). Compared to the "self" projected by Westerners, the Asian "self" is more extensively and significantly influenced by the assumptions and beliefs about face, and emphasizes involvement with other.

As proclaimed by Markus and Kitayama (1991, 1994), Asian cultures support the "interdependent conception of the self" more than Western cultures. An "interdependent self" is defined by the person's relations with others in specific contexts (Markus and Kitayama 1991, 1994). The interdependent construal of self is more likely to pay attention to the group when forming opinions and attitudes, to attach importance to preserving their own and others' "face", and emphasize harmony and cooperation in the ingroup. The other-orientation is therefore essential to an interdependent self. Congruous with the notion of an interdependent self, the Chinese self, in the Confucian sense, is defined by a person's surrounding relations. The Chinese self involves multiple layers of relations with others, and needs to be recognized, defined and completed by others. The self's orientation to others' needs, wishes, and expectations is essential to the development of the Chinese self (King and Bond 1985; Sun 1993; Gao 1996). The importance of "other" in defining the Chinese self is also reflected in cultural norms such as modesty and humility (Bond et al. 1982; White and Chan 1983), reserve and formality, as well as restraint and inhibition of strong feelings. The Western culture supports the "independent conception of the self" more than Asian cultures. The "independent self" is more likely to be willing to enter into confrontation and competition; be willing to express open criticism; and be disposed to express individual, unpredictable views (Markus and Kitayama 1991, 1994).

In the West, egalitarianism in relationships is a valued cultural ideology; while in Asia, hierarchical human relationships are valued. Westerners and Asians hence differ in the way they conceive face. Westerners emphasize the independence aspect of face. They respect the rights of the addressee to freedom of choice, autonomy, territory, and so on. For Asians, due to the valued hierarchical human relationships as a cultural ideology, they tend to emphasize the involvement aspect of face; and that is, the importance of "being a normal and contributing participant in communicative events" (Scollon and Scollon 1995: 36–37). Involvement is demonstrated by taking the point of view of other people, by supporting them in the views they take, and by any other means that the speaker wishes so as to uphold a commonly created view of the world.

The notion of "face" of an individual is derived from that of Goffman (1967) which links face with notions of being embarrassed or humiliated, or "losing" face. Thus face is something that is emotionally invested and that can be lost, maintained or enhanced, and must be constantly attended to in interaction. Based on Goffman's notion of "face", Brown and Levinson (1978, 1987) propose that face as a public self-image is composed of two specific face-wants: positive and negative face. "Positive face" refers to the positive consistent self-image or "personality" (crucially including the desire that this self-image be appreciated and approved of) claimed by interactants. "Negative face" refers to an individual's basic claim to territories, personal preserves, rights to non-distraction, i.e. to freedom of action and freedom from imposition (Brown and Levinson 1987).

Face systems and politeness values in Chinese are different from those in Anglo-American cultures (Hu 1944; Gu 1990; Kasper 1990; Mao 1994). Chinese "face" has two aspects: 'miànzi' which refers to one's need to conform to social conventions and to express one's desire to be part of the community (Hu 1944; Mao 1994), and 'lian' which defines one's need to show a moral sense of place and role. Both roles revolve around an individual's desire for others to recognize his or her social prestige, reputation or sanction (Hu 1944; Mao 1994).

Chinese politeness centres on self-denigration and other elevation (Gu 1990). The Chinese word for "politeness" is 'limào', the word-for-word translation of which is "polite appearance" (Gu 1990: 238). 'Limào' is formulated by Confucius (551 B. C. – 479 B. C.) and is derived from the Chinese word 'li', which refers to "the social hierarchy and order of the slavery system of the Zhou Dynasty (dating back to 1100 B. C.)" (Gu 1990: 239). 'Li' itself conceals two meanings: social hierarchy and order and politeness, which are closely connected to each other. Social hierarchy and order give rise to politeness, and politeness expresses and helps to maintain social hierarchy and order (Gu 1990).

The social structure and social relationships of the Chinese have changed over time. Consequently, the Confucian meaning of 'limào' has acquired a broader meaning. Gu (1990) posits that in modern Chinese culture, 'limào' is composed of four notions: respectfulness, modesty, attitudinal warmth and refinement. Respectfulness is to give concern to others' face and social status by showing positive appreciation and admiration. Modesty is to denigrate self. Attitudinal warmth is to show consideration, kindness and hospitality to others. Refinement is to behave in order to meet certain standards. Other than these four notions that constitute 'limào', in modern Chinese culture, sincerity and balance are very important values.

Dissimilar face systems and notions of politeness of the Chinese (Gu 1990), compared to those of the West, have contributed to differing purposes of language use in communication. As noted by Scollon and Scollon (1995: 40), "the choice of language in discourse is not simply a matter of practical choice governed by efficiency of communication of information. Every such choice is also a matter of the negotiation of the face of the participant". Westerners consider language to be a major aspect of the ongoing negotiation of the relationship, and they take particular care to seek continual growth in the relationship through language and communication (Scollon and Scollon 1995). Westerners respect each other's rights to their own autonomy and freedom of choice. In an English-speaking context, redressive language is usually performed using "independent face strategies" (Scollon and Scollon 1995: 40–41), or in Brown and Levinson's (1987) term "negative politeness strategies". For Asians, the purpose of language is for affirming or ratifying relationships that have already been established, and they take particular care to ratify existing relationships. In communication, Asians usually place greater emphasis on the harmony of the interactions and use more "involvement face strategies" (Scollon and Scollon 1995: 40–41), or in Brown and Levinson's (1987) term "positive politeness strategies".

The social orientation and public self-image of Chinese face converge more with Goffman's (1967), rather than Brown and Levinson's (1987), notion of face. Goffman conceives face as a public image that is on loan to the individual from society, whereas Brown and Levinson regard face as evolving around an individual's private face "wants". The facework proposed by Brown and Levinson is unidirectional with the speaker taking redressive action to address the hearer's face. The social parameters of power, social distance and the ranking of imposition are indices by which the speaker assesses particular situations of interaction for using linguistic strategies to manage the face wants of the hearer. As Mao (1994: 19) observes, "to be polite" in Chinese discourse is "to know how to respond to each other's *lian* and *miànzi* as well as to perform speech acts appropriate to and worthy of such an image". For the Chinese, "the interactional dynamic of facework" is "positively reciprocal with both parties engaged in mutually shared orientation to negotiate, elevate, and attend to each other's face as well as one's own face" (Zhang 1995: 85). Hence, central in Chinese facework is "face-balance", which means giving face to others' face simultaneously enhances one's own face and depriving others' face simultaneously damages one's face (Zhang 1995: 85).

Chinese culture is characterized by a strong emphasis on the group, which can be traced to both traditional norms that encourage the Chinese "to perfect oneself, family, country, world" (Confucius), to depend on each other for support and protection, and to preserve the extant social order. Such characterization is reflected in the communist government's advocacy that "serving the people" (the Party) is a national ethic (Weiss with Stripp 1998). Jandt (1998) observes that for the Chinese, respecting the relationship is achieved through group harmony, avoidance of loss of face to others and oneself, avoidance of saying what one actually thinks when it might hurt others in the group, and a modest presentation of oneself. In a group, for instance, one does not say what one actually thinks so that others will not be hurt. Hence, communication, which is pervasively influenced by Confucianism, will be defined as "an infinite interpretive process where all parties are searching to develop and maintain a social relationship" (Jandt 1998: 34). In a similar vein, Yum (1988) concludes from her study that in Confucian societies the main functions of communication are "to develop and maintain social relationships and to maintain face through indirectness, so that meaning depends on the receiver's interpretation".

Contrary to the position that supports a dichotomy between Asian and Western cultural patterns, other studies suggest that Asian and Western cultures are not as distinct from each other as one would normally assume. For instance, it is noted by Yamada (1992) that for Americans, talk is regarded as a medium for communicating sincere and cooperative intentions, for clarifying and disambiguating the ongoing conversation, for reaching mutual understanding, and for building rapport. Recent evidence from a survey by Japan's Dentsu Institute for Human Studies in 1998 (*Herald Tribune* 1999) suggests that the values that are cherished by Asia's various peoples (2.7 billion), nations and cultures are very diverse. According to the survey, on the whole, values cherished in Asia are markedly similar to those in the West; and these values include financial wealth, acquiring high-quality goods, success in work, mental relaxation, living for the present, striving to achieve personal goals, and having good relationships with others. In fact, on some values, such as good relations with others, Asian people seem to diverge more from one another than they do from Americans and the Western Europeans. Asians differ significantly from Westerners only on two dimensions of value; they place greater importance on family relationships and less importance on leisure activity.

Similarly, Weiss with Stripp (1998) caution against adopting a lop-sided view of cultural characterization, which maintains that Chinese as a culture has "a longstanding cultural aversion to openly confronting conflict, a tendency complemented if not caused by hierarchy in social relationships and Confucian norms". Weiss with Stripp (1998: 65–71) argue that in intercultural negotiations, the Chinese can be engaged in "emotionally overt, intense conflicts", and this could be attributed to the communist ideology, which espouses dialectics, and Deng Xiao Ping's policy changes, under which individual aspirations and accomplishments are gaining much more attention.

The perspective which emphasizes broad cultural variability dimensions, such as the cultural taxonomies proposed by Hall and Hofstede, in order to identify and account for communicative differences in intercultural encounters has been criticized for being overdeterministic (Fant and Grindsted 1995), and being normative and prescriptive (Holliday 1999: 252). By overdeterministic, it means that such a perspective tends to over-emphasize linguistic and cultural differences, particularly those associated with the non-native speakers of the target language, but not enough attention is paid to "interactants both in terms of their cultural attributes and in the context of their societal and institutional role-relationships" (Sarangi 1994: 424). Taking solely cultural factors into consideration in analyzing intercultural interactions runs the risk of making stereotypical statements and presenting rigid views about intercultural communication at best, or will even lead to potential discrimination and denial of social justice. In many cases, cultural influences are expressed through far-reaching generalizations (Littlewood 2000). Such a perspective also assumes a normative and prescriptive position, representing a "deficit" view of intercultural communication (Holliday 1999). When a deficit view is adopted, normative communication behaviour is assumed and the dominant or majority culture is invariably perceived as representing the norm, while the non-dominant or minority culture is consistently viewed as deviating from the norm, and how such deviation may lead to communication breakdown.

The present research argues against a position which unquestioningly employs a deficit view of intercultural communication although it acknowledges the potential usefulness of the taxonomies for characterizing cultural patterns in behaviour and for categorizing the effects and phenomena observed in the intercultural discourses analyzed. Therefore though the study begins by working on the assumption that there are cultural differences between the East and the West in norms, values, beliefs and practices which impact the behaviours of the people, it will not "indulge in the 'analytic stereotyping' of intercultural encounters as mainly characterized by the intercultural differences present" (Sarangi 1994: 409). Instead through examining actual use of language by actual people from different cultures doing actual things with language in actual social situations, the study endeavours to provide interpretations and explanations to the conception that discourse represents both an embodiment of the culture-language relationship and a process of creation and recreation of language and culture. In other words, the study focuses on finding out how individual conversationalists mediate, negotiate and modify the values, beliefs, norms, attitudes and language that they bring along into the conversation.

The context of Hong Kong

Asian cultures are characterized by a rapid pace of change and a greater responsiveness to global cultural influences. In Asian societies such as Singapore, Taiwan and South Korea, social redistribution and economic development have led to awareness of human rights, the eradication of poverty and want, and increasing self-esteem and empowerment, with the ensuing evolution of a more open and participatory society (Chan 1992). Apart from growing prosperity and heightened self-esteem, East Asian societies also possess a distinctive and unique set of Asian values, or "The Asian Way" (Becker 1996: 1–2). In various Asian societies, these values include a new sense of pride and achievement, a specific Asian identity based on their own traditional moral values. Hong Kong is a unique and vibrant city, and is one of East Asia's most productive economies. Hong Kong, as the gateway to China and China's "window to the West", witnesses the coexistence of traditional Chinese beliefs and customs and Western technologies, values and beliefs (Becker 1996: 2–3). According to Ng (1998), despite being highly cosmopolitan due to its international trade ties, Hong Kong has a very deep-rooted Chinese culture.

As reported by Bacon-Shone and Bolton (1998), a sociolinguistic survey conducted in 1993 has shown that 81.6% of the total population of Hong Kong speaks Cantonese, and 65.8% of the population claimed that they can speak some English. Among those, "33.7% would claim to speak 'quite well', 'well', or 'very well'. And of those, 16.1% would consider themselves to be 'bilingual'" (Bacon-Shone and Bolton 1998: 79). In Hong Kong society, the English language and English-speaking community are characterized as a "constant and persistent, but psychologically distant, force" (Pennington 1994: 149). English is used for restricted, functional and formal purposes where "there is a power differential among the interlocutors or between the interlocutors and some other relevant groups (e.g. high-level executives vs. middle-level managers and low-level employees)" (Pennington 1994: 149). Hong Kong Chinese associate English with such external attributes as attractiveness and stylishness, success and sometimes wealth, and academic achievement and intelligence. They view English in Hong Kong as part of an "outwardly oriented, non-in-group, non-home, and non-family values" culture (Pennington 1994: 86).

Regarding their native language, Cantonese, Hong Kong Chinese associate it with positive inner values, including certain traditional Chinese traits, family values, Hong Kong characteristics, and strength of personality (Pennington 1994). Pennington also observes strong "ethnolinguistic vitality" (Giles, Bourhis and Taylor 1977) and strong intragroup cohesion in the Cantonese-speaking community in Hong Kong.

Hong Kong is becoming an increasingly multicultural city, which brings numerous challenges and opportunities to Hong Kong Chinese, particularly in the settings in which they conduct their social and professional lives. In personal exchanges in institutional settings and in any non-institutional contexts, Cantonese is likely to be used except in the presence of a non-Cantonese speaker. The choice of English among Cantonese speakers in informal interaction (apart from occasional code-mixing) will be a highly marked choice creating extreme social distance. In their professional lives, most educated Cantonese speakers in Hong Kong are also relatively proficient in English and may make extensive use of English in formal functions.

In intercultural encounters in Hong Kong, English is the predominant language of communication, used by Hong Kong Chinese either as a second language, when interacting with a native speaker of English; or as a lingua franca, when interacting with another non-native speaker of English who does not speak Cantonese. The difficulty level of communication between cultural groups depends on how much the communicators share in common (Jandt 1998). The challenges that Hong Kong Chinese are faced with in intercultural communicative settings are both communicating in another language and communicating with culturally different individuals. Hong Kong Chinese (henceforth referred to as HKC) and native English speakers (henceforth referred to as NES) examined in this study speak, as their native language, languages that differ in features at all of the phonological, morphological, semantic, syntactic and pragmatic levels. HKC and NES also differ in beliefs, values and norms (see, for example, Hall 1977; Hofstede 1980, 1983, 1991; Yang and Bond 1990; Triandis 1995; Becker 1996; Markus and Kitayama 1991, 1994; Weiss with Stripp 1998; Lustig and Koester 1999).

Defining conversation

Among different speech events, conversation is the most prevalent form of discourse, accounting for more than 90 per cent of all spoken language, and is considered "the quintessence of spoken discourse" (Svartvik 1980). Swales (1990) maintains that conversation, as the pre-eminent form of language, is a pre-genre in the sense that all genres, both spoken and written, are derived from it. Similarly, Fillmore (1981) maintains that conversational language constitutes the benchmark against which other forms of the language can be compared and contrasted and that "once the syntax, semantics, and pragmatics of these basic types of discourse have been mastered, other types of discourse can be usefully described in terms of their deviation from such a base" (Fillmore 1981: 165).

Conversation is often described as ranging somewhere between casual talk in everyday settings and being synonymous with spoken interaction in general. This use of the term "conversation" as a catchall for any type of spoken discourse is quite commonplace. McGregor (1984: 72–73), for instance, states that although researchers of various disciplines, including ethnomethodologists, insist on using and examining "'everyday' language use", their data of "conversation" rarely meets the requirements of their own terms of reference. The sources of data, which are described as conversation, include "job interviews, telephone calls, joke and story telling episodes, teacher-pupil exchanges, ritual insults, and a range of reported and recorded psychiatric, psychotherapeutic and psychological investigative activities" (McGregor 1984: 73). In Ricento's (1987: 757–758) study on multiparty conversation, for instance, "spontaneous conversations " are on a par with "conversational re-telling" of a film. Francis and Hunston (1992) consider telephone conversation a form of everyday conversation. To Eggins and Slade (1997: 20), the term 'conversation' encompasses both "casual conversation" and "pragmatic conversation" such as a "buying-and-selling transaction" that achieves a "pragmatic goal".

For the purposes of the present study, such non-specific use of the term "conversation" is unsuitable. Conversations do constitute a distinctive form of spoken discourse and to conflate them with spoken discourse in general is to suggest that there are no criteria for distinguishing conversations from what is termed "specialized discourse types" after Abercrombie (1965: 2–9). To date, there has not been any generally accepted definition of a conversation as a speech event. Goffman (1967) offers the following definition, which very clearly sets conversation apart from institutionalized discourses, or interactions for instrumental purposes:

> ... conversation, restrictively defined, might be identified as the talk occurring when a small number of participants come together and settle into what they perceive to be a few moments cut off from (or carried on to the side of) instrumental tasks; a period of idling felt to be an end in itself, during which everyone is accorded the right to talk as well as to listen and without reference to a fixed schedule ... and no final agreement or synthesis is demanded, differences of opinion to be treated as unprejudicial to the continuing relationship of the participants. (Goffman 1967: 264)

The study of conversation

The study of naturally occurring conversation produced by English native speakers was begun in the early seventies by a group of sociologists (see, for example, Duncan 1972; Sacks 1974; Sacks et al. 1974; Schegloff 1972; Schegloff and Sacks 1973) who looked at how participants manage the organizational and social aspects of conversation. More recent research includes studies by Bublitz (1988), Nofsinger (1991), Warren (1993), Tsui (1994), Stenström (1994) and Eggins and Slade (1997).

Sacks, Schegloff, Jefferson and others were early conversation analysts who examined the fine detail of talk, which represents materials collected from naturally occurring instances of everyday interaction. In fact, one of the strengths of conversation analysis is its emphasis on using recorded data of naturally occurring interactions as the object of research. Conversation analysis objects to other methods of data collection such as interviewing, taking field notes, native speaker intuition, experimental methodologies and other forms of elicitation in which participants' verbal behaviour is manipulated or directed (Atkinson and Heritage 1984; Heritage 1984). Conversation analysis also objects to the use of invented speech samples, which is "a practice by certain schools of linguistics and applied linguistics", such as Widdowson (1978, 1983) (Nunan 1993: 85).

The aim of conversation analysis is to study "small phenomena" that "may give an enormous understanding of the way humans do things" (Sacks 1984: 18). A characteristic feature of conversation analysis is the "very elaborate analysis of relatively small samples of language" (Nunan 1993: 86). Conversation analysis is oriented to examining talk as social, multi-party, interactional, and meaning-making practices. It focuses on the underlying structures of social action, as perceived and oriented to by participants. The central question of conversation analysis is: "How is it that conversational participants are able to produce intelligible utterances, and how are they able to interpret the utterances of others?" (Nunan 1993: 84).

In conversation analysis, a wide range of aspects of conversation has been investigated. These include openings and closings (Schegloff and Sacks 1973), turn-taking (Sacks et al. 1974), adjacency pairs (Schegloff and Sacks 1973), sequential organization (Jefferson and Schenkein 1978), sequencing rules and coherence (Tsui 1991a), opening sequences (Schegloff 1972), preference organization (Sacks 1987), assessments (Pomerantz 1978, 1979, 1984), topic shift (Jefferson 1984), and conversational pairs (Schegloff, Jefferson and Sacks 1977).

Conversation analysis recognizes that conversation is fundamentally a turn-taking activity, where taking a turn is regarded as the speaker's right and obligation. Sacks et al. (1974) suggest that speakers organize their talk in units, which they call Turn Construction Units (TCUs). There are four different-sized TCUs: words, phrases, clauses and sentences. Sacks et al. (1974) also observe that a minimum of two participants is required for a conversation to take place and that this necessitates the speakers taking turns.

Apart from the importance given to the turn-taking organization of talk or who gets to be speaker, conversation analysis recognizes that topic is a distinct aspect of conversational organization, as demonstrated in earlier studies of topic generation (Button and Casey 1984, 1988) and topic shift (Jefferson 1984). Conversation analysis proposes such notions as step-wise topic progression, topic shift, and topic change to account for the smooth procedures individuals take to progress from one topic to another (Sacks et al. 1974; Schegloff and Sacks 1973; Jefferson 1984).

According to Sacks et al. (1974), the organization of conversation is both "context-free" and "context-sensitive". Conversation is "context-free" in that the basic mechanism of turn-taking is applicable to all forms of talk, regardless of physical and socio-cultural contextual features such as place, time, and identity of participants. Conversation is "context-sensitive" in that the turn-taking system can accommodate features of specific context. Sacks et al. (1974) recognize that social factors such as the identity of conversationalists can influence the distribution of speaker rights; and consequently, the systematic organization of conversation. Despite that, Sacks et al. (1974) focus on the "context-free" nature of conversation, the main reason being that they think that analysis of the internal structure of conversation should precede analysis of its social features.

This conception of conversation analysis is reinforced in later studies. Schegloff (1987), for example, argues that analysis of the micro-structure and organization of conversation, such as interruption and repair, should take precedence over analysis of its macro-structure such as gender, age and class. What he objects to is linking conversational actions and social variables in the initial stages of analysis, without examining micro-level mechanisms that are involved in the performance of conversational actions. In fact, Schegloff (1987) suggests that detailed examination of micro-mechanisms of conversation would ultimately enable the researcher to explore the relationship between conversational features and social variables.

Conversation between Hong Kong Chinese and native English speakers

In Hong Kong, the interest of local academics and researchers in examining and describing the English produced by HKC in different contexts for different purposes has been growing in recent years. Little attempt has, however, been made to date to offer systematic descriptions of naturally occurring English conversations involving HKC (i.e. mother tongue speakers of Cantonese). A glance through the research work undertaken in Hong Kong in the fields of discourse analysis, conversation analysis, the use of English in Hong Kong, and the nature of the English in Hong Kong has revealed a wide range of interest and activities. There have been studies of classroom talk and academic discourses (see, for example, Flowerdew 1994; Lockhart 1994; Pennington 1995; Tsui 1985, 1987, 1991c, 1994); and spoken business, professional, public and broadcast discourses (for example, Leung 1996; Bilbow 1997a, 1997b; Scollon and Flowerdew 1997; Flowerdew 1997; Kong 1998a, 1998b; Grundy 1998). There have also been studies adopting a conversation-analytic approach to examining an aspect of the spoken discourse produced by local HKC as, for example, the study of responses to compliments between British and Chinese speakers (Loh 1993) and conversational sequences in English and Chinese (Luke 1996). Regarding the nature of the English spoken by Hong Kong people, Bolton and Kwok (1990) provide a sketch of the Hong Kong accent, which is based on recordings of radio and television news, Legislative Council speeches (i.e. parliamentary speeches) and interviews with employees of various companies and with university students.

Studies that are based on naturally occurring English conversations between HKC and NES are much in need. Research that analyses features of Hong Kong conversational English has been rare, except for a few studies conducted by the researcher and her colleagues. Cheng (1999), for example, describes the ways in which Hong Kong Chinese speakers construct and negotiate ideologies of race and ethnicity in conversations with native speakers of English. Cheng (2001, 2003) investigates the process, functions and techniques employed by Hong Kong Chinese and native speakers in jocular interactions in intercultural conversation. Cheng et al. (1997) and Cheng and Warren (1999a) describe the Hong Kong Corpus of Conversational English and delineate the features of conversation. Cheng and Warren examined features of non-specificity and imprecision in conversation, namely inexplicitness (Cheng and Warren 1999b) and vague language (Cheng and Warren 2001b). In another study, the relative use of vagueness, inexplicitness and indirectness observed in the intercultural conversational corpus (Cheng and Warren 2001a) was analyzed. Other studies include the grammar of speech through analyzing the use of tags (Cheng and Warren 2001c), the use of discourse markers as discourse organizational devices in the Hong Kong Corpus of Conversational English (Cheng and Warren 2000), and intonational aspects (Cheng and Warren, forthcoming). Each of these studies, however, has focused on describing discrete discoursal, linguistic or prosodic features in the intercultural conversation, but has not encompassed a broader and more comprehensive approach by collectively examining a range of interrelated conversational features in such discourses.

The present study investigates a very important genre of communication, i.e. naturally occurring conversation, in the context of Hong Kong. Conversation is not only perceived as the optimal discourse for studying everyday structures of social interaction, but also as the optimal discourse for investigating linguistic interaction to encode, enact, negotiate and modify the cultural values and norms of individual speakers.

Chapter 2

Literature review and descriptive framework

Culturally-laden features of conversation

The research question of the present study is: How do Hong Kong Chinese and native speakers of English, being culturally divergent participants, manage the organizational and interpersonal aspects of English conversation? The study investigates the ways in which HKC and NES interact verbally to initiate and organize conversational contributions, to sustain conversation, to manage interpersonal relationships, and to negotiate meanings. It also examines the way in which cultural identities and ideologies permeate conversational interactions.

Conversation Analysis studies ordinary conversation and talk-in-interaction, which are the primary sites of social interaction. Talk occurs between groups of individuals, whose participation in conversation is one form of engagement with the world. Conversation Analysis is oriented to examining talk as social, interactional, and meaning-making practices, and focuses on the underlying structures of social action, as perceived and oriented to by members (i.e. participants).

Through examining the ways in which participants locally manage talk, Conversation Analysis has revealed "organized patterns of stable, identifiable structural features" (Heritage 1984: 241). Conversation Analysis is a search for order in talk and structures of talk. As such, Conversation Analysis has investigated a wide range of aspects of conversation, including openings and closings (Schegloff and Sacks 1973), turn-taking (Sacks et al. 1974), adjacency pairs (Schegloff and Sacks 1973), sequential organization (Jefferson and Schenkein 1978), sequencing rules and coherence (Tsui 1991a), opening sequences (Schegloff 1972), preference organization (Sacks 1987), assessments (Pomerantz 1978, 1979, 1984), topic shift (Jefferson 1984), conversational pairs (Schegloff, Jefferson and Sacks 1977), and topic development and management (Wilson 1987; Geluykens 1993; Bublitz 1988). In determining the conversational features which will throw light on understanding the management of conversation in intercultural communication, the studies in the Conversation Analysis literature were drawn on. The present study has confined itself to features that are likely to be affected by cultural factors.

This study is at the same time an investigation of intercultural communication. Cultural variations in the structure and management of conversation have been observed by researchers in cultural studies; for example, Lustig and Koester (1999) list a number of important dimensions that differentiate one conversation from another, including the length, the nature of the relationship between the conversationalists, the kinds of topics discussed, and the way information is presented. The importance that culture plays in conversational processes has been widely examined. Cross-cultural pragmatics (Gumperz and Hymes 1972; Thomas 1983; Blum-Kulka et al. 1989; Collier and Thomas 1988) focuses on the study of different expectations among different cultures and communities regarding how meaning is constructed and negotiated. In conversations, meanings are negotiated between the speaker and the hearer, and negotiation is dependent on the context of situation (i.e. physical, social and linguistic contexts) and the meaning potential of what is spoken (Thomas 1995). Participants in intercultural conversations may make different cultural assumptions about the context of situation, and about appropriate behaviour and intentions within the context. As Yule (1996: 113) states, "Although the pragmatic conditions of communicative tasks are theoretically taken to be universal, the realizations of these tasks as social practices are culturally variable." This study hence focuses on features of conversation which are likely to be affected by cultural differences, particularly the cultural assumptions made by the participants and the cultural values and orientations specific to the participants, as observed by studies in the fields of cultural and communication studies and cross-cultural pragmatics.

In order to capture the dynamics of conversational interaction and culture-specific conversational behaviour, the study has chosen to examine five conversational features that are susceptible to cultural influences. The features chosen are all fundamental in terms of being either organizational or interpersonal aspects, or both organizational and interpersonal aspects, of conversation, which have been well documented in studies of native English speakers and, although to a lesser extent, studies of native speakers of other languages. These features are seen as not only fundamental to conversation but also as potential sites for culturally divergent behaviour, and are therefore appropriate for the purposes of this study.

These features are namely preference organization realized in disagreements; compliments and compliment responses; simultaneous talk that exemplifies potential violation of "one at a time" turn model (Sacks et al. 1974); discourse topic management in terms of strategies of topic introduction, orientation of topic subject contents, and managing culturally sensitive topics in conversations; and lastly, discourse information structure. Each of the features will be elaborated on below. On the basis of the literature reviewed, the descriptive framework for characterizing each conversational feature will be proposed at the end of the discussion of each feature.

Preference organization: Disagreements

As pointed out by Mey (2001: 166–167), "the phenomenon of '(dis)preferred response sequences is probably universal, the way (dis)preference is realized is not", and individual manifestations of the probably universal phenomenon of conversational organization in different languages may vary a great deal. What constitutes a dispreferred response could, therefore, be culture specific. This study has chosen disagreement as an aspect for investigation as disagreement is very face-threatening and is something that a culture which seeks convergence tries to avoid. The way members of a culture manage disagreements in talk-in-interaction is very much motivated by preserving the "face" (Goffman 1955) of the participants, particularly avoidance of face-threat and conflict (Heritage 1989), and hence the amount of redressive language expected. Cultures, nonetheless, differ in the extent to which they are geared toward verbal confrontation.

Disagreement can be either a preferred or dispreferred response. Disagreement is considered a preferred response following self-deprecation, and a dispreferred response following assessment, or following a question, as in the case of a negative answer. In this study, instances of disagreement given by HKC and NES as a dispreferred response are examined to find out to what extent structural and linguistic realizations of disagreement as a dispreferred response vary. Explanations will be offered to account for similarities and differences observed.

The notion of preference organization

In adjacency pairs, a first pair part is typically made in the expectation of a certain second pair part; for example, an apology is typically made in the expectation of an acceptance. It is, however, possible that an apology is met with a refusal. In Conversation Analysis, acceptance of an apology as a responding utterance is "preferred", while refusal as a responding utterance is "dispreferred" (Schegloff et al. 1977: 362). Structurally, a dispreferred response differs from a preferred response. A dispreferred second pair part is marked and made structurally complex, while a preferred second pair part is unmarked and typically structurally simple (Schegloff et al. 1977).

Due to these preferences, preferred second pair parts of adjacency pairs are sometimes delivered "not only without delay but actually in partial overlap" (Levinson 1983: 334) and are relevant for all utterance-types. Yule (1996) also lists characteristic features of a dispreferred response, including delay/hesitation, preface, expression of doubt, token 'yes', apology, mention of obligation, appeal for understanding, making the dispreferred response non-personal, giving an account, hedges and mitigators.

In Tsui's (1994: 58–59) characterization of responding acts, preferred and dispreferred responses are called "positive" and "negative responding acts" respectively. Tsui also identifies a third type of responding act, "temporization", which is a dispreferred response but is neither a positive nor a negative responding act. It functions as postponing giving an answer and contains typical linguistic features of delay. An example of a temporization is given below:

(33) [BCET: A: 22]
C: Could I stay at your place for a bit Rob?
⇒ D: um I don't know. (Tsui 1994: 59)

Motivations for preference organization

From the perspective of Conversation Analysis, "preference" demonstrates conversational organization manifested in turn-taking (Schegloff et al. 1977; Sacks 1987; Yule 1996). "Preference" is not a psychological notion in the sense that it does not relate to any mental, psychological or emotional desires of the interlocutors. Nonetheless, from the perspective of pragmatics, preference organization is motivated. As remarked by Thomas (1995: 183), pragmatics "is **motivated**: people have reasons for speaking as they do, for choosing one grammatical form rather than another, for preferring one lexical item over another, for employing indirectness and politeness." An overview of the literatue has found studies that have investigated the reasons for and the psychological and social function of preference organization. Taylor and Cameron (1987), for example, suggest that in conversation, preference organization is motivated by preserving the "face" of participants, and therefore the use of "preferred" and "dispreferred" seconds is psychologically or functionally based. Heritage (1989) considers preference to be strongly associated with avoidance of face-threat and conflict, which can be accounted for by the notions of face-work (Goffman 1955) and politeness phenomena (Brown and Levinson 1987).

Research on politeness in the West very often examines the way the interpersonal relation (distance, power, etc.) is constructed and negotiated during the course of interaction. In accounting for politeness behaviour in interaction, Brown and Levinson's (1987) politeness model has been most influential. Central to politeness phenomena are the notions that in most instances of human interaction, language behaviour is inherently face-threatening, and speakers will make use of various linguistic strategies to protect and enhance each other's face. Brown and Levinson's (1987) linguistic politeness theory expounds that the ways utterances are formulated can often be explained by way of interlocutors trying to temper or diffuse a "Face Threatening Act" (FTA). Brown and Levinson (1987: 74) opine that "in many and perhaps all cultures", the assessment of the seriousness of an FTA involves three sociological variables:

(i) the "social distance" (D) of S and H (a symmetric relation)
(ii) the relative "power" (P) of S and H (an asymmetric relation)
(iii) the absolute "ranking" (R) of impositions in the particular culture.

Politeness is the use of redressive language to reconcile face-want and face-threatening behaviour in interaction. When a speaker is faced with an FTA, depending on the estimated weightiness of the FTA, he or she can choose among four strategies to temper or diffuse FTAs, arranged from the lowest to the greatest estimated face loss (Brown and Levinson 1987). The four strategies are ranked from (1), which has no linguistically encoded compensation, through a succession of strategies of increasing politeness to (4), where the danger to face is great.

> (1) Bald-on-record without any redress. S is concerned about clarity and ignores the FTA aspect of the imposition.
> (2) On record with positive redressive action. S can pay H positive face.
> (3) On record with negative redressive action. S can pay H some negative face.
> (4) Off record. This strategy is chosen when the danger to face is great. It affords S the opportunity of evading responsibility altogether, and simultaneously allows S to give H an option to satisfy more of H's negative face in negative politeness. (Brown and Levinson 1987: 74–75)

As discussed in Chapter 1, the universality of the notion of "face" has been challenged (see, for example, Gu 1990; Scollon and Scollon 1991; Mao 1994; Zhang 1995). Chinese "face" is a public self-image, and so to be polite on every social, personal and interpersonal level requires the participants to observe each other's face. Western "face", however, evolves around an individual's private face wants. Concerning the notions of positive face and negative face, it seems that people all over the world have both positive and negative face-wants. But apart from these generalizations, people will agree that "there are innumerable differences as to the nuances and details appropriate to the individual cultures, and consequently as to the way these universal rights are expressed in language" (Mey 2001: 269). Culture members' preference for "positive" or "negative" facework depends more on their cultural value orientations than on their linguistic abilities or competence (Mey 2001). Similarly, facework is "a symbolic front that members in all cultures strive to maintain and uphold", but the modes and styles in which the members express and negotiate face-need vary from one culture to the next (Gudykunst and Ting-Toomey 1988: 86).

Research studies on disagreements

Among representative studies of disagreements in conversation are Schegloff et al. (1977), Pomerantz (1984) and Sacks (1987). Pomerantz's analysis of conversational data has shown that disagreements are dispreferred and thus marked in various ways, and agreements are preferred and thus unmarked.

Sacks (1987), in his work titled 'The preference for agreement and contiguity in sequences in conversation', describes a general preference for agreement as an answer to a question, rather than a disagreement. This is motivated by the combined influence of the "preference for contiguity" and the "preference for agreement". For instance, there is "a strong preference for contiguity between question and answer, and for agreement between question and answer" (Sacks 1987: 58) such that "answerers are constrained to construct their turns in a way that ensures that 'agreeing' answers come early in their turns and are thereby contiguous with their questions" (Sacks 1987: 65). Sacks (1987) notes that a dispreferred second pair part, such as a disagreement, generally gets pushed back into the turn. It may be marked by a variety of features such as linguistic features of delay (*hehh*, *hh*, *uhm*), mitigation, giving a reason, preface marking such as *well*, and so on.

A few studies have been conducted on disagreements in discussions (see, for example, Conroy and Sundstrom 1977; Trimboli and Walker 1984; Morgan and Krueger 1993) and letters written by biochemists (Mulkay 1985). Disagreements found in dyadic discussions are characterized by high rates of verbalization, increased numbers of turns, more frequent interruptions and reduced back channels (Trimboli and Walker 1984). Myers (1998: 99) found that in focus group discussions, participants manage disagreements by means of "markers of dispreferred turns, hedges, concessions, and attributions". Myers also observed that even for a direct disagreement between participants, the disagreement is often presented within a shared view, namely by agreeing with one aspect of the previous turn, using repetition, concessions, or repair.

Disagreeing with an addressee is regarded as a face-threatening act as it threatens both the positive face and the negative face of the addressee. Disagreement can threaten the addressee's positive face because the speaker is not taking his or her point of view. It can threaten the addressee's negative face because the speaker is imposing a view that is different from, or contradictory to that of the addressee.

Cultures differ in the extent to which they are geared toward verbal confrontation, in that some cultures are "extremely averse to such conflicts and prefer silence to a heated, tendentially interesting (but also potentially face-damaging) conversation" (Mey 2001: 270). In the literature on conflict management, such sociocultural factors as individualism-collectivism, societal values of harmony, "face" and the loss of "face", and power distance have been attributed to orientations to conflict and conflict management (Yuen 1992). According to Yuen, Asian societies stress collectivism, face and harmony; and the "preferred conflict-resolution styles are likely to be compromising (the middle ground, with neither side having to suffer a loss of 'face'), avoiding (not address the conflict, a strategy used to avoid a possible loss of 'face'), or collaborating (satisfy the concerns of both parties)" (Yuen 1992: 376). Kirkbride et al. (1991) investigated the conflict styles of 981 Chinese respondents in Hong Kong. The findings conform to the researchers' predictions based on Chinese cultural values. The conflict management styles of the Chinese in Hong Kong are, in order of preference: compromising, avoiding, accommodating (satisfy the other party's demands even at the expense of his/her personal concerns), collaborating, and competing (pursue his/her own concerns at the expense of the other party). In contrast, Western cultures do not avoid conflict or confrontation, but when disagreeing, a speaker is expected to employ negative politeness as redress action.

Analysis of disagreements in the intercultural conversations

In this study, each disagreement found in the 25 intercultural conversations will be examined within its specific context of use in order to understand how a speaker disagrees with the other speaker in conversation. The most important context-dependent factors are the cultural values and orientations of HKC and NES regarding disagreeing with the other, the purpose for a speaker to disagree, and the subject matter to which disagreement is directed. All of these factors have important implications for understanding the way a speaker perceives disagreement as a response in the immediate context of situation, the structural organization of disagreement, and the linguistic strategies that he or she adopts to present the disagreement.

The politeness linguistic strategies respectively employed by HKC and NES to maintain their own and their interlocutor's face when giving disagreement as a dispreferred response will be compared. Culture-specific values such as individualism-collectivism, and face systems and politeness underscore the communicative behaviours of individual speakers. Based on previous conflict management studies (Yuen 1992; Kirkbride et al. 1991), the hypotheses are that compared to their NES interlocutors, HKC tend to do less disagreeing; and that in disagreement situations, HKC will prefer the communicative styles of compromising, avoiding and accommodating, but not confrontational, to prevent either party from suffering a loss of face. In addition, when disagreeing with the other, HKC speakers are more likely to redress their disagreements so that neither of the participants will suffer a loss of face. Compared to NES, HKC are more likely to demonstrate a greater concern for face management.

Compliments and compliment responses

Under Searle's (1969) classification of speech acts, complimenting can be defined as an "expressive" that has the function of making known the speaker's psychological attitude towards a past act performed by the recipient that was beneficial. Leech (1983) adds that speech acts such as complimenting have a "convivial" function, and are therefore intrinsically polite. Speech acts have a goal that coincides with the "social goal of establishing and maintaining comity" (Levinson 1983: 104–106). Holmes (1986) defines a compliment as "a speech act which explicitly or implicitly attributes credit to someone other than the speaker, usually the person addressed, for some good (possession, characteristic, skill, etc.) that is positively valued by the speaker and the hearer" (Holmes 1986: 485). A credit may be directed to the hearer (Example 1), or to a third person (Example 2) (Holmes 1988: 447).

Example 1
What a polite child.

Example 2
Two elderly women discussing a new TV news-reader
A: Oh but you must admit she's got a lovely voice.
B: She certainly has.

Cases like Example 2, where the credit is directed at a third person, are not considered compliments by Holmes (see Holmes 1988). Similarly, Lewandowska-Tomaszczyk (1989) distinguishes between "complimenting" (utterances like Example 1) and "praising" (utterances like Example 2), stressing the importance of the "motivation" of "satisfying the addressee's expectations" (i.e. complimenting) "rather than expressing a positive judgement for a referential/ informative reason" (i.e. praising).

Compliments and compliment responses are culture-specific speech acts in social interaction. Patterns of compliments and compliment responses observed in different cultures can, in part, be accounted for by their perception of the notions of "face" and "politeness" (see, for example, Chen 1993; Creese 1991; Herbert 1986, 1989, 1991; Holmes 1986, 1988; Loh 1993; Manes and Wolfson 1981; Pomerantz 1978; Wolfson 1981, 1983, 1984).

Research studies on compliment topics and compliment responses

Socio-cultural and linguistic complexities are very often involved in the encoding and decoding processes of giving and responding to a compliment in compliment-response interchanges. In intercultural communication, a high level of "compliment competence, i.e. the linguistic and cultural competence" (Herbert 1989: 8) in giving and responding to compliments is required of a non-native speaker.

Previous studies that explored speech acts in different languages or social groups have broadened our understanding of the pragmatic norms of different cultures and provided evidence for cross-cultural and intercultural comparisons. The speech event of compliment and compliment response has been quite extensively studied. It has not only given insights into the rules of language use and organization of conversational utterances, but has also shown the value system specific to individual speakers, the context of culture, and the context of situation. Compliment and compliment response also embody the notion of face and politeness that are characteristic of the social and cultural group from which speakers come.

Previous studies on compliment and compliment response have shown that cross-cultural differences are manifested in the topics, structure, lexical choice, functions, response types, distribution, and intent in the complimenting behaviour (see, for example, Chen 1993; Creese 1991; Herbert 1986, 1989, 1991; Holmes 1986, 1988; Knapp et al. 1984; Manes and Wolfson 1981; Pomerantz 1978; Wieland 1995; Wolfson 1981, 1983, 1984). Wolfson (1981, 1983, 1984) and Wolfson and Manes (1980), for instance, conducted a series of studies on compliments in American English, focusing primarily on compliment formulas and functions. Holmes's (1984, 1986, 1987) studies on New Zealand English cover a range of aspects of compliments, namely the sex-preferential, functions, topics, syntactic structure and lexical predictability of compliments, as well as the semantic and functional features of compliment responses. Similarly, Creese (1991) collected naturalistic data from teachers' rooms in the United States and Britain, which comprised 73 compliments and compliment responses, and compared them in terms of "lexical predictability, compliment response, syntactic categories and compliment topic" (Creese 1991: 48). The following summarizes the findings of compliment topics and compliment response types that have been examined by these studies. These two aspects, which are sensitive to cultural values and assumptions, are examined in this study of intercultural conversations.

Compliments vary from culture to culture in terms of acceptable or preferred compliment topics, and yet within a culture or speech community, there is strong agreement as to the relative importance of compliment topics. Chinese speakers tend to compliment people most on performance (Ye 1995). In America, compliments are given in certain situations; and yet in similar situations in some other cultures, complimenting will be considered inappropriate (Wolfson 1981). In Western cultures, compliment topics are often related to personal appearance, ability, performance and possessions (see, for example, Holmes 1984; Wolfson 1989; Creese 1991). Manes (1983) found that in American compliments, all compliments made on personal appearance are made by American female speakers, which reflects American cultural values, namely a concern about both their and others' appearance and perceiving these compliments as an expression of solidarity. Egyptian speakers have been found to favour the topic of personality (Nelson, El-Bakary and Al-Batal 1993).

Herbert's (1991) study suggests that Polish compliments are predominately related to possession, which appears to contradict the belief that the Poles attach less importance to material possessions than Western Europeans. This finding is attributed to "the ethnography of everyday life in Poland at the time of the fieldwork (1983–1988)", when acquisition of goods was considered an accomplishment in pre-democratic Poland (Herbert 1991: 381). This phenomenon has underscored the importance of examining speech act behaviours in the immediate context of interaction.

Compared to compliments, compliment responses serve much more complex functions. Compliment responses vary from culture to culture in terms of what constitutes an appropriate response. In English-speaking cultures, for instance, the social etiquette is that accepting a compliment by saying 'Thank you' is the only response necessary; however, many English speakers feel a simple 'Thank you' is not adequate as a response to a compliment.

Pomerantz (1978) is the first researcher to study compliment responses. Working with American data, Pomerantz (1978) has noted that responding to a compliment can pose a dilemma for the speaker. Most of the compliment responses in American English depart from the model or standard norm of acceptance; instead there is a "prevalence of rejections and disagreements" (Pomerantz 1978: 88). The non-accepting behaviour, which may constitute "noticeable, reportable, puzzling, troublesome" phenomena, has been found to be predominant. As revealed in her data, compliments are repeatedly either rejected, downgraded, or only accepted with qualification. When responding to a compliment, a speaker is therefore caught between the two maxims of speech behaviour — "agree with the speaker" and "avoid self-praise" conflict with each other (Pomerantz 1978: 71–72).

Pomerantz's (1978: 79–112) taxonomy of compliment response types, which has been most frequently quoted by other researchers (for example, Herbert 1989; Loh 1993), is presented below.

Response Type	*Example*
I. Acceptances	
1. Appreciation Token	A: That's beautiful. B: Thank you.
2. Agreement	A: Oh it was just beautiful. B: Well thank you. I thought it was quite nice.
II. Rejections	
1. Disagreement	A: You did a great job cleaning the house. B: Well, I guess you haven't seen the kids' room.

III. Self-praise Avoidance Mechanisms

1. Praise Downgrades

a. agreement	A: That's beautiful. B: Isn't it pretty?
b. disagreement	A: Good shot. B: Not very solid though.

2. Referent Shifts

a. reassignment	A: You're a good rower, Honey. B: These are very easy to row. Very light.
b. return	A: Ya' sound really nice. B: Yeah, you soun' real good too.

Herbert (1986) examined 1,062 compliment responses collected from American students in a university in New York, and found that speakers are "almost twice as likely to respond with some response other than acceptance" (Herbert 1986: 80). Although the prescribed norms of American speech behaviour state that the appropriate response to a compliment is 'Thank you', speakers usually downgrade the compliment or return it to the complimenter. His findings indicate that "non-agreement" and "request interpretations" are as frequent as "appreciation tokens" and "comment acceptance". In another study, Herbert (1989) attributes the low frequency of "Acceptance" by American English speaking university students to American notions of equality and democratic idealism.

Some studies indicate otherwise. Holmes's (1986) study, for example, shows that the most common New Zealand compliment response is to accept it (61%), followed by deflecting the credit (29%), while overtly rejecting compliments is very rare (10%). Similarly, Creese (1991) found accepting a compliment as the most common response among British and American teachers, followed by deflecting and rejecting, despite differences in the percentages: for the British, "accept" (54%), "deflect" (29%) and "reject" (17%); and for the Americans, "accept" (45.9%), "deflect" (40.6%) and "reject" (13.5%) (Creese 1991: 51).

Compliment responding behaviour has been observed in intercultural communicative contexts. In a study examining seven dinner conversations in French between French and American speakers of French, it has been found that mitigated responses and transferring the credit to something or someone else are common among French native speakers due to the cultural value of modesty (Wieland 1995). Han (1992) compared the compliment responses of Korean females in English interactions and in Korean interactions. Korean females respond differently when speaking in Korean compared to speaking in English. In Korean interactions, they are more likely to reject or deflect compliments in order to avoid self-praise. In English interactions, they are more likely to accept compliments by saying 'Thank you' because they believe that Americans are direct and frank and always accept compliments upon receiving them.

Cultural differences are apparent in compliment responses given by American and PRC Chinese college students when answering a questionnaire, which elicited their responses in four situations: looks, clothes, achievement, and possession (Chen 1993). Analysis of the 339 responses given by American subjects has demonstrated that four Super Strategies are employed: Accepting (39.28%), Returning (18.5%), Deflecting (29.5%), and Rejecting (12.7%). The Chinese subjects produced a total of 292 responses which fall into three Super Strategies: Rejecting (95.73%), Thanking and Denigrating (3.41%), and Accepting (Thanking only) (1.03%). What is striking about the PRC Chinese college students is the overwhelming use of Rcjecting (95.73%) as a strategy to deal with compliments.

Loh (1993), employing the survey methods of questionnaires and interviews, compared the compliment responding behaviour of the British and the Hong Kong Chinese. Her subjects were 40 undergraduate and post-graduate students — 20 British and 20 HKC, with ages ranging from 16–30. Cross-cultural differences are evident in the behavioural patterns of compliment response. The British group responds to compliments more frequently by giving an agreement. The Hong Kong Chinese subjects, when responding to compliments in English, tend to adopt the textbook etiquette, a kind of "taught knowledge" (Loh 1993: 50). They are much more inclined to accept compliments with a mere thank you or thanks (i.e. appreciation token), without agreeing or making reference to the compliment (i.e. agreement) in order to reduce potential blunders and communication difficulties. Loh (1993) attributes the phenomena to the fact that Hong Kong Chinese had been taught that in English, the normative response to a compliment is an acceptance, and yet the cultural constraint for them to be modest puts them in a dilemma. The solution is therefore a mere 'thank you' without agreeing to the compliment or making reference to it.

However, when her Hong Kong Chinese subjects respond to compliments given in Chinese, they respond in a Chinese manner; and that is, they "appear to show greater 'deflection' and even 'denial' of the praise" (Loh 1993: 58). Loh (1993) opines that different ways of speaking or different norms upheld are connected to culturally specific values. Besides, the language in which the compliment is given affects the compliment response of the Hong Kong Chinese subjects. When compliments are given in English, the subjects adopt a British style, whereas when given in Chinese, they respond in a Chinese manner. This differing behaviour is attributed to the educational background of the subjects. The fact that they are bilingual with both languages in their "schemata" enables them to shift from one set of cultural values to another.

Chen (1993) compared compliment response behaviour between Americans and the Chinese. American English speakers are less likely to reject compliments on appearance than ability (or "achievement" in Chen's word) and possessions, as they associate appearance with their self-image, and are reluctant to damage it by declining compliments on their appearance. Conversely, the Chinese tend to accept compliments on possessions, but reject compliments on appearance and achievement, as "looks are more intimate and private to a person than achievement and possession" (Chen 1993: 69). The Chinese feel that being modest helps to enhance their face and self-image. When being constrained by the conditions of "agree with the complimenter" and "avoid self-praise", the Chinese subjects tend to adopt the "self-praise avoidance" strategy such as shifting credit to the complimenter (Chen 1993: 59).

Motivations for compliments and compliment responses

What counts as a compliment and an appropriate compliment response differs from culture to culture, and involves "complex cultural-linguistic skills" (Creese 1991: 47). Giving and responding to compliments reflect cultural values and norms of behaviour (Manes 1983). Compliments in spoken discourse are primarily social in function, and hence they are a positive speech act to create, maintain or consolidate the solidarity between interlocutors by expressing admiration or approval (Wolfson 1983; Holmes 1988). Other functions performed by compliments include reinforcing desired behaviour; strengthening or replacing other speech acts such as apologies, thankings and greetings; and softening criticism, or even sarcasm.

The notion of "face" is central in describing complimenting behaviour (Wieland 1995). Face is defined as "an image of self, delineated in terms of approved social attributes" (Goffman 1967: 5). Goffman (1967) views social interaction rituals such as giving and receiving compliments to be social norms. Participants in an interaction try to act according to social norms to avoid generating negative feelings from any of the participants. Negative feelings may come from a perception of loss of face. Goffman contends that a person "tends to conduct himself during an encounter so as to maintain both his own face and the face of the other participants" (Goffman 1967: 11). Goffman's notion of the "response act" has the property of "telling about the individual's position or alignment in what is occurring" and is "meant to be given attention by other, i.e. to be assessed, appreciated, understood" (Goffman 1976: 280). As a response act, a compliment response will reflect the recipient's perception of the compliment-giving situation, and will provide insights into the understanding of the structure and values of the respective societies or cultures.

The giving of compliments, which very often involves positive evaluative comments, is a verbal manifestation of addressing the positive face of the addressee. The speaker tries to elevate the FTA by anointing the compliment-recipient's positive face, by attending to the recipient's "interests, needs and wants" (Brown and Levinson 1987: 103). Giving a compliment can threaten the recipient's negative face in some cases, as the speaker indicates that he or she would like to have the recipient's wants, or to possess something belonging to the addressee (Holmes 1988). Responding to compliments may intimidate the speaker's positive face, that is, "the want of every member that his wants be desirable to at least some others" (Brown and Levinson 1987: 62).

The Chinese notion of politeness, which takes the forms of "self-denigration" and "other elevation" (Gu 1990) and "reciprocity" (Hong 1985), explains why the Chinese do not accept compliments often. In Chinese culture, being modest and respectful as a manifestation of humility is considered ideal in daily communication among the Chinese (Gu 1990). Chen (1993) found that Gu's (1990) Chinese politeness model can best account for the overwhelmingly high percentage of "Rejecting" Super Strategy (95.73%) adopted by his PRC Chinese college students in response to compliments.

According to Loh (1993), the proper response from the perspective of Hong Kong Chinese is to deny the compliment by means of disagreement, a downscaling of compliment, or a shifting of credit, and simultaneously to upgrade the complimenter, saying that he or she is much better (Loh 1993). The Chinese give an impression of humbleness because they tend to act modestly in order not to exaggerate their ability or accomplishments, for fear that if he or she is later discovered by others as idly boasting, or if something turns out differently, they would lose face (Brunner and You 1988). "Reciprocity" is another politeness principle for the Chinese (Hong 1985), implying that a recipient is indebted to repay something received (e.g. goods and services). In situations of complimenting, a recipient is obliged to pay back, or "return", what he or she has received. To return a compliment also allows the recipient to give "face" back to the complimenter (Brunner and You 1988).

Analysis of compliment topics and compliment responses in the intercultural conversations

In this study, instances of compliments and compliment responses will be analyzed to identify any characteristic features in the giving and receiving of compliments by HKC, and how such features compare to those of their NES interlocutors. Compliment topics and compliment response types will be examined in relation to possible motivations for their usage. The analysis will aim to find out whether or not, and in what manner, HKC and NES differ in these areas examined, and what could have caused the differences. It is hypothesized that HKC and NES will differ in the aspects that are complimented on, i.e. compliment topics. They will also differ in their respective ways of dealing with compliments, i.e. compliment response types. Specifically HKC will use rejections and self-denigrating responses more frequently when being complimented on, and NES will use acceptances and self-praise avoidance mechanisms more frequently as compliment responses.

Simultaneous talk

Turn organization, as manifested in simultaneous talk, in conversation is not only sequentially and linguistically constituted, but also socially and culturally constituted. Simultaneous talk occurring in intercultural communication is often perceived as revealing the dynamics of a relationship or discerning patterns of control and submission (Bargiela-Chiappini and Harris 1995, 1997; Beebe and Giles 1984; Scarcella 1983; Zuengler 1989; Murata 1994), and, again, is a relevant site for a study into culturally-laden features of discourse such as the present one.

Turn organization in conversation

In conversation, turn organization refers to turn-taking, turn-yielding and turn-holding. A minimum of two participants is required for a conversation to take place and this necessitates the speakers taking turns. Sacks (1971) argues that he has substantial evidence, based on a study of American English conversation, that "at least and not more than one party talks at a time". He observes that turn-taking usually occurs with little overlapping speech and few silences, and that if two or more speakers are talking or if there is silence, this state of affairs is recognized by the speakers who then quickly return to a situation where there is one speaker.

Many explanations have been offered regarding how turn-taking is successfully performed, such as the system for the organization of turn-taking in conversation proposed by Sacks et al. (1974):

(i) For any turn, at the initial transition-relevance-place of an initial turn-construction unit:
   (a) If the turn-so-far is so constructed as to involve the use of a 'current speaker selects next' technique, then the party so selected has the right and is obliged to take next turn to speak; no others have such rights or obligations, and transfer occurs at that place.

(b) If the turn-so-far is so constructed as not to involve the use of a 'current speaker selects next' technique, then self-selection for next speakership may, but need not, be instituted; first starter acquires rights to a turn, and transfer occurs at that place.

(c) If the turn-so-far is so constructed as not to involve the use of a 'current speaker selects next' technique, then current speaker may but need not continue, unless another self-selects.

(ii) If, at the initial transition-relevance-place of an initial turn-constructional unit, neither (i)(a) nor (i)(b) has operated, and, following the provision of (i)(c), current speaker has continued, then the rule-set (a)–(c) reapplies at the next transition-relevance-place, until transfer is effected.

The system for the organization of turn-taking in conversation proposed by Sacks et al. (1974) is attractive as long as turn-taking occurs smoothly; and that is, speakers and hearers alternate their roles only at the "possible completion point". However, naturally occurring conversation can be messy. Interruption, overlap and silence often occur in conversations for which Sacks et al.'s system may not be able to account for satisfactorily.

Defining simultaneous talk

Simultaneous talk, meaning two or more speakers talk at the same time, is a prevalent phenomenon in conversation. Many studies in conversation analysis have used increasingly sophisticated definitions in their examination and classification of simultaneous talk. They usually look at the position of simultaneous talk in the turn of the current speaker, the functions it serves in the on-going conversation, whether or not it has successfully fulfilled the intended functions, the readiness of the current/primary speaker to relinquish the floor when being interrupted, and the different motivations that give rise to simultaneous talk.

Based on the notion of the organization of turn-taking in conversation, simultaneous talk in everyday conversation is broadly classified into "interruption" and "overlap". An "interruption" can be of variable size and of various construction unit types. It may occur "by competing self-selectors for a next turn" (Sacks et al. 1974: 706–707). Sacks et al. (1974) maintain that from the perspective that conversation is rule-governed, organized and is locally managed by the participants, "simultaneous starts" are produced when a participant projects his start to the earliest possible start at some possible transition-relevance-places. Schegloff (1987) defines "interruption" as simultaneous talk that does not occur at or near a Transition Relevance Place (TRP). "Interruption" occurs when a participant begins to talk when the current speaker is still taking his or her turn-at-talk, but not yet approaching a TRP (Schegloff 1987).

In contrast to simultaneous talk that involves the apparent violation of the rules of the turn-taking system (i.e. interruption), another type of simultaneous speech, "overlap", is resultant from participants' orientation to those rules. "Overlap" can arise in several ways: premature self-selection related to the upcoming TRP, occurring in conjunction with the current TRP, and self-selection at the same time as the current speaker elects to continue (Sacks et al. 1974). This type of simultaneous talk occurs within a syllable or two of the TRP where interactional participants are entitled to take turns.

Functions and perceived meanings of interruptions and overlaps

Apart from defining and labeling "interruption" and "overlap" in terms of their positional relations with the TRP, other classification systems and labels have been used. For instance, clause-final and transition-device interruptions are called "co-operative" and mid-clause ones "uncooperative" (Schiffrin 1986: 369–71). In the past, psychologists viewed interruption as indicative of dominance and gender effects in communication (Beattie 1983; Grimshaw 1987; Kennedy and Camden 1983; Zimmerman and West 1975; West and Zimmerman 1983). Disruptive interruption of a speaker's talk is, for instance, considered "blatant non-cooperation", which is indicative of lack of care about the speaker's negative- or positive-face wants (Brown and Levinson 1987). To some researchers, interruption can convey negative meanings, as evident in expressions such as "inconsistent and nonlistening" (Ng, Brooke and Dune 1995: 65), "disorderly" (Speier 1972), "confrontational" (Hutchby 1992), "a violation of turn-taking rules" (Sacks et al. 1974: 706–707) and "a violation of another speaker's right" (Bilmes 1997: 520). Interruption is very often considered unsolicited, unhelpful, intrusive and obtrusive. Murata (1994) identifies three functions of "intrusive interruptions", namely topic-changing, floor-taking and disagreeing.

Some researchers highlight the positive motivations and functions of simultaneous talk. Heightened involvement (Long 1972), an expression of enthusiasm (Ferguson 1977) and a need for social approval (Nathale et al. 1979) have been incorporated into research on simultaneous talk. In fact, simultaneous talk in conversations is very often considered to be laden with affective and attitudinal meanings. Simultaneous talk can indicate active involvement, active and continued listenership, camaraderie, mutual interest, support, co-operation, encouragement and rapport (for example, Bennett 1981; Ervin-Tripp 1979; Goldberg 1990; Levinson 1983; Murata 1994; Tannen 1994).

Other researchers have examined simultaneous speech from the perspective of "interactional pressures" in conversation (Goldberg 1990). These interactional pressures are due to demands of the evolving conversational structure, satisfying both the self (i.e. interrupter) and the addressee (i.e. current speaker). First, the turn-allocation nature of conversation makes it important for a participant to immediately get the turn-space at the end of the ongoing turn to ensure that he or she makes an utterance that is relevant to the ongoing talk. Second, the expectation of "active and continued listenership" may lead the listener to produce overlapping speech in order to indicate comprehension, reception and agreement, or otherwise (Goldberg 1990: 886–7). Third, interrupting a current speaker to seek clarification would not constitute infringing the current speaker's rights, but will rather satisfy the interrupter's want for an answer, the current speaker's obligations to the interrupter to answer, and also the interrupter's wants to appear competent and cooperative. Finally, a hearer may interrupt and present his or her own issues and views due to a need to satisfy his or her own face wants, irrespective of topical fit or effect upon the speaker's face (Goldberg 1990).

Some discourse analysts (see, for example, Stenström 1984) even go so far as to argue that in fact most instances of simultaneity in conversations, even interruptions, are a product of co-operative behaviour, if viewed in the widest sense of the intention of the interrupter is to continue the conversation with the active participation of his or her hearer in pursuit of a successful outcome (personal communication, Sinclair 1991; cited in Warren 1993).

From the discussion above, it is apparent that simultaneous speech is a much more complex conversational phenomenon than that suggested by Sacks et al. (1974). Many researchers have cautioned against the simplistic view that interrupting others serves to violate their speaker's rights (for example, Houtkoop and Mazeland 1985; Murray 1985, 1987; Thomas 1985). Rather, they point out that conversationalists' decisions about simultaneous talk are made based on their own and other's interactional rights and obligations of the moment, and personal or interactional needs or face-wants (Sacks et al. 1974; West and Zimmerman 1983; Goldberg 1990; Tannen 1994; Schiffrin 1986; Makri-Tsilipakou 1994). Participants also "make strategic and normative decisions on the basis of how overlap occurs and their interpretation of it" (Nofsinger 1991: 104).

Cultural and contextual factors relating to interruptions and overlaps

As discussed above, simultaneous talk in conversation is more than indicative of conversational structure. It very often demonstrates complex interactional and management strategies. Strategy use is very often determined by the goals for a speaker to initiate simultaneous speech, and the ways the current speaker reacts to the initiation of simultaneous speech, namely whether or not the current speaker relinquishes the turn as a result. Individuals who come from different cultures can attach divergent values and meanings to simultaneous speech. As remarked by Mey

(2001: 277), not only the rules that allow a speaker to "jump into" the ongoing conversation at a TRP vary from culture to culture, the notion of what constitutes a valid TRP can be different across cultures.

The reasons for and motivations behind interruption and overlap are complex and dependent on organizational, interactional, interpersonal, contextual and socio-cultural factors. Every instance of simultaneous talk is culturally, socially, sequentially and linguistically constituted. Simultaneous talk occurring in intercultural communication is often conceived as revealing the dynamics of a relationship or discerning patterns of control and submission due to differences in language proficiency, topical knowledge and context of interaction (Bargiela-Chiappini and Harris 1995, 1997; Beebe and Giles 1984; Scarcella 1983; Zuengler 1989). Some social contexts are more conducive to the occurrence of interruptions. Beattie (1981), for instance, found that in a tutorial group, students interrupt their tutors significantly more than the other way round. Beattie explains that "students seem forced to cut in on tutor's and other student's speech in order to make some contribution to the discussion", and this shows that certain contextual factors may "encourage" some speakers to use interruption for certain reasons (Beattie 1981: 31).

Tannen (1994) also points out that in order to differentiate overlap from interruption, the researcher needs to consider the context, speaker's habitual styles, and the interaction of their styles. When interactional contexts such as a conversation between friends and a job interview are compared, the former is more likely to produce more "cooperative" overlapping. Such factors as familiarity with each other and the conversational or interactional style of the speakers can affect the occurrence of interruptions (Tannen 1989). Tannen's research has revealed that the number of interruptions in a conversation may increase as participants feel more comfortable with one another. Speakers of the "high involvement" style frequently begin speaking while another speaker is still speaking because the strategies of these speakers place a higher priority on the need for positive face and to show involvement. Conversation is not disrupted if high involvement speakers are talking with each other and "the fast pacing and overlapping served to grease the conversational wheels" (Tannen 1994: 63). However, when high involvement speakers use the same strategies with "high considerateness" speakers, the speakers will feel that they are being interrupted and dominated as "their strategies place relatively more emphasis on serving the need for negative face, not to impose" (Tannen 1994: 63).

Interruption and overlap have been examined in relation to dominance and control (Grimshaw 1987) and facework (Brown and Levinson 1987), which are culture- and context-specific elements. Studies in second language acquisition (Beebe and Giles 1984; Scarcella 1983) have found that the native speakers often dominate the non-native speakers in interactions. Scollon and Scollon (1981) compared conversations between White Men and Athapaskans, noting that due to differences in the pace of speech, White men tend to interrupt Athapaskans. White men hence appear to be aggressive and the Athapaskans inarticulate. Bargiela-Chiappini and Harris's (1995, 1997) study contrasted the interruptive strategies used in British and Italian business meetings. They found cross-cultural and linguistic differences in the interruptive strategies adopted by British and Italian speakers in business meetings. Power relationships have been shown to be an important variable in the discourse.

How interruption is perceived may vary drastically across cultures (Murata 1994). In some cultures, the use of interruption may be welcomed or encouraged, and viewed as the interrupter's willingness to participate in the ongoing conversation. This type of culture is considered to defer more to the "co-operative imperative", which "provides for the need for social interaction". This means that the use of interruption may be interpreted as a device for maintaining social relationship between speakers. However, in other cultures, interruption may be interpreted as rude, aggressive or disrespectful to the speaker. This type of culture is said to defer more to the "territorial imperative", which "provides for individual security" (Murata 1994: 386–387). Speakers from these cultures may place greater emphasis on the right of a speaker to finish or complete his or her turn. In cultures where "territorial imperative" is highly valued, even "co-operative interruption" could be interpreted as disturbing or threatening. An interruption may therefore be perceived as either intrusive or co-operative, depending on whether the current speaker being interrupted defers more to the territorial imperative or the co-operative imperative.

In Murata's (1994) intercultural study of Japanese and English speakers, native speakers of Japanese (NSJ) initiate more interruptions, as they adjust their Japanese conversational style that "seems to prefer not to have interruptions" to the English conversational style that "seems to show conversational participation and listenership by way of interruption". Nevertheless, compared to their NES interlocutors, NSJ still do not interrupt as much as NES, probably because they want to show respect and give deference to their interlocutors, and to show that they are listening (Mentis 1994). In the NSJ-NSJ interaction, intrusive interruptions occur very rarely, due to the traditional Japanese attitude towards conversation, namely "one must not start talking before the conversational partner has completed his/her utterance, especially when one is talking to one's senior" (Murata 1994). NES speakers have been found to use both cooperative and intrusive interruptions equally in both NSE-NSE and NSJ-NSE interactions. Murata (1994) concludes that cultural variations in the interpretations and values given to interruption may influence the conversational style of the speaker (c.f. Tannen 1985), and hence asserts that the use of interruptions is culture-specific.

Itakura (1998, 2000) investigated the influence of gender on Japanese speakers' conversations in Japanese and in English. She examined interruptions as a means of "conversational dominance", and proposed that the act of interrupting alone is not indicative of dominance. Rather, it is only when the person being interrupted relinquishes the floor that the interrupter can be considered to have successfully controlled the floor.

To date, no studies on simultaneous talk in conversation, particularly in intercultural conversation, have compared cultural groups in terms of resistance to relinquishing the floor when being interrupted, and persistence in getting the floor from the current speaker when initiating simultaneous talk; and no research has been conducted on simultaneous speech in naturally occurring conversational interaction between Hong Kong Chinese and native speakers of English.

Analysis of simultaneous talk in the intercultural conversations

In this study, the neutral term "simultaneous talk" (ST) is used to refer to all instances where two speakers talk at the same time. Such terms as "interruption" and "overlap" are not used, as these terms have very often been used for various meanings, have been subjected to a range of interpretations, as well as laden with value judgement (Houtkoop and Mazeland 1985; Murray 1985, 1987; Thomas 1985; West and Zimmerman 1983; Goldberg 1990; Nofsinger 1991; Tannen 1994; Schiffrin 1986; Makri-Tsilipakou 1994; Murata 1994). Simultaneous talk is classified into three types (Sacks et al. 1974). Type A, which starts at a non-TRP of the current speaker's turn-at-talk, is what Sacks et al. (1974) term "interruption". Type B, which starts at or near a TRP of the current speaker's turn-at-talk, is "overlap". Type C simultaneous talk starts at turn beginning, representing the two speakers self-selecting at the same time.

Analysis of intercultural conversations can track which categories and relationships were actively invoked. In this study, investigation is carried out into the nature of simultaneous talk and the functions of various forms of simultaneous talk in naturally occurring intercultural conversations; as well as the effects of social, cultural and contextual factors on the tendencies of HKC and NES both to initiate simultaneous talk and to relinquish the floor when simultaneous talk occurs. Stereotypical beliefs about the Chinese are that they are a collectivistic and hierarchical culture (Hofstede 1980, 1983, 1991), and they conceive the self as an interdependent being (Markus and Kitayama 1991, 1994). One would therefore expect that the Chinese would be similar to Murata's (1994) Japanese subjects, who defer more to the "territorial imperative". In other words, when engaging in social interaction, HKC are assumed to be vigilant and controlled in their verbal behaviours. They will show greater care about their interlocutor's negative-face and positive-face wants. They will, therefore, be more mindful about not violating the speaker rights of their interlocutors. In terms of turn-organization in conversation, HKC will tend to initiate simultaneous talk at the "rightful" location, i.e. at the TRP, of the interlocutor's turn-at-talk, rather than out of the TRP. In other words, HKC will tend to initiate "overlap" rather than "interruption". Interpersonally speaking, HKC will tend to initiate simultaneous talk that is cooperative and supportive, rather than uncooperative and intrusive.

The assumption is also that NES, as far as simultaneous talk is concerned, may dominate HKC, as non-native speakers, by initiating simultaneous talk more frequently. Also, when HKC initiate simultaneous talk, NES will be less likely to relinquish their current turn. Based on the cultural assumptions made about HKC and NES, three hypotheses are formulated:

1. On the whole, HKC will initiate fewer instances of simultaneous talk than NES.
2. Compared to NES, HKC will be more likely to initiate simultaneous talk at or near a TRP (Type B) than at a non-TRP (Type A), as a non-TRP is not considered a rightful position for initiating simultaneous talk.
3. Compared to NES, HKC will yield more readily, irrespective of the turn positions at which simultaneous talk is initiated, and irrespective of whether they are a Current Speaker or an Initiator of Simultaneous Talk.

In order to test the hypotheses, a "Typology of Initiation of and Yielding to Simultaneous Talk" has been devised to capture and describe the major types of simultaneous speech. The typology also describes the relative verbal behaviours regarding initiation of ST at various positions in the current speaker's turn-at-talk, and the relative verbal behaviours regarding yielding to, as well as not yielding to, simultaneous talk that is initiated by the interlocutor, exhibited by HKC and NES when they act as a Current Speaker (CS) and an Initiator of Simultaneous Talk (IST) respectively.

Each type of simultaneous talk is then further categorized to allow for yielding and unyielding verbal behaviours of HKC and NES, in their respective roles of CS and IST. Yield, in this study, is used to refer to the talk of both CS and IST. When a speaker yields, he or she stops the utterance and relinguishes the turn to his or her interlocutor. Conversely, when a speaker does not yield, he or she holds on to the turn and continues speaking, but does not relinquish the turn.

Specifically, the typology will be applied to:

1. compare the relative frequencies of occurrence of Type A simultaneous talk (non-TRP) and Type B simultaneous talk (at or near a TRP) initiated by HKC and NES respectively;

2. compare the relative tendencies for HKC and NES to yield, as well as not to yield, in situations of simultaneous talk when the "one-at-a-time" (Sacks 1971) model of conversation is being violated (i.e. all of the three types of simultaneous talk in the typology); and
3. explore data qualitatively with a view to accounting for the observed similarities and differences between HKC and NES when they produce simultaneous talk in conversation, as deduced from their acts of initiating simultaneous talk, yielding to initiation of simultaneous talk, and unyielding to initiation of simultaneous talk.

Discourse topic management

The strategies and practices regarding discourse topic management are considered culture-specific, reflecting differences in the cultural value orientations specific to the participants (Young 1982; Scollon and Scollon 1981; Scollon 1985; Scollon and Scollon 1991; Tannen 1986, 1990), such as social relations orientation and self orientation (Hofstede 1987; Markus and Kitayama 1991, 1994), and the notions of face and politeness (Brown and Levinson 1987). The ways in which conversationalists manage such discourse topic strategies as topic introduction, orientation to topic subject contents, and management of culturally sensitive topics are all indicative of the speakers' cultural value orientations.

The notion of topic in conversation

In everyday conversation, speakers sequence their utterances in an orderly, connected, coherent, meaningful and acceptable manner. One of the ways in which utterances are organized is through the topic, among other things such as the form and function of the discourse. Topics in conversation are considered different from topics in specialized discourse types. Bublitz (1988: 7–8), for example, suggests that topics in conversation are characterized by the absence of predetermination in their contents, order and direction of occurrence, unlike in specialized discourse such as committee meetings, or candidate interviews, where one participant "controls topics, topical actions and (the distribution of) participant roles".

Different discourse analysts deal with the analysis of topic in spoken discourse differently. This applies both to the approach and the terminology employed. Topic can be a semantic field, or a stretch of talk bounded by phonological and/or lexical markers or connected by means of chains of lexical cohesion (McCarthy 1991). Change in discourse topics is identified as "referential expressions" (realized as NPs) which have complete or low "irrecoverability" in relation to the preceding context, and some degree of "persistence" in relation to the following context (Geluykens 1993: 187). Topic is defined as "what the speakers talk about" (Stenström 1994: 150).

Yule (1980) defines discourse topic as "what is generally being talked about", and likens the "multifeatured" aspect of discourse topic to the topic "framework" characterized by Chafe (1976) and Haiman (1978). Topic framework, which is "the contextual framework within which the topic is constituted", comprises "those aspects of the context which are directly reflected in the text, and which need to be called upon to interpret the text" (Brown and Yule 1983: 75). Topic framework and context are intricately linked. "Topic framework" refers to the areas of overlap in the speaker's contributions to a discourse, and serves to lay down a set of constraints for a speaker to comply with so as to continue "speaking topically" (Brown and Yule 1983: 75).

Managing topics in conversation

Different approaches to discourse analysis deal with topic management in discourse differently, among which are conversation analysis and dialogical studies. Conversation analysis posits symmetries between speakers (Drew and Heritage 1992; Sacks et al. 1974; Schegloff 1987, 1992). It maintains that in conversation, topics are neither pre-planned nor predictable in their number and in the scope and development of their content by any one party. The rules of English conversations, according to Conversation Analysis, allow an equality of speaker rights to initiate and develop topics, but the rules sanction such uncooperative behaviours as overt topic control and domination. In most interchanges, topics are negotiated through the turn-taking process with the cooperation between speaker and hearer. Such collaborative topic management by all speakers can be motivated by the needs and priorities of conflict-avoidance, mutual and balanced interest, consideration of the interlocutor, creation and maintenance of common ground, cooperation and agreement (Wilson 1987; Geluykens 1993; Bublitz 1988). Bublitz (1988), for instance, gives a comprehensive account of discourse topics in English conversation by the educated sector of British society. He posits that participants' "discourse topic" and the "accompanying topical actions" serve to assert joint interests and to establish a continuous flow of talk, and for the individual participant to assert his or her own interests by means of steering the direction of conversation.

However, dialogical studies, which have established an analytical framework specific to investigating conversational dominance, consider asymmetries between speakers to be inherent to any kind of interaction (Marjovà and Foppa 1990). Dialogical studies see language as inseparable from cultural, socio-historical or situational contexts, and suggest that interlocutors are bound to differ in their control of the content, as well as the quality and quantity of their dialogical contributions. Topic dominance is viewed as a dimension of conversational dominance (Linell 1990; Luckmann 1990).

Other studies, nevertheless, do not make a priori assumptions about symmetry or asymmetry between conversational participants; they emphasize the importance of interplay of different factors in the specific context of situation. Mentis (1994), in examining topic management, suggests that successful topic management, which is a necessary prerequisite for the establishment of conversational coherence, involves an interaction between situational, social, textual, topical, interpersonal, linguistic and cognitive conditions that are specific to the context of situation. According to Mentis (1994), a speaker will fail to contribute to conversational coherence under a few conditions, namely if he or she changes the topic of conversation abruptly without signalling the transition to a new or related topic, or introduces inappropriate tangential topic shifts or noncoherent topic changes, or makes contributions that provide information unrelated to the topic under discussion, or is unable to share responsibility for the introduction and propositional development of a topic.

Mentis's (1994: 32) "multidimensional model of topic coherence" comprises essential parameters of topic introduction, topic maintenance, linguistic factors, and cognitive factors. First of all, topic introduction is concerned about the number of topics and subtopics introduced that is indicative of the extent to which a speaker initiates topics for discussion, the manner of topic/subtopic introduction (change, shift, etc.), and type of topic/subtopic introduction (new, related, or reintroduced, and whether the content is concrete or abstract). Second, topic maintenance is related to the length of topic/subtopic sequence, and the type of topic maintenance contribution (whether or not it gives new information). Finally, topic-related areas of cognition, including general world knowledge and underlying organizational knowledge structures such as scripts and schemas, attention and memory also contribute to topic coherence in conversation.

Intercultural differences in discourse topic management

Intercultural communication studies on discourse topic management have investigated cultural differences in various aspects of discourse topic management. In intercultural conversation, discourse topic management strategies and practices are often culture-specific (Young 1982; Scollon and Scollon 1981; Scollon 1985; Scollon and Scollon 1991; Tannen 1986, 1990). In the literature relating to intercultural conversation, three aspects of topic management which are believed to reflect differences in the cultural value orientations specific to the conversational participants have been discussed. These are employment of topical strategies in introducing topics, orientation of topic subject contents and management of culturally sensitive topics.

Strategies of topic introduction

Topic introduction can be achieved by means of a set of "topical strategies" (Stenström 1994: 151–160), or "accompanying topical actions" (Bublitz 1988: 16). Stenström (1994: 151–160) describes a total of six "topical strategies" that British speakers use to deal with topics in conversation, namely changing, shifting, drifting, digressing, resuming and terminating. Except for termination, all of the topical strategies represent different forms of topic introduction. Accordng to Stenström, changing a topic involves "abandoning the current topic in favour of a new, related, topic". Shifting a topic involves "moving from one topic to a related topic or from one aspect of the current topic to another". Both topic changes and shifts may be initited by a marker; the marker found in topic shifts marks the transition between two related topics rather than, as in topic changes, introduces an entirely new topic (Stenström 1994: 156). Examples of informal topic change markers are "what else, did I tell you, do you know, I wonder" and informal markers include "can I ask you, let me tell you, let me ask you" (Stenström 1994: 155). Examples of shift markers are "actually, by the way, in (actual) fact, incidentally, now, talking about, that reminds me, well, what about". Topic drifts, the third topical strategy, are "common when the main aim of conversation is being social" (Stenström 1994: 158), and involve "moving almost imperceptibly from one topic to another", and are regarded as topic "shifting in an inconspicuous way" (Stenström 1994: 157). Topic drifts are linguistically (and prosodically) unmarked but the old and the new topic is usually linked in some ways. Topic digressions, the fourth topical strategy, occur when a speaker initiates a move away from the current topic. When either of the speakers is prompted by a greater momentary interest in the new topic, the previous topic is then suspended, one-sidedly or temporarily. A new topic is introduced and then closed before the old topic is re-adopted. Topic digressions may or may not be related to the current topic. Some digressions are spontaneous, for example, when a speaker suddenly remembers that he or she has to pass on some information to the other participant. Other digressions are deliberate, resulting from speakers seeking and receiving clarification or additional information. The participant who began the digression has been found to often take the initiative to resume the old topic. Digression markers include "actually, as a matter of fact, by the way, I mean, incidentally" (Stenström 1994: 159). Finally, topic resumption happens when a digression is ended and the previous topic is returned to. Topic resumption markers, or "return markers" (Stenström 1994: 160), include "all right, right, OK, (well) now, now then, anywy, so" (Stenström 1994: 160).

Stenström's classification of topical strategies will be adopted in the present study because her five topical strategies can be usefully categorized into interdependent topical strategies and interdependent ones. In this study, topic shift, topic drift and topic resumption are considered interdependent topical strategies as the topic introduced is semantically or propositionally relevant, or connected to, the previous one. Topic digression is classified as an interdependent topical strategy; only digressions that are related to the current topic are examined. Digressions that are unrelated to the current topic are regarded as topic changes. Topic change is considered an independent topical strategy as the topic introduced is unrelated to the previous topic.

Orientation of topic subject contents

In intercultural conversation, the types and nature of topics discussed can reveal important cultural variations. In Lustig and Koester's (1999) cross-cultural study comparing opening topics, they have found that in Hong Kong, common conversational topics among males include inquiries about the hearer's health and business affairs, and that in Denmark, people's incomes are taboo topics. They have also found that in Algeria, the weather, health, or the latest news is acceptable, but only among male family members. In Ecuador and Chile, it is appropriate, almost obligatory, to inquire politely about the other person's family; whereas Africans are expected to first inquire about a person's well-being before making a request. Lustig and Koester (1999) have also observed that in social conversations, compared to Westerners, Japanese spend more time on finding out about the interlocutor.

In intercultural conversation, the respective cultural value orientations of the speakers are likely to have an impact on the nature of the topics each speaker initiates. Specifically, the individualism-collectivism dimension (Hofstede 1987) and the conception of interdependent self and independent self (Markus and Kitayama 1991, 1994) can influence discourse topic management in conversation. Gudykunst (1998), for instance, posits that collectivists organize topics interdependently, whereas individualists organize topics independently. In other words, members of the collectivistic culture make greater attempts for their topic to be, or to appear to be, semantically or propositionally relevant, or connected to the previous one. Relatively speaking, members of the individualistic cultures, who stress independent activities more than they stress other people and relationships among people, tend to organize topics without paying as much concern about their interlocutors. Similarly, Klopf (1991) notes cultural differences in how a speaker perceives the relation of his or her utterance with the preceding one. Klopf has observed that Japanese, for example, expect comments in a conversation to be related to previous ones, while European Americans express their views without necessarily responding to what the other has just said.

Managing culturally sensitive topics in conversation

In social interactions such as conversation, the immediate concerns for the speakers are very often to have a pleasant and mutually satisfying talk with each other, to keep the conversation going and developing, and finally to close it smoothly. However, when the conversational topic is culturally sensitive and potentially face-threatening, the speakers will have to deal with it with care.

In conversation, when topics that are concerned with racial and ethnic stereotypes or even racial discrimination arise, the speakers take on the role of social members who engage in the invocation, formulation and expression of their ideological assumptions, values, attitudes and position. Such topics involving delicate and sensitive content are potentially face-threatening to the speaker and the hearer in at least two ways. First, when a speaker is constructing and delivering racial and even discriminatory prejudiced talk, his or her own positive face and the hearer's negative face are being threatened simultaneously (Goffman 1967; Brown and Levinson 1987). The positive face of the speaker is being threatened as he or she may be seen as mean and prejudiced, and hence falls short of being likable and respectable. The hearer's negative face may be threatened as the speaker is imposing socially undesirable ideational messages on him or her. Second, the degree of face-threat becomes greater when the race or ethnicity to which one, or both of the participants, belongs is being discussed. In other words, the face-threatening effect is greater when participants can identify themselves with what is being remarked upon, or even criticized.

When speakers are engaged in racial and ethnic talk, their verbal behaviours are influenced by a complex system of social constraints, rules, norms, information and situational variables (van Dijk 1984), and they tend to adopt a range of pragmatic and interactional strategies to fulfill various social functions of the discourse (van Dijk 1984; Shi-xu 1994; Kleiner 1998). A strategy is defined as "a partial plan about the way a goal can or should be reached" (van Dijk 1984: 115). In van Dijk's (1984) study, Dutch interviewees were asked about minority groups. The discourse represents the interviewees' informal expression and diffusion of ethnic beliefs, opinions and attitudes in the multiethnic community. The strategies identified include "narrative and argumentative strategies, local semantic strategies, and various strategies of stylistic and rhetorical formulation" (van Dijk 1984: 147). van Dijk (1984) also examines interactional strategies, which include turn-taking, pauses, hesitations, repairs, false starts and corrections, to communicate the ideological assumptions made of racial and ethnic stereotypes, to handle social information about ethnic groups, and to resolve beliefs and opinions that conflict with those of the interlocutor. In other words, the goal of employing these interactional strategies in racist talk is to fulfill various social and communicative functions.

Apart from interactional strategies, a range of social functions has been identified in topics that involve prejudice, including socializing personal experiences, self-expression, camaraderie and amusement (van Dijk 1984). First, socializing personal experiences occurs when one talks with others about one's personal experiences, opinions, attitudes, evaluations and actions concerning other racial and ethnic groups. Such personal experiences are generalized to become shared experiences based on which further talk and opinions are generated. The second is self-expression when the speaker expresses his or her assumptions, opinions and experiences relating to such topics. In the case of racial and ethnic talk in intercultural conversations, speakers display their relationships both with the interlocutor and with members of the racial or ethnic group being talked about. Engaging in talk about racial and ethnic stereotypes enables speakers to show how much they know about such groups in terms of their norms, values, behaviour, characteristics, and so on (though may be mistaken or distorted) (van Dijk 1984). The third social function is camaraderie, which is an essential element in social interaction. Camaraderie can be strengthened by means of constructing a common basis of talking about and evaluating other groups. Finally, a speaker may present stereotypical descriptions of certain racial and ethnic groups in order to amuse the conversational partner, to signify "the 'funny', 'stupid' people or ways of behaviour of these people as well as the 'interestingness'" of the speaker himself or herself (van Dijk 1984: 52).

Collaborative argumentation was examined by Kleiner (1998) who compared the structural and functional features between his "pseudo-argumentative discourse" (PA) on issues of race between college friends and "ordinary argumentation" (OA). Despite superficial similarities in the sequential organization of the ideational units (positions, supports and disputes) configured within larger units (arguments), Kleiner (1998) found that there are clear differences between PA and OA. In PA, there is no opposition or disagreement between the participants. Two identifying patterns of ideational units have been noted in PA. The first one involves the collaborative support for a mutually accepted position (making a case together), and the second involves the collaborative dispute of an absent antagonist's imported position and support. Kleiner (1998) notes that the function of collaborative argumentation is mainly for identity management, i.e. to avoid negative inferences (to avoid the attribution of "racist"), not for the purposes of persuasion, but rather to reinforce their mutually held non-normative beliefs as well as to reassure each other of their ideological alliance and solidarity.

Face-to-face conversation between interactants from different racial and sociolinguistic backgrounds constitutes an even more unique and richer interactional context for examining the way these interactants deal with culturally sensitive topics, as the conversation will often enlist a range of norms, beliefs, values, views and background knowledge deriving from and embedded in more than one sociocultural and linguistic world. Intercultural conversation therefore constitutes a fundamental source of linguistic data for investigation into and analysis of discourse and ideology.

Analysis of discourse topic management in the intercultural conversations

In this study discourse topic management refers to the way conversational participants contribute towards the topic subject contents and the direction and organization of the topical framework, both informed by the goals for conversational interaction and reflecting the context of conversation. The ways in which HKC and NES manage discourse topics in the unfolding conversation will be investigated through examining topical strategies in topic introduction, orientation of topic subject contents and management of culturally sensitive topics.

Topical strategies

First of all, the relative numbers of topical strategies used by HKC and NES will be compared in order to find out whether NES have a tendency to control and dominate HKC by means of initiating a greater number of topics into the conversation. The analysis of topical strategies will then focus on verifying whether HKC and NES are different in their respective ways to initiate and organize topics, particularly whether HKC are inclined to organize topics interdependently and NES independently. This hypothesis is based on intercultural communication studies (Gudykunst 1998; Klopf 1991) comparing collectivistic and individualistic cultures.

If that is the case, the topic initiated by HKC will be more likely to be propositionally connected to the previous one. In other words, compared to NES, HKC will initiate topic shifts, topic drifts and topic resumption more frequently, but will not necessarily initiate topic changes and topic digressions more frequently. In a similar vein, compared to NES, HKC will be more likely to initiate resumption of the old topic, after a topic shift, drift, digression, or even a change has taken place, but less likely to initiate topic digressions. Regarding topic resumption, HKC will be more likely to initiate resumption to the old topic that was initiated by their interlocutor (the Addressee) than to that initiated by themselves (the Speaker), the rationale being that HKC are more concerned about aligning their contributions with those of their interlocutor.

Topic content orientations

In everyday conversation, the choice and introduction of topics by any one speaker may reflect his or her cultural inclinations. If such cultural dimensions as individualism-collectivism (Hofstede 1983, 1984, 1991) impact on the conversational behaviour and style of HKC and NES, these conversationalists will tend to initiate topics with varying topic orientations. A taxonomy that consists of three types of topic subject contents orientation is proposed, and these are:

1. Speaker and Addressee-oriented topic contents
2. Speaker-oriented topic contents
3. Addressee-oriented topic contents

Based on the assumption that for the Chinese, the self is an "interdependent self" (Markus and Kitayama 1991, 1994) and the Chinese tend to orient themselves to others' or the group's needs, wishes and expectations (King and Bond 1985; Gao 1996; Hofstede 1984, 1987, 1991), it is hypothesized that in conversation, HKC will initiate topic subject contents that are more concerned with the other (i.e. the Addressee) and all of the participants in the immediate context of situation (i.e. Speaker and Addressee-oriented). It is also hypothesized that NES will initiate topic subject contents that are more concerned with themselves (i.e. Speaker-oriented). This is based on assumptions that NES focus more on individual autonomy (Hofstede 1991) and they are relatively less concerned about mutuality and interdependence in activities and less inclined to perceive demarcation between "self" and "other".

As a result, with respect to topic content orientations, two hypotheses are formulated:

1. HKC will initiate topics in descending order of frequency as follows: Addressee-oriented, Speaker and Addressee-oriented, and Speaker-oriented.
2. NES will initiate topics in descending order of frequency as follows: Speaker-oriented, Speaker and Addressee-oriented, and Addressee-oriented.

Culturally sensitive topic management

In social interactions such as conversation, when the topic is related to racial and ethnic stereotypes or even discrimination, the speakers are engaged in the formulation and expression of their ideological assumptions, values and attitudes concerning some delicate and sensitive, and potentially face-threatening, topics. The more a participant identifies himself or herself with the topic of talk, the greater the degree of face threat. Politeness strategies are very often adopted by the participants to compensate for face loss. As Hernández-Flores (1999) puts it, "politeness is based on a social ideology, i.e. on a set of ideas about behaviour which are shared by a community and, hence are recognized as appropriate in the community."

In modern society, of which Hong Kong is an example, where egalitarianism is upheld and racial equality is promoted, for a person to openly express views and beliefs which contradict social norms implies that facework is required to rectify any resultant negative impressions. In this study, conversational interchanges between HKC and NES concerned with socially and culturally restricted topical propositions will be investigated, with a view to examining:

1. the way the speakers invoke cultural knowledge and cultural identity in presenting and negotiating ideational messages related to cultural stereotypes and prejudice in discourse;
2. the strategies employed by HKC and NES to express and organize ideologies related to cultural stereotypes and prejudice in discourse; and

3. the strategies employed by HKC and NES to address the face needs of both the speaker and the addressee so as to manage interpersonal relationships.

Discourse information structure

Discourse information structure, whether deductive or inductive, is a realisation of the degree of directness/indirectness in interpersonal communication. The way conversationalists structure discourse information can be accounted for by cultural values, norms and beliefs, namely the use and perception of messages in communication, clarity and topics in conversation, social relations orientation and self orientation (see, for example, Hall 1977; Hofstede 1987; Gudykunst and Ting-Toomey 1988; Gudykunst 1998), and the notions of face and politeness (Brown and Levinson 1987).

The notion of indirectness

As pointed out by sociologists (see, for example, Gumperz and Hymes 1972; Hymes 1972; Sacks 1971; Saville-Troike 1982; Schegloff 1972; Gumperz 1982), language use is situated, depending on social variables such as relative status, social distance and power of communicators on language production and comprehension in general. Indirectness in conversations is a way of conveying desired messages by means of an interrelationship of social variables and linguistic content (McQuiddy 1986). Indirectness is mainly expressed by means of lexical choice, syntactic structure, conversational implicature and discourse structure (Miller 1994: 39). Research on communicative style (Lakoff 1973, 1976), speech act theory (Austin 1962), conversational implicature (Grice 1975), politeness phenomena (Brown and Levinson 1987) and discourse organization patterns (Kaplan 1987; Kirkpatrick 1991; Scollon and Scollon 1991) have all contributed to the discussion that most communication is characterized by indirectness.

People on occasion do not use words to say what they mean. They insinuate and hint at what they mean. They try to get an idea of what the other person might think of what they might mean, and be ready to adjust or take back what they might have meant (Tannen 1985; Holtgraves 1998). Indirectness, according to Dascal (1983), is costly and risky. Indirectness is costly as it usually takes longer for a speaker to produce an indirect utterance and for the listener to process the expressed meaning to understand the implied meaning. It is risky as the speaker risks being misunderstood. As Thomas (1995) states, indirectness is rational behaviour, through which the speaker obtains some social or communicative advantage or avoids some negative consequence.

Cultural variations in indirectness

Cultural patterns and their associated cultural values, beliefs and norms very often account for degrees of directness/indirectness in interpersonal communication. Specifically, high-context and low-context cultural patterns (Hall 1977) are associated with indirectness and directness in communication. High-context communication is indirect, ambiguous, understated with speakers being reserved and sensitive to listeners; low-context communication is direct, explicit, open, precise and consistent with one's feelings (Gudykunst 1998).

Cultural differences clearly exist in how much and what type of indirectness is expected in particular settings, and what has motivated the use of indirectness (Young 1982; Tannen 1985; Gudykunst and Ting-Toomey 1988; Gudykunst 1998). According to Gudykunst and Ting-Toomey (1988), people in individualistic, low-context cultures, such as European Americans, prefer a direct style and talk explicitly about their true intentions and desires. People in collectivistic, high-context cultures, such as African Americans, Japanese and Koreans prefer the indirect style and use ambiguous statements to mask their true wants and thoughts.

Research has found that Japanese differ from Americans in that they organize their ideas, persuade others and structure their conversations differently (Okabe 1983). According to Okabe (1983), Japanese favour synthetic thinking that focuses on the whole, resulting in high-context messages, and U.S. Americans favour analytic thinking that involves looking at parts. According to Okabe, when talking or writing, Americans construct low-context messages which specify how the parts are related to each other and use explicit words in communication which reflect the cultural value of precision. They also use categorical words such as *absolutely*, *certainly* and *positively*. Further, the English syntax requires the absolute *I* be placed at the beginning of the sentence in most cases and the subject-predicate relation be constructed in an ordinary sentence (Okabe 1983).

Indirectness in conversation is very much caused by cultural differences in the importance people assign to values such as rapport and harmony versus independence, as well as clarity and topics in conversation (Wierzbicka 1991). Greeks, for instance, are considered highly indirect; the Israelis are highly direct; and the Anglo-Americans are in the middle (Wierzbicka 1991). Japanese cultural assumptions of interdependence and harmony require that Japanese speakers limit themselves to implicit and even ambiguous use of words, avoid leaving an assertive impression, and use qualifiers such as *maybe*, *perhaps*, *probably* and *somewhat*. These differences are often manifested even when Japanese speak in English and U.S. Americans speak in Japanese (Gudykunst 1998).

Yamada's (1992, 1994) study of Americans and Japanese in intercultural meetings found that Americans are direct in their talk because they regard talk as a medium for communicating sincere and cooperative intentions, for clarifying and disambiguating the ongoing conversation, for reaching mutual understanding and for building rapport. The Japanese are indirect due to the Japanese ideal of implicit communication and talk-distancing. They achieve indirectness by means of subject ellipsis, stretch-talk and exemplification. Subject ellipsis is a grammatical feature characteristic of Japanese and can serve the discourse function of obscuring talk ownership. Stretch-talk, i.e. drawing out the talk by pausing, hesitating and lengthening syllables, is another means of talk-distancing. Exemplification is employed to soften criticism, and thereby distancing personal ideas and downplaying the talk (Yamada 1992: 1994).

Another cultural dimension — individualism-collectivism — also contributes to the degree of directness and indirectness in interpersonal communication. Individualistic cultures, compared to collectivistic cultures, are more concerned about clarity in conversations (Kim 1994) and view clarity as necessary for effective communication (Kim and Wilson 1994). Clarity in conversations is linked to directness (Kim 1994; Kim and Wilson 1994). In the case of making requests, for example, individualistic cultures consider direct requests the most effective strategy for accomplishing their goals, while collectivistic cultures consider direct requests the least effective (Kim and Wilson 1994).

The motive for a speaker to convey meanings in an indirect way can be unintentional due to inadequate linguistic competence; for instance, when speakers do not know the correct word for some object in their own or a foreign language (Thomas 1995). But very often, being indirect in meaning is intentional, and in fact pragmaticists are only concerned with intentional indirectness though "it is not always possible to say with certainty whether indirectness is intended or not" (Thomas 1995: 120).

Motivations for indirectness include the desire to make one's language more, or less interesting; to increase the force of one's message; competing goals (generally a clash between the speaker's propositional goal and his or her interpersonal goal); and regard for face (Thomas 1995). In interpersonal interactions, indirectness can be motivated by the considerations of "mutual sensitivity to the thoughts and feelings of one another" (Holtgraves 1998: 72). Other motivations for being indirect in interaction include promoting friendship or intimacy between speakers (Ghim 1992), and expression of sarcasm (Slugoski and Turnbull 1988) or humour and wit (Roberts and Kreuz 1994; Kreuz, Kassler and Coppenrath 1998).

Politeness, which is laden with cultural values, beliefs and norms, is a widely discussed and examined motivation behind indirect language use (Searle 1975; Leech 1983; Brown and Levinson 1987). Leech (1980) makes the relation of indirectness and politeness even clearer by remarking that given the same propositional content, it is possible "to increase the degree of politeness by using a more and more indirect kind of illocution. Indirect illocutions tend to be more polite (a) because they increase the degree of optionality, and (b) because the more indirect an illocution is, the more diminished and tentative its force tends to be" (Leech 1980: 108). Similarly, Brown and Levinson (1987) maintain that people often prefer to express their wants and opinions off record, that is, indirectly if they perceive what they say as face-threatening. The authors posit that indirectness is an apparently universal strategy for achieving this goal.

Chinese inductive pattern and Western deductive pattern

Chinese culture has very often been characterized as favouring indirectness in language and communication. "The inscrutable Chinese" are described by Young (1982) as "a speaker merely fulfilling the Chinese expectation that one start somewhere off the point and work in to the point by indirection. Getting right to the point seems hopelessly rude or foolishly childlike, or is to be an indirect way of implying something else". In the last ten to fifteen years, "the stereotypical perception of 'frank' and open westerners and 'inscrutable' and enigmatic orientals has been systematically investigated" in order to show "culture-specific ways of speech behaviour and patterns of communicative interaction" (Zhang 1995: 72).

In a survey on intercultural communication at a large airline in Hong Kong, respondents were asked to make judgements about "typical" Westerners and Chinese in the meeting they attended (Bilbow 1996). Most of the Chinese managers felt that expatriates were more "direct", "aggressive" and "rude" than were Chinese members of staff; whereas most expatriate managers in the survey felt that local Chinese staff was more "evasive", "cautious" and "non-confrontational" than expatriate staff. The prevalence of indirection and reading between the lines in the Chinese communication context is attributed to the culture's preference for harmonious and positive interpersonal communication (Weiss with Stripp 1998).

Cultures are perceived to differ in their valued rhetorical strategies. Inductive and deductive rhetorical strategies are said to characterize Asian and Western cultures respectively. According to Scollon and Scollon (1995: 84), "the inductive rhetorical strategy" works by "presenting the evidence one has first, and progressively leading the listener (or reader) to the conclusion one would like him or her to accept", and 'the deductive rhetorical strategy" is employed to show the listener or reader "how one has arrived at a foregone conclusion" or an idea that is taken for granted (Scollon and Scollon 1995: 84).

Asians, and particularly Chinese, are postulated as having their own valued, or preferred and specifiable rhetorical patterns in discourse; and that is, inductive or delayed introduction of the first or main topic in the discourse. Conversely, a deductive pattern, i.e. early introduction of the topic, is used in Western culture

(Kaplan 1987; Young 1982; Scollon and Scollon 1991, 1995). Scollon and Scollon (1991) examined information sequencing in Asian speech act utterances. They have observed the use of lengthy small talk preceding and following the main topic, for example, request in a requestive event, which functions as "a kind of extended facework", gauging the mood and attitude of the participants, adjusting the distance and relationship between them and creating an amicable atmosphere to conduct transactions. Scollon and Scollon (1991, 1995) found that the Chinese and other Asians generally defer the introduction of the topic until after a considerable period of small talk. They called this speech behaviour "inductive" as opposed to "deductive" style where topics precede explanations (see also Young 1982).

Similar observations were made by Kirkpatrick (1991) who examined Chinese politeness manifested in the structure of forty English letters of request written by mainland Chinese. He observed an overwhelming use of an "indirect way" of making request by the Chinese. The structure of those letters is schematically represented as Salutation, Preamble (facework), Reasons for request and Request. Kirkpatrick attributed the structure to a syntactic analysis of Chinese complex sentences with subordinate clauses, which have a "because … therefore" sequence as the preferred unmarked order. Kirkpatrick (1991: 70) hypothesizes that "it is possible that this sequence is also the preferred sequence at discourse and text levels". Generally speaking, Asian cultures are marked by circularity, implicitness and digressiveness; whereas Western cultures are characterized by linearity and explicitness (Kirkpatrick 1991).

Similar findings have been obtained in journalistic writing. Li et al. (1993) conducted a contrastive analysis of a Chinese news article and an English one on the same topic, and found an exact mirror image reflected from the ways information is organized in the headlines, the first paragraphs and the news articles. Specifically, the Chinese news article is characterized by an inductive discourse pattern and the English one a deductive discourse pattern. Zhang (1995) compared requestive strategies in Chinese and English by means of Discourse Completion Test and interviews, and found differences in how indirectness manifests itself in the languages. Zhang (1995: 82) suggests that Chinese indirectness is associated with "information sequencing" and explains:

> Whether or not A's speech is more indirect than B's depends on first, whether A prefaces his/her intended proposition with any small talk or supportive moves, and second, how much of it A employs to convey his/her communicative intention before explicitly bringing it up. The degree of indirectness is determined by the length of the supportive moves which do not contain explicitly the intended proposition. The more one beats around the bush, the more indirect one's speech becomes (interview data). To define indirectness in Chinese, and to realize it in interaction, external modification of (request) utterances is mandatory, utterance internal modification is not. (Zhang 1995: 82)

Chinese indirectness is hence achieved through framing the utterance in the larger discourse context by "external build-ups, i.e., small talk or supportive moves" (Zhang 1995: 82) preceding and oriented toward the proposed action, rather than achieved through how a particular speech act utterance is realized. According to Zhang (1995: 97), supportive moves that preface the main topic (in this case, the request) are utterances that inquire about preparatory conditions for the request to be made, for example, "expressing worries and problems, seeking advice, offering sympathy, stating wishes, self-criticism", and supportive moves that follow the main topic (the request) include self-criticism, promising and thanking. Linguistic indirectness manifested in small talk and supportive moves is considered a strategy to "constantly assess the situation so as to make appropriate face adjustments to others and self" (Zhang 1995: 85).

Zhang (1995) also points out that requesting in British English, German and Danish, on the contrary, is characterized by optional external modification of requesting utterances, but mandatory internal modification of the propositional content of the utterance, by means of modals, particles, pronouns, etc. (see also Faerch and Kasper 1989). Zhang (1995) further discusses that in English, modifying the internal structure of an utterance such as 'Open the door' to become 'Could you open the door please?' is moving from directness towards indirectness. For British English, German and Danish, an indirect structure as such is for the speakers to ensure that they will not perform an impolite act, or they will perform an impolite act in a non-conflicting way; in other words, for the speakers to observe, balance and negotiate each other's face in the course of the discourse.

Scollon and Scollon (1995: 139) maintain that Asians are more concerned about establishing and maintaining good relationships, even at the expense of the right amount of information getting exchanged, and that "the average Asian is somewhat more skeptical about the value of direct, informational communication and place a higher value on thinking deeply about a subject". For this reason, Asians tend to adopt an indirect pattern. The Chinese inductive pattern can be adopted by a Chinese person to show that he or she is rather sensitive to other participants by delaying the introduction of the topic until the moment is right for it, even if that Chinese person has the right to introduce the topic. This is opposite to Western culture which uses a deductive rhetorical pattern for the introduction of topics, as the main purpose of communication is to exchange information (Scollon and Scollon 1995).

Direct and indirect cultures

Stereotypical assumptions made about particular cultures and their preferences for directness and indirectness in speech should be guarded against. Condon (1984), for instance, has noted that indirect communication is also found in individualistic cultures such as the United States, though it is motivated by reasons different from those in collectivistic cultures such as Japan. Americans are usually indirect when something very sensitive is being discussed, or when they are nervous about how the other person might react. For Japanese, indirectness is a part of their way of life as they often worry about other's reactions toward what they say (Condon 1984). In a similar vein, both indirect and direct communication could be found in collectivistic cultures (Gudykunst 1998). Indirect communication will be used to maintain harmony and not to offend another member of the in-group; and direct communication will be used when maintaining harmony is not a primary concern, for instance, in interaction with a member of the out-group.

Similarly, based on her analysis of American and Japanese in workplace communication, Miller (1994) argues against the prevailing conceptions that polarize the communicative styles of the Japanese and American which characterize the Japanese as "always indirect, non-verbal and ambiguous" and Americans as "always forthright, direct and clear" (Miller 1994: 37). She argues that, contrary to prevailing stereotypical assumptions, both direct and indirect forms of communication are appropriate to both cultural groups. According to Miller (1994: 52), neither direct nor indirect uses of language are a regular feature of any culture or any language, but are "speech behaviours employed in some contexts for particular interactive functions". Miller also observes that although social harmony is a treasured value in Japanese society and individualism in American society, both cultures value "saving face" by using indirect speech acts and such mitigating devices as hedging. Miller (1994) suggests that how a speaker interprets directness and indirectness is dependent on a number of factors, including the social relationships of the participants, the assumptions and understanding about the nature of the communicative task at hand, and the contextual-based cultural and linguistic differences in the manifestation of indirectness.

Debate has been going on as to whether or not valued rhetorical patterns in discourse, that is, delayed introduction of the main topic for the Chinese and early introduction of the topic for Westerners, are free variation or culturally motivated. Kaplan (1987) suggests that preferred interaction patterns depend on the participant's perception of functional appropriateness to the context, but are not strictly culture constrained.

Similarly, Scollon and Scollon (1995: 80) point out that despite a superficial observation that indicates a strong preference for the inductive pattern in Asia (namely Taiwan, Hong Kong, Guangdong, Korea and Japan) and for the deductive pattern in the West, "this apparent cultural difference lies not in a cultural template for the introduction of topics in discourse, but in differences in the cultural structuring of situations and participant roles". They explain that it is this difference in expectations on participant roles, or face, which leads to the frequently observed differences in the introduction of topics in Asian and Western discourse.

Consequent to analyzing Chinese and English business letters, Kong (1998a) asserts that both inductive and deductive strategies are used by people of both Eastern and Western cultures. In other words, irrespective of culture or first language, all speakers will use an inductive rhetorical strategy in situations where the speaker wants to show that he or she does not want to impose upon others. It is therefore the different "expectations" of the participant role, rather than the different motive or imposition of writers, which cause the apparent differences in the ways in which a topic is introduced in Chinese and Western discourses.

This study adopts the view that the stereotypical perspective of dichotomy made about particular cultures and their preferences for directness and indirectness should not be taken for granted and remain unchallenged. Such generalizations should best be put to the test through studying naturally occurring intercultural communicative events, particularly examining the differences in "the cultural structuring of situations and participant roles" (Scollon and Scollon 1995: 83) and the resultant notion of face and politeness.

Analysis of discourse information structure in the intercultural conversations

In this study, HKC and NES will be compared in the way they sequence information in their discourse as a realization of indirectness, as well as the cultural values and motivational factors regarding indirectness. The discussion on what determines indirectness in speech and how indirectness is linguistically realized has never been simplistic. One would imagine that the discussion becomes even more complex when indirectness in discursive interaction in intercultural communication settings is described. Any communication involving negotiation between the participants coming from different cultural backgrounds needs to take into consideration such factors as information sequencing (inductive and deductive styles) (Scollon and Scollon 1991; Kirkpatrick 1991), the meaning of indirectness and its manifestation in different contexts (Scollon and Scollon 1991; Kirlpatrick 1991), the length and types of supportive moves (Færch and Kasper 1989; Zhang 1995), and the face implications of speech acts (Brown and Levinson 1987; Gu 1990).

The purpose of the analysis is three-fold, and these are:

1. To investigate whether or not, and to what extent, indirectness in conversation is culture-specific;
2. To compare the forms in which indirectness is realized in the HKC discourse and the NES discourse in conversation; and

3. To compare the ways in which HKC and NES sequence the information in the discourse to perform different functions.

Considering the overriding factors of cultural background at play, the study hypothesizes that compared to NES, HKC will be more likely to use the inductive discourse pattern, or will use it more frequently. The use of the deductive discourse pattern, which is a form of directness, will also be examined in order to compare the two groups of speakers from a reverse perspective. Possible reasons that may have contributed to the speakers' indirectness in conversation will be offered.

Chapter 3

Research methodology and data collection

Approach to data analysis

The assumption that underlies this study is that there are cultural differences between the East and the West in norms, values and beliefs which impact on the behaviours of the people. The study takes as its starting point purported cultural attributes specific to HKC and NES that are portrayed in the fields of cultural and communication studies. These cultural attributes include such cultural dimensions as individualism-collectivism and uncertainty avoidance, the conceptions of self and other orientations, the notions of face systems and politeness. Conversational behaviours encode cultural attributes and cultural attributes are invoked in conversational behaviours. This study analyzes discoursal and pragmatic features found in the intercultural conversations, which involves a complex, interactive and collaborative process of communication. The study thus looks at what goes on in the context of situated discourse, and considers discourse as the concrete expression of the language-culture relationship.

The study has situated the intercultural conversations both in their wider context and in their immediate conversational context. This is achieved by describing the features, structures and organization exhibited in the intercultural conversations in order to gain insights into how meaning is created in the immediate context. The features manifested in the intercultural conversations were quantitatively analyzed to investigate patterns of verbal behaviour across HKC and NES. The intercultural conversations were then analyzed qualitatively and triangulated with the findings of the quantitative analysis. Both quantitative and qualitative findings were corroborated to see the extent to which the purported cultural attributes specific to the participants have impacted on the way the participants manage conversations, as well as the extent to which management of conversation is subject to the moment by moment context-specific negotiation between participants.

Nature of conversational data

This study argues that the data for any study of conversation should best be "real occurrences of talk" rather than "invented decontextualized sentences" (Channell

1994: 38), or verbal behaviour that is elicited by means of such experimental procedures and instruments as role-play (Blum-Kulka et al. 1989), questionnaires, interviews and observations. These procedures have been challenged on the grounds that people do not behave in role-play as they would in real-life communication (Blum-Kulka et al. 1989). Similarly, self-reported verbal behaviour fails to reflect spontaneous speech behaviour. It biases "the response toward less negotiation, less hedging, less repetition, less elaboration, less variety and ultimately less talk" (Beebe 1985: 3).

Warren (1993) states that in order to enhance the credibility and to increase the degree of generalizability of the findings of a study, the data described should be spontaneous naturally occurring conversations. Such data is preferred also because it is more representative of talk in the real world (Taylor and Cameron 1987). The interlocutors in natural contexts of use have genuine control over the discourse (Roger 1989) and are free from the influence of the researcher or linguist's demands on their behaviour and the resultant discourse. Holding similar views, Tsui (1994: 6) argues that conversational data that is "produced by the linguist's intuition" is "not representative of the normal use of language".

Some studies have examined recordings of spontaneous communication (Gumperz 1982; Milroy 1987; Warren 1993). The main merit of obtaining spontaneous and naturally occurring conversation is that such data provide information about the context of an ongoing face-to-face interaction and represent what occurs in real-life interaction. As naturally occurring data are contextualized and reflect interactions unfolding in real time, the phenomena observed can be more credibly extended to real-life communication in general. It is for all of these reasons that this study has avoided using elicited speech as data. As this study aims to describe the ways in which language is used for communicative purposes in everyday social situations, data were obtained from naturally occurring conversations in which the interlocutors may be assumed to be behaving normally. In order to ensure that the data under study were genuine exchanges of conversation, there was no control or manipulation of any kind over the conversations by means of experimental techniques, role-play, the researcher's introspection, fabrication and on-the-spot note-taking. The conversations collected occurred spontaneously, without any advanced prompting or planning.

Data collection procedures

The study examines how HKC interact with NES in conversations. Social variables which affect the HKC participants' linguistic and conversational competence in English, namely their educational background, first language, place of residence and social status, were controlled. All HKC were adult Chinese raised, educated and working in Hong Kong. They had Cantonese as the first language and English as a second language. All of them were educated to tertiary level. None of them had been educated or had lived in an English-speaking country. Educational background is a variable because in Hong Kong, "English is almost entirely a 'learnt'

Table 3.1. Summary record of the participants in the HKC-NES intercultural conversations

Code	HKC: gender & age	HKC: occupation/ profession	NES: gender & age	NES: occupation/ profession	NES: nationality
001	m/30-39	Administrative Officer (AO), Civil Service	M/40–49	Engineer	Australian
002	f/40–49	Education Officer	M/40–49	Stage Manager	British
003	m/18–29	Trainee Solicitor	M/20–29	Engineer	British
004	f/40–49	School teacher	M/30–39	Officer, advertising agency	British
005	f/40–49	Education Officer	M/40–49	Pastor	American
006	f/40–49	Education Officer	M/40–49	Missionary	American
007	f/30–39	Audio-visual Support Officer	M/50–59	Education Dev. Officer	Australian
008	m/40–49	Engineer & Director of company	M/40–49	Manager	British
009	f/40–49	Education Development Officer	F/30–39	Private Tutor	Irish
010	m/40–49	Education Development Officer	M/40–49	University teacher	British
011	m/30–39	Police Inspector	M/40–49	Police Inspector	British
012	m/30–39	School teacher	F/50–59	School teacher	British
013	f/30–39	Training Officer	M/20–29	Training Officer	American
014	f/30–39	Nurse	F/30–30	Anaesthetist	Scottish
015	f/30–39	Senior Staff Officer, Training and Development	M/40–49	Senior Investigator	British
016	f/30–39	Senior Staff Officer, Training and Development	M/40–49	Senior Investigator	British
017	f/40–49	A. O., bank	M/40–49	Electrical Engineer	British
018	f/40–49	Police Inspector	M/50–59	Police Inspector	British
019	m/30–39	Accountant	M/30–39	Officer, advertising agency	British
020	m/20–29	Manager	M/20–29	Manager	American
021	f/40–49	Administrative Officer	F/50–59	Finance Officer	British
022	f/40–49	Accountant	F/50–59	Finance Officer	British
023	f/30–39	Executive Officer	M/40–49	University teacher	British
024	f/20–29	Social worker	M/30–39	University teacher	British
025	f/30–39	Executive Officer	M/30–39	University teacher	British

language" (Bolt and Bolton 1995: 3) and Hong Kong people mainly learn the language at school. It is thought that educational experience in an English-speaking country is likely to affect the nature of the language used, the ways in which it is used, and possibly the language proficiency of the speaker. At the time the recordings were made, these participants were employed in a variety of professions.[1] Table 3.1 presents the background information of the participants in each of the conversations, namely the ethnicity, gender, age group and occupation of the participants.

Given the need to control the characteristics required of HKC and NES, as well as the private nature of the conversations, it was deemed to be more feasible if the HKC participants were, either directly or indirectly, known to the researcher. The relationship between HKC and NES, in terms of social distance and power, was also controlled. The majority of the participants were friends or colleagues of each other and only in two conversations were the relatives of the participants. In the case of colleagues and relatives, care was taken to ensure that they were not in any hierarchical relationships. For all of the dyads, there was no perceived difference in social status and power relations.

It is important to point out that this study did not examine gender differences in conversational processes and behaviours. The gender of the participants was not controlled as it would have been very difficult if not entirely possible. Adding the gender variable would have required pairing up specific genders in the dyadic conversations which would have proved to be extremely difficult to achieve. Soon after data collection had started, it was realized that data were not easy to come by. It had also proved to be very difficult to constrain the HKC participants in terms of the gender of his or her interlocutor. As a result, gender distribution in the intercultural conversations was not monitored. As it turned out, twelve of the 25 conversations were of same gender, and thirteen were of mixed gender. Among the mixed gender intercultural conversations, twelve of the thirteen had a female HKC and a male NES. There was only one conversation in which there are a male HKC speaker and a female NES speaker (012) (see Table 3.2).

Neither did this study attempt to distinguish NES into different cultural or ethnic groups, despite the fact that first, the participants came from different

Table 3.2. Gender distribution in the data set

Gender composition	Number of conversation
male HKC & male NES	7
female HKC & female NES	5
male HKC & female NES	1
female HKC & male NES	12
Total	25

countries, namely Britain, the United States of America and Australia; and second, cultures represented by these countries have been found to differ in such cultural variability dimensions as Power Distance, Uncertainty Avoidance and Individualism-Collectivism (Hofstede 1980, 1983). There were several reasons for not differentiating NES. First, an assumption was made that linguistically and culturally, native speakers of English will have a greater affinity with each other than with HKC. Second, the focus of the study is on the first language of the NES being English, as opposed to the first language of the HKC not being English. It is, therefore, neither important nor necessary to differentiate NES in terms of the variety of English they speak. Third, as explained in the data collection procedure below, HKC assisted the study in identifying a suitable NES conversational partner. It was already difficult enough to find 25 suitable HKC participants, and so it would have been even more difficult to specify the English-speaking community to which the NES should belong. Finally, the small sample size of NES (N=25) means that differentiating British from Americans from Australians was neither essential nor worthwhile.

Once a suitable HKC participant was identified, he or she was approached and the aim of the research study explained. No mention was made of the research question, lest this would affect the ways in which the participants conduct the conversation. In fact, the potential participant was told that there would be no parameters set on the location, subject matter and length of the conversation.

Each potential HKC participant was then asked whether there was a native English speaking friend or colleague with whom he or she socialized with on a regular basis; and if there was, whether it would be possible to obtain permission to record one of their conversations on a social occasion. The researcher also suggested speaking to the participant's friend to explain that the recording was made for research purposes, where necessary. Most of the HKC participants being approached had been able to make an arrangement with a friend or a colleague, such as a lunch or tea gathering, which they would normally do together for socializing purposes.

In this study, all the data were audio-recorded with the prior knowledge and consent of the participants concerned. Permission to use the data for the purposes of research was sought from both HKC and NES. To comply with ethical standards for research studies involving human subjects, certain safeguards were built in. All of the participants in the conversations were asked to sign a consent form, which states the purpose of the research. The consent form was also a means of acquiring demographic details about the participants, namely age, gender, place of birth, first language, educational background, residence patterns and occupation.

The researcher was not present in any of the conversations recorded. The equipment used in collecting the data was a Sony MD recorder and a Sony microphone which provided maximal sound recordings and minimal obtrusion. Before the recording took place, individual HKC participants were given the recording

Table 3.3. Summary record of the data set: HKC-NES conversations

Code	Place of recording	Duration of conversation	Number of words
001	Oliver's	63 min 10 sec	10,136
002	Church common room	10 min	1,973
003	Private club	13 min 50 sec	2,610
004	Home of NES	24 min 41 sec	4,670
005	Church common room	10 min	3,685
006	Church common room	22 min	4,100
007	Office of NES	18 min 38 sec	2,183
008	Western restaurant	15 min 38 sec	2,139
009	Home of HKC	25 min 12 sec	5,374
010	Chinese restaurant	75 min	9,725
011	Chinese restaurant	24 min	5,475
012	School playground	17 min 7 sec	3,612
013	Western restaurant	36 min	4,833
014	Car of HKC	19 min 6 sec	3,848
015	Office of HKC	45 min	8,962
016	Office of HKC	37 min 31 sec	6,937
017	Home of NES	35 min 34 sec	8,827
018	Office of HKC	20 min 38 sec	4,324
019	Home of HKC	11 min 34 sec	2,438
020	McDonald's restaurant	17 min 19 sec	2,351
021	Japanese restaurant	22 min 24 sec	3,945
022	Office of HKC	21 min	3,852
023	Chinese restaurant	82 min	9,928
024	Restaurant in a university	27 min	2,844
025	Restaurant in a university	20 min	3,997
Total		**13 hours**	**122,768**

equipment and a couple of mini-discs and then told how to operate the equipment. The participants were instructed to place the mini-disc recorder and the microphone in the immediate vicinity. The physical contexts in which the conversations were recorded included private homes and places where groups of HKC and NES would be expected to gather, such as social areas in the workplace, restaurants, cafeterias, sandwich shops and exclusive clubs in Hong Kong.

The kinesic aspects of conversation are not available since the data was based on audio recordings only. This has, to a certain extent, limited the kinds of description which are possible by excluding non-verbal behaviour such as direction of eye gaze, gesture, posture of the participants, and the like. However, filming of the participants would have been required if the kinesics of the conversational behaviour had been examined. This could not have been done in this study since the conversations had not been conducted in a studio setting with technical set-up and assistance. Employment of a video camera would have been incongruent with the procedures involved in collecting naturally occurring data for this study.

Table 3.4. Relative number of words spoken by HKC and NES

Code	Gender of speaker	Words spoken by HKC		Words spoken by NES	
		Tokens	%	Tokens	%
001	1m 1M *	6,842	67.5	3,294	32.5
002	1f 1M	1,039	52.7	934	47.3
003	1m 1M	1,064	39.4	1,546	60.6
004	1f 1M	1,707	33.6	2,963	66.4
005	1f 1M	2,088	56.7	1,597	43.3
006	1f 1F	2,121	51.7	1,979	48.3
007	1f 1M	896	41	1,287	59
008	1m 1M	1,017	47.7	1,122	52.3
009	1f 1F	2,747	51	2,627	49
010	1m 1M	5,121	52.7	4,604	47.3
011	1m 1M	2,888	52.7	2,587	47.3
012	1m 1F	946	26.2	2,666	73.8
013	1f 1M	2,113	43.7	2,720	56.3
014	1f 1F	1,707	44.4	2,141	55.6
015	1f 1M	3,703	41.3	5,259	58.7
016	1f 1M	2,025	29.2	4,912	70.8
017	1f 1M	5,114	58	3,713	42
018	1f 1M	2,336	54	1,988	46
019	1m 1M	1,293	58.2	1,145	41.8
020	1m 1M	839	35.7	1,512	64.3
021	1f 1F	2,385	60.5	1,560	39.5
022	1f 1F	1,990	51.7	1,862	48.3
023	1f 1M	4,863	49	5,065	51
024	1f 1M	1,486	52.3	1,358	47.7
025	1f 1M	1,521	38.1	2,476	61.9
Total		**59,851**		**62,917**	

* "M" and "m" are short for male; "F" and "f" for female. Upper case refers to native speakers of English and lower case refers to Hong Kong Chinese.

The HKC-NES intercultural conversations

The intercultural conversations consisted of 25 dyadic intercultural conversations, amounting to thirteen hours of data, and all the data had been transcribed verbatim. No names were transcribed in order to provide the participants and others with a degree of anonymity. The transcripts of the conversation recordings totalled at least 122,000 running words. Table 3.3 provides information of each of the recordings in terms of the place of recording, the duration of conversation and the number of words.

Table 3.4 compares the relative number of words spoken by HKC and NES. The number of words spoken by HKC is very close to that by NES: HKC (59,851) and NES (62,917). It is important to note that, in terms of amount of talk, there is no obvious pattern of dominance of NES over HKC or vice versa. Of the 25 conversations, HKC speak more than 50% in 13 conversations, and NES speak more than 50 % in 12 conversations.

The following five chapters describe and analyze each of the conversational features investigated in this study, namely preference organization in the form of disagreements (Chapter 4), compliments and compliment responses (Chapter 5), simultaneous talk (Chapter 6), discourse topic management (Chapter 7) and discourse information structure (Chapter 8).

Note

1. Scollon and Scollon (1995: 5) provide a list 'professional communicators' and these are accountant, account executive, assistant auditor, assistant manager, copywriter, designer, editor, executive, executive secretary, manager, marketing executive, media executive, teachers (at all levels), merchandiser officer, receptionist, reporter, sales executive, senior administrative assistant, senior clerk, senior engineer, tour guide, trainee manager, trainee programmer, and translator.

CHAPTER 4

Preference organization

Introduction

This chapter on preference organization presents findings on the way HKC and NES manage disagreement, realized both in the structure of the disagreement and the politeness strategies, or redressive language employed to present disagreements. Compared to NES, HKC were predicted to have communicative styles that are compromising, avoiding and accommodating, and not confrontational, all of which aim to prevent either party from suffering a loss of face. It was hypothesized that HKC are inclined to disagree with their NES interlocutors less often. When HKC disagree with NES, they will avoid making direct, blunt disagreements and will use a greater amount of redressive language. Consequently, three hypotheses were tested:

1. HKC will disagree with NES less frequently than the other way round, that is, NES disagreeing with HKC.
2. HKC, compared to their NES interlocutors, will use fewer bald-on-record strategies in their disagreements.
3. HKC, compared to their NES interlocutors, will use more redressive language in their disagreements.

Analysis of disagreements in the intercultural conversations

The 25 intercultual conversations were examined to identify instances of disagreements by HKC and NES. Each instance of disagreement was classified according to whether it is a bald-on-record disagreement without any use of redressive language, or whether it is presented with the use of redressive language. Extracts 1–4 below exemplify each type of disagreement examined in this study, as follows:

Extract 1: HKC's bald-on-record disagreement
Extract 2: HKC's disagreement with redressive language
Extract 3: NS's bald-on-record disagreement
Extract 4: NS's disagreement with redressive language

The participants in Extract 1 were colleagues and the conversation took place in a Chinese restaurant. A popular topic in conversations in Hong Kong is the price of residential property which is either soaring or plunging in dramatic fashion. As it happens in Extract 1, the price of residential property is a serious topic for the HKC where prices are discussed with perhaps a greater expectation of precision and accuracy than might be the case in other cultures. The speakers are discussing the prices at a housing development where the NES is currently completing the purchase of a flat.

(1) 023
a: female Hong Kong Chinese B: male British
1080. a: [what's the price that you bought per
1081. per square [per per
1082. B: [four square feet about four thousand
1083. eight four thousand nine nearly four nine
1084. a: four nine per square feet you mean
1085. B: yea
1086. a: but the price now is more than five thousand five
1087. thousand per square feet
1088. B: well that's the average [I think it depends what
1089. a: [yea
1090. direction you're facing

On lines 1080–81, the HKC asks what the NES is paying *per square feet* (it is not considered taboo in Hong Kong culture to ask directly and precisely what someone is paying for a property). On lines 1082–1083, the NES responds with *four about four thousand eight four thousand nine nearly four nine.* The HKC confirms the NES's meaning (line 1084), and then baldly on record disagrees with the figures given by the NES, saying that this cannot be correct because *the price now is more than five thousand five thousand per square feet* (lines 1086–1087). This utterance by the HKC is interesting in two ways. First, it is the NES who is currently purchasing a flat and yet the HKC confidently and directly disagrees with his approximations as to the current purchasing price of flats at this particular housing development. Second, it becomes clear that the HKC has a very good grasp of the prices as the NES is seen to concede to her figures and saves his own face by talking about average prices, the direction the flat faces, and so on.

The HKC's bald-on-record disagreement could be face-threatening to the NES in two ways. First, as it is the NES who is buying the flat, openly disagreeing with him implies that he does not know what he is talking about, and also implies that the HKC is more up-to-date and knowledgeable about flat prices at the housing development. Second, the fact that the NES concedes to the HKC's figures, saying that the price the HKC is quoting is 'the average' and then justifies the price he is paying. To do so, he is put himself into the situation where he has to explain that the flat he is buying does not fall within the upper price range of the better flats at this particular housing development with superior locations and views.

The cultural attribute being examined here is that the Chinese are expected to stress cooperation, face-balance and harmony, and so are inclined not to disagree; and when disagreeing, they will use redressive language. The discussion so far has shown the complex interplay between the local and the wider context of interaction. Analysis of the situated discourse has shown that the conversational behaviour of the HKC, which does not conform to the expected cultural attribute, is very likely due to the nature and proposition of the topic at hand. Elsewhere in the conversation, it is clear that flat prices are something that the HKC has been monitoring over the past few years, as in 1997 she and her then fiancé bought a flat in Yuen Long, the price of which has since dropped 30%. This can explain why she is so well-informed and feels so strongly about the topic.

In Extract 2, the participants were colleagues working in the Hong Kong Police Force. They were having a conversation in an office in a police station. The NES has just described to the HKC an unpleasant experience of having seafood in a restaurant on an outlying island in Hong Kong.

(2)	015	
	B:	male British a: female Hong Kong Chinese
327.	B:	erm (.) I I but there is a general I love seafood
328.		especially when it's done with all these garlics and
329.		and spices that that you can put on them (.) but
330.		[I did get er but I did I did
331.	a:	[oh you spoil (.) I've been you spoil the seafood you
332.		shouldn't [put so many seasonings ((laugh))
333.	B:	[yea ((laugh))
334.	B:	yea (.) well you know the the (pause) a popular food
335.		in U.K. it's not actually er seafood it's actually er
336.		er it's actually a slug that's in the garden it's
337.		called l'escargot which is actually a snail
338.	a:	mhmm

The topic is then shifted to the NES saying how much he enjoys seafood *especially when it's done with all these garlics and spices.* The HKC disagrees that this is the best way to prepare seafood. Her disagreement is *you shouldn't put so many seasonings* (lines 331–332), prefaced by a reason *you spoil the seafood* (line 331). Giving reasons is a positive politeness strategy, as "the H is thereby led to see the reasonableness of S's FTA" (Brown and Levinson 1987: 128). The HKC's word 'seasonings' corresponds to the NES's 'garlics and spices'. The HKC is claiming that far from enhancing the taste, adding so many seasonings actually spoils it. In Chinese culture, where culinary expertise is widely claimed and appreciated, food is a topic which is frequently the source of disagreement, criticism or advice. Here we see the meeting of two different eating cultures — a British native speaker who happily drowns any dish with spices and seasonings and a HKC who views such behaviour as spoiling the food and who is not reluctant to point this out.

In Extract 3, the participants were friends and were having a conversation in the NES's flat. Before the Extract begins, the NES has said that he paid a visit to Guangzhou in China fifteen years ago but since then he has not been to China.

(3) 017

a: female Hong Kong Chinese B: male British

271.	B:	[I haven't been since
272.	a:	never been to [China
273.	B:	[(inaudible) because (.) the problem is
274.		(.) I mean this is where I think the the Hong Kong
275.		tourist board is going wrong because they should be
276.		(.) looking at Hong Kong as a gateway for China (.)
277.		they could make visa applications a lot easier get
278.		the visa er at the border which we can't do (.) [if I
279.	a:	[mm
280.		want to go to to China I've got to go to Chi- China
281.		Travel Agency with my passport (.) I've got to pay
282.		three hundred dollars I've got to wait (pause) five
283.		days I think (.) [five working days
284.	a:	[no you can apply for a visa at the
285.		border I think
286.	B:	no
287.	a:	no [no you must apply the visa [beforehand
288.	B:	[no [yea I've got to go
289.		for a visa beforehand I've got to wait five days I've
290.		got to go back to the China Travel Agency collect my
291.		passport five [days later
292.	a:	[oh that's why [you don't you don't go

The NES is complaining about the logistical problems concerning travelling into Mainland China from Hong Kong. On lines 279–283, the NES is explaining that it takes five working days to get an entry visa. The HKC disagrees and states that it is possible to get a visa at the border (i.e. there and then without a five day wait) (lines 284–285) although this is mitigated with a hedge *I think* (line 285). The NES is adamant, however, and disagrees baldly on record with a direct and blunt *no* (line 286). The HKC then backs away from her prior assertion and paraphrases what the NES has said previously (*no [no you must apply the visa [beforehand*, line 287). As the HKC is speaking, the NES again says *no* (line 288) overlapping with the HKC and then emphatically repeats the procedure that has to be gone through to acquire an entry visa into mainland China (lines 288–291).

The speakers in Extract 4 were colleagues working in a hospital. The conversation took place in the car of the HKC who was giving the NES a lift home. The NES tells the HKC that she will be going to the Christmas party in her husband's office in Sydney in Australia.

(4) 014
A: female Scottish   a: female Hong Kong Chinese
339. a: [are you taking the children with you
340. A: I'm taking O_
341. a: uh huh
342. A: I'm not taking the other two
343. a: oh he is [lucky
344. A: [((clear throat)) he is lucky
345. a: he is always lucky
346. A: oh no that's not true because I when I went back to
347. England when my poor mom was ill (.) I took E_ (.)
348. and (.) we were there for a week she was thoroughly
349. spoilt (.) so it's O_'s turn this time (.) poor a
350. little H_ he doesn't just get a look in
351. a: he is too young
352. A: he is too young he wouldn't really (.) appreciate it
353. and he would be a nuisance (.) he's my sweetex and I
354. love him

The participants in this extract are discussing the NES's impending overseas trip, and on line 339, the HKC asks if the NES is taking her children with her. The NES responds that she is only taking one of her three children and the HKC states that the child going on the trip *is lucky* (line 343). The NES agrees with the HKC that the child is lucky (line 344). The HKC then asserts that the child going on the trip is *always lucky* (line 345). The implication that this particular child is consistently treated better than his siblings is challenged by the NES, who starts by directly saying *oh no that's not true* (line 346), and then mitigates this with reasons and examples to illustrate her evenhanded parenting (lines 346–350). It would appear that the HKC has backed off from her earlier assertion, when her friend strenuously claims to the contrary. The HKC offers a reason (*he's too young*, line 351), which the

NES accepts and incorporates into her utterance to justify not taking one of the children on the trip (lines 352–354).

Table 4.1 presents the quantitative findings concerning HKC and NES's disagreements in the 25 intercultural conversations. The disagreements are classified into bald-on-record disagreements and disagreements with redressive language.

Table 4.1. Disagreements by HKC and NES

Strategies	Hong Kong Chinese		Native Speakers	
	Tokens	%	Tokens	%
Bald-on-record	10	11.1	23	27.3
Use of redressive language	80	88.9	63	72.7
Total	90	100.0	84	100.0

Contrary to expectations, HKC actually disagree slightly more than NES do — 90 instances for HKC and 84 for NES. Hypothesis 1, which predicted that HKC will disagree less often than NES is therefore not supported. Both Hypotheses 2 and 3 are, nevertheless, confirmed, as HKC use fewer bald-on-record strategies (11.1%) and more redressive language (88.9%) in their disagreements, compared to NES. For NES, bald-on-record disagreements constitute 27.3% and disagreements with redressive language 72.7% of the total disagreements. The quantitative findings indicate that the HKC participants in this study are not at all shy to disagree with their NES interlocutors. But when they disagree, they pay greater concern to address the face-want of both themselves and their NES addressees by using redressive language and mitigating devices. This finding converges with the Chinese conception of "face-balance" which means giving others' face simultaneously enhances one's own face and depriving others' face simultaneously damages one's face (Zhang 1995: 85).

The importance of understanding the way a disagreement is produced in its immediate context of situation is essential. In real-life communication, especially in intercultural conversations, every single instance of disagreement is a unique occurrence. The acts of disagreement are "pragmatically founded in the social set-up of the language users" (Mey 2001: 279). Every act of disagreement is situated in both its linguistic and its intercultural context. It provides rich information that throws light on the complex interrelationships and interaction among various linguistic, social and cultural variables.

The four most extended extracts in the intercultural conversations which contain instances of disagreements will be discussed. The speakers in each of these extracts have been found to collaboratively develop a topic framework, in the course of which multiple instances of disagreements occur. Extracts 5 and 6 illustrate disagreements respectively given by a HKC and a NES. Extracts 7 and 8 show disagreements given by both speakers.

In Extract 5, the female NES was the English private tutor to the two daughters of the female HKC. The women had become friends, and usually had a chat over tea and biscuits after the lesson. When the extract begins, the NES woman initiates a topic relating to a new theory about teaching children.

(5) 009
A: female Irish a: female Hong Kong Chinese
112. A: I read an article in the newspaper when I was in the
113. States about teaching erm children and it mentions
114. the in the erm s- the University of California had a
115. new theory about teaching children and it said that
116. you must start from a very early age from two or
117. three [yea teaching children and [they said
118. a: [((laugh)) [so this interests
119. you very much you are going to have a baby ((laugh))
120. A: [that's right (.) yes and it it said er you know
121. a: [((laugh)) eh
122. starting erm starting that early with the children
123. (.) erm is er very er is a great advantage for them
124. later in life for learning do you think this is true
125. a: I totally believe that it is true and in fact er two
126. or three er is already too late
127. A: that's what they [what they said actually they said
128. a: [((laugh))
129. it starts
130. a: because the er the theory about the early childhood
131. learning as er actually suggest that the child er
132. baby starts learning er right from the beginning when
133. it is born yea yea
134. A: that's right it said one of the professors er what
135. the very minute the baby was born he started hand
136. signals and signs [and waving and (.) he felt that
137. a: [yea yea yea
138. the baby was learning from the very mo- moment it was
139. born
140. a: uh huh uh huh uh huh [yea
141. A: [and in fact some people
142. believe that they play music to the baby when it's

143.		still in the womb
144.	a:	((laugh)) yea yea
145.	A:	do you think this is [going a bit too far
146.	a:	[this this
147.	a:	this this er I mm yea I do have some doubts about
148.		this ((laugh))
149.	A:	yea yea
150.	a:	yea in in Chinese we have a similar saying [huh huh
151.	A:	[er
152.		we we say er yea teach yes teach your baby when it's
153.		still in the womb but er [this I don't know [but
154.	A:	[yea [yea
155.		perhaps it's sort of affecting the mother's er you
156.		know the mood if you listen to music [you will keep
157.	A:	[yes
158.		yourself happy all the time then the mother is in a
159.		better [mood and that is good for the ba[by yes
160.	A:	[mood [baby yes er
161.		[so it's more relax[ing and you think it's something
162.	a:	[but [yea yea
163.		to do more with er
164.	a:	I think it's something more like that rather than
165.		really the the edu[cating or the tea[ching and the
166.	A:	[yea yea [yea
167.		learning [the er yea (.) it seems [but I don't
168.	A:	[yea [to be yea
169.		know it still needs to be researched ((laugh))
170.	A:	yeah that's right it's it seems to me like it's going
171.		a little bit too far
172.	a:	yea ((laugh))

Extract 5 demonstrates both speech acts of agreement and disagreement in a context that involves more than two parties, and hence entails complex power relationships and social distance among the different parties. Apart from the HKC and the NES who are conversing with each other, there are two other parties, namely *one of the professors* (line 134) and *some people* (line 141), as quoted by the NES. The NES reports theories pronounced by a professor about the learning capacities of babies and educating fetuses (*one of the professors er what they very minute the baby was born he started hand signals and signs and waving and (.) he felt that the baby was learning from the very mo- moment it was born*, lines 134–139). The

NES continues reporting some people's practices, saying *and in fact some people believe that they play music to the baby when it's still in the womb* (lines 141–143).

Professors are supposed to have "expert power" (Thomas 1995: 127), that is "some special knowledge or expertise that other person needs". In her utterance, the NES does not state the racial and cultural backgrounds of the professor and those people. However, judging from the fact that the HKC later on compares what these people say with a Chinese saying (lines 151–153), the tacit understanding between the speakers seems to be that these people are non-Chinese, and very likely Westerners whose work the NES has read.

The NES, after her quotations, asks the HKC *do you think this is [going a bit too far* (line 145), to which the HKC responds by saying *this this er I mm yea I do have some doubts about this ((laugh))* (lines 147–148). In her response, the HKC is responding to the NES obviously, but on a different level she is also giving her response to the theories proclaimed by experts and people out there. The HKC's response is in fact a disagreement with the theory proposed by the professor. The disagreement is marked by false starts, verbal fillers, hesitations and reformulations, which may indicate that she is busy planning what to say as she goes along. Some kind of thinking aloud process is seen to be at work.

The argument for the latter interpretation is that the HKC is aware that what she is going to say contradicts the expert's views and beliefs, and so her hesitance indicates that it is difficult for her to perform the action of disagreeing with the expert. It is also probably because when the NES cites the theory, the HKC is not sure whether or not the NES shares the expert's view. If the NES did, it would be face-threatening.

The HKC's disagreement *this this er I mm yea I do have some doubts about this* (lines 147–148) is quintessential of a typical dispreferred response. The response sounds like an effort to minimize imposition, i.e. her 'doubts' about Western professors' views, as compared to 'I don't agree with this' or 'I disagree with this', either of which would have been a bald-on-record disagreement. She also mitigates her 'doubts' (disagreement) by using 'some'. The imposition in the HKC's utterance is her action of disagreeing with the expert's view and some people's practices. Both hedging and minimizing imposition are examples of redressive action of negative politeness (Brown and Levinson 1987). Negative politeness strategies are likely to be employed when referring to someone who has power, and in this context "expert power" (Thomas 1995: 127–128), over them than when they are referring to equals or individuals over whom they have power (Brown and Levinson 1987; Scollon and Scollon 1995).

What is interesting is the way in which the HKC further contributes to the topic by offering to her NES friend, in a reciprocal way, what her culture says about the topic — *yea in in Chinese we have a similar saying [huh huh we we say er yea teach yes teach your baby when it's still in the womb* (lines 150–153). By using *a similar saying*, the HKC is trying to claim "common ground" with the Western expert in order to show that the speaker and the addressee "both belong to some set of persons who share specific wants, including goals and values" (Brown and Levinson 1987: 103). Here, by drawing a parallel between what the Western expert says and what the Chinese say, the HKC, as part of the Chinese group, claims a common perspective with the Western group. By doing so, the HKC is effectively trying to minimize the face-threatening effect caused by her disagreement with the view of the Western expert.

The HKC goes on giving a more sophisticated interpretation of the benefits of music — *but er [this I don't know [but perhaps it's sort of affecting the mother's er you know the mood if you listen to music [you will keep yourself happy all the time then the mother is er in a better [mood and that is good for the ba[by yes* (lines 141–147). Giving a reason is a positive politeness strategy (Brown and Levinson 1987), but the HKC quite heavily hedges her reasoning (*but er [this I don't know [but perhaps it's sort of*, line 140) which may indicate that she is cautious about imposing her reason on her NES interlocutor. The HKC uses 'I don't know' to indicate her tentative position. As observed by Tsui (1994), 'I don't know' can be used to avoid commitment.

In fact, the NES has followed the reasoning offered by the HKC and comprehended the reason. This is evident in her interpretive statement *[so it's more relax[ing*, and checking with the HKC about her interpretation *and you think it's something to do more with er* (line 148). Not waiting until the NES has finished her turn, the HKC introduces simultaneous talk and agrees with the NES 's interpretation — *I think it's something more like that rather than really the the edu[cating or the tea[ching and the learning [the er yea (.) it seems [but I don't know it still needs to be researched ((laugh))* (lines 150–154). The HKC also reiterates what it is that she disagrees with, but tries to minimize imposing her view on the NES, by saying *[but I don't know it still needs to be researched.* This second instance of 'I don't know' functions to avoid committing oneself to a position (Tsui 1991b: 612).

The NES agrees with the HKC, saying *yeah that's right it's it seems to me like it's going a little bit too far* (line 155). Her utterance, which echoes her initial question put to the HKC *do you think this is [going a bit too far* (line 135) is interesting, as the NES neither gives her view nor assessment relating to Western experts on child care and education, but rather solicits the HKC's view. This shows the NES explicitly selecting the HKC to contribute towards topic development, particularly towards developing a topic that potentially lends itself to the sharing and exchange of cultural ideologies and beliefs.

Below the sequential structure of the HKC's disagreement (lines 137–154) is analyzed:

1. State disagreement with Western theories prefaced by false starts, verbal fillers, hesitations and reformulations.
2. Offer a similar Chinese saying.
3. Hedge the certainty she expressed regarding Western theories and the Chinese saying.
4. Give reasons to justify her disagreement.

To sum up, the HKC's disagreement with Western theories, and similarly with the Chinese theories later on, regarding educating babies is heavily redressed. No bald-on record strategy is used. The redress action includes assuming the addressee's knowledge regarding the referent for 'this' (line 137); asserting reciprocity when she draws a parallel with theories in the West in order to build rapport and involvement with the NES (*in Chinese*, line 139); claiming common ground (*a similar saying*, line 139); giving reason regarding the function of music in order to establish common ground with the NS; use of hedging to mitigate imposition; stating the FTA as a general rule; and two instances of avoiding committing oneself to a position. 'I don't know' can be said to be further evidence that the HKC is concerned about face management in this particular context of intercultural conversation. As knowledge is one aspect of power, such strategy use does not only equalize the power differential between herself and Western experts, but also addresses interpersonal relations with the NES interlocutor. By making herself sound less like an expert, the HKC can be seen as more interested in establishing solidarity and involvement with her NES interlocutor.

In order to contrast the way HKC and NES manage disagreement, Extract 6 below shows an explicit disagreement given by the NES. The two speakers were colleagues teaching in a secondary school: the female NES teaching English and the male HKC Mathematics. In Extract 6, they are exchanging opinions about the sixth-form students they teach.

(6) 012
b: male Hong Kong Chinese A: female British
7. b: oh so you like the sixth forms very much
8. A: yeah I think it's er a little bit more demanding so
9. you enjoy it more and [their English is better of
10. b: [mhmm
11. course
12. b: yes
13. A: I think there's a good rapport as well cos you can
14. be you can have fun it's humorous and they can talk
15. to you whereas the other forms I think are a little

16. bit restricted because of their English so [it takes
17. b: [mhmm
18. longer to get to know them [I mean that's one of the
19. b: [mhmm
20. problems
21. b: I teach half the classes but I found they er some of
22. them are very passive (.) but they are very attentive
23. in class
24. A: er I don't think they're passive erm maybe some of
25. the girls but maybe that's the subject
26. [because I mean for you it's very hard to have them
27. b: [yes mm hmm yea ((laugh))
28. active and running round the classroom but I mean for
29. me that's part of the teaching process yeah I
30. encourage them to be active and to stand up move
31. around whereas for you that wouldn't work [would it
32. b: [yes sure
33. it would be chaos [you know so I think that's a good
34. b: [mhmm
35. aspect for me about being here is that I can let them
36. relax so they probably enjoy it more [than they are
37. b: [mhmm
38. sitting doing Maths
39. b: but during this this past week many of my students
40. in the secondary six class they're going to do some
41. activities [so some

The HKC expresses his opinion that some of the F. 6 students are passive, though attentive, in his Maths class (lines 19–21), which is very different from their attitudes and behaviours in the English class taught by the NES. The NES disagrees with him directly and explicitly, though with a marker of hesitation 'er' (*er I don't think they're passive*, line 22). After giving a verbal filler (*erm*), the NES continues and says *maybe some of the girls* (lines 22–23). Tentativeness is hence expressed through a hedge 'maybe' and changing 'they' to 'some of the girls'. The tentativeness is qualifying, or softening her disagreement with the HKC that some of the girls may be passive. In this way, modifying the bald-on-record disagreement shows that the NES is trying to minimize the imposition; in other words, the face-threatening effect of her disagreement with her HKC colleague.

The NES continues her turn, trying to account for the different behaviours of those students in her class and in the HKC's Mathematics class. Her reason focuses on conveying the message that it is *the subject* and *the teaching process*, rather than the teacher that have caused the differences. Encouraging students to be *active and to stand up move around* is *part of the teaching process* of her English lessons. In the case of the HKC, *it's very hard to have them active and running around the classroom* and *that wouldn't work ... it would be chaos* (lines 24–31). The NES works at face management, and specifically, she is trying to minimize the face-threatening effect by means of explicitly attributing some students' passiveness to the nature of the subjects and the teaching process, by showing understanding of the situation that is inherent in the subject that the HKC teaches, and by explicitly comparing the different kinds of class activities that are logistically permitted and academically effective in the HKC's Maths class and in her English class respectively. Giving reasons in this context refers to the NES's accounting for the passiveness of some students in the HKC's lessons.

The NES takes care to hedge her utterances to increase the tentativeness of her views and opinions, in order not to impede on the HKC. The strategies employed show that she is careful to avoid claiming credit for the relatively active classroom behaviour of her students. At the same time, she attributes student passiveness to the nature of the subject rather than the teaching method of the HKC.

During the course of the NES's disagreement, the HKC gives a number of back-channel responses (*mhmm, yes mm hmm yea*). At one point, he says *[yes sure* (line 30), during the NES 's turn to show agreement with her view. "Back-channelling" (Yngve 1970; Duncan and Fiske 1977) is considered to be supportive feedback used by hearers as an indication of their attention, interest and/or understanding. Schegloff (1982) examines the employment by hearers of vocalizations such as 'uh huh', 'yea' and so on, while an utterance is being produced. Schegloff (1982) offers an additional explanation which is their employment as "continuers". The use of "continuers" serves to demonstrate that the hearer recognizes an extended unit of talk is underway and indicates his or her support and compliance. The back-channelling given by the HKC seems to serve all of these functions. In other words, his back-channelling serves as active support for the NES to proceed, and signals that he remains a willing participant in the conversation.

By way of summing up, the NES's disagreement with the HKC consists of one bald-on-record strategy and a lot of face-redressive strategies. As noted by Levinson (1983), a dispreferred second pair part is marked and made structurally complex, and may be marked by a variety of features such as delay, an explanation as to why the preferred second pair part cannot be performed, and preface markers. The sequential structure of the NES's disagreement as a dispreferred response is, therefore, atypical, in the sense that the disagreement is not pushed back into the turn. Nevertheless, the disagreement bears some characteristics of a typical dispreferred response, and that is, hedging and giving reasons or explanations. Giving reasons, which constitutes an attempt to convey that S and H are cooperators, clearly indicates the NES's effort in managing relationships with the HKC, by means of which shared meaning is created.

Below Extract 7 illustrates an interactive, collaborative process of sharing, negotiating and constructing experiences and ideologies, which involves many instances of disagreements and agreements. Both speakers were police officers of the Hong Kong Police Force. In the conversation, the female HKC is describing to the male NES a charity walk, organized by the Community Chest. The Police Force is going to ensure safety along the route on that day. On the previous Sunday, the HKC and her colleagues went to check out the route.

(7)	018	
a:	female Hong Kong Chinese B: male British	
78.	a:	no it start from (.) the toll (.) the toll
79.	B:	toll booth
80.	a:	the toll booth er of route three
81.	B:	yea
82.	a:	and then it's about one point two kilometre before
83.		you reach the erm (.) the tunnel [and then for the
84.	B:	[yea
85.		tunnel itself it's about four kilometre
86.	B:	and you (.) you're walking through the tunnel
87.	a:	we didn't we didn't we [just use our er our ima-
88.	B:	[yea
89.	B:	imagination
90.	a:	yea [we just pretend
91.	B:	[the the the the actual walk will go through the
92.		tunnel
93.	a:	right ye [a
94.	B:	[that will be very very boring
95.	a:	right exactly [and
96.	B:	[four kilometres (.) with nothing to
97.		look at
98.	a:	right [((laugh))
99.	B:	[er I don't envy you if you're going on the
100.		walk yourself
101.	a:	but [if
102.	B:	[very uninteresting
103.	a:	((laugh)) I totally agree and then after the walk I
104.		mean after the tunnel it it would it becomes quite
105.		interesting (.) because it will be the Tsing Gu

106. Bridge (.) and a lot of you know [to see
107. B: [oh you're going
108. that way through
109. a: yea from Yuen Long out to er Tsing Yi
110. B: uh huh
111. a: so it's er it's actually quite a nice walk half and
112. half [the first bit is nice
113. B: [where will you you'll miss so much of Tai Tam
114. Country Park
115. a: ahh ((laugh)) well there is no comparison between the
116. two I think but er (.) anyway I think er people are
117. are are really upset with er so many Walk for Million
118. these days (.) so last Sunday it was a very very er
119. (pause) boring one
120. B: I I always find that to be er rather sterile (.)
121. [to be (.) just walking along the road and somebody
122. a: [mmhm
123. (.)paying me ridiculous amounts of money per step
124. taken or [per mile walked or per kilometre walked erm
125. a: [right
126. (.) I always feel that the energy [could be so much
127. a: [mhmm
128. better harnessed to do something more positive
129. a: oh it is positive I mean by doing some sort of
130. charity walk and (.) when you walk you feel like er
131. somebody is sponsoring you and then somebody will be
132. er benefited in the long run in due course
133. B: yea
134. a: it would be nice but er (.) I'll I'll rather they
135. change the format these days because somany Walk
136. for Million now
137. B: I I just wish the effort which people are putting in
138. be more focused
139. a: uhmm
140. B: I I'd rather (.) be (.) going out into a country park
141. and planting trees spend the day [working to improve
142. a: [uh huh
143. a trail possibly er (.) doing some work on a trail
144. [so that there would be something [permanent to show
145. a: [right [I see I see I see
146. that this particular section of a (.) country park

147.	a:	your point
148.		road or track [is maintained by the efforts of
149.	a:	[it's my effort mm
150.		volunteers [who are being (.) also collecting money
151.	a:	[right yea
152.		for the amount of effort they put in [for the for the
153.	a:	[yea
154.		hours that they've worked on it and [this sort of
155.	a:	[yea yea yea it
156.		thing they would be
157.	a:	would be a good idea actually
158.	B:	to my mind there there'd be more benefit
159.	a:	uh huh
160.	B:	then again mean the administration would be
161.		phenomenally difficult
162.	a:	it's true but it depends whether there are people
163.		interested in doing all these (.) always is er you
164.		need somebody to do the back-up job behind (.) before
165.		things can be done (.) perfectly well
166.	B:	yes [well
167.	a:	[so wo- well it's a good idea actually I think
168.		you can write to the Community Chest (.) and make up
169.		your suggestion (.) and see maybe you'll become the
170.		first one who do this [((laugh))
171.	B:	[((laugh)) they'll make me run
172.		it if I do that
173.	a:	uh huh
174.		(pause)

The NES very explicitly expresses his disapproval of walking in a tunnel as a form of charity walk by saying *[that will be very very boring* (line 94), *[four kilometres (.) with nothing to look at* (lines 96–97), *[er I don't envy you if you're going on the walk yourself* (lines 99–100), and *[very uninteresting* (line 102). Note that his disapproval is directed at charity walks rather than his HKC interlocutor, and so in theory it does not constitute an FTA aimed at her. However, as the object of disapproval is derived from the topic initiated by the HKC as well as arranged by the department to which she belongs, the NES's criticism indirectly constitutes an FTA addressed to the HKC. The few utterances of the NES are analyzed below.

In his disapproval, the expression the NES uses is face-threatening. Much more than stating the FTA with a bald-on-record strategy, namely with no redressive action, the NES has actually used an intensifier (*very*), repetition of the intensifier (*very very*), a negative word (*nothing*) and a negative prefix (*un-*) to strengthen the degree of his disapproval. The NES holds on to his turn and persists in finishing his expression of disapproval, despite the HKC's attempts to cut in on his turn. In lines 99–100, the NES says *er I don't envy you if you're going on the walk yourself*, which is used to distance the HKC from the charity walk, meaning that it is not the HKC's doing, and thereby reduces the face-threatening effect.

In response to the NES's disapproval of the walk, realized in *that will be very very boring, four kilometers (.) with nothing to look at,* and *very uninteresting,* the HKC appears to agree with these criticisms, as reflected in her responses in the sequence *right exactly and* (line 95), *right ((laugh))* (line 98), and an exaggerated agreement *I totally agree* (line 103). However, a close analysis shows that the HKC actually disagrees with her NES colleague. It is quite difficult to categorize *right exactly* and *right.* If the HKC's disagreement actually starts here, these expressions would become token agreements. A "token agreement" functions to pretend to agree or to hide disagreement (Brown and Levinson 1987: 113–114). The analysis has adopted this view and considers these expressions ('right exactly', 'right') as signs of a dispreferred response. Disagreement is also signalled in *but if ((laugh)) I totally agree* (lines 101 and 103), followed by a conjunction 'and' that is likely to carry an adversative function (McCarthy 1991) in *and then after the walk I mean after the tunnel it it would it becomes quite interesting (.) because it will be the Tsing Gu Bridge (.) and a lot of you know [to see* (lines 103–106).

This part of the utterance shows the HKC trying to offer more information about the route of the charity walk, so as to contradict the NES's critical view. Her *quite interesting* (lines 104–105), which acts as a hedged contradiction to her colleague's *very uninteresting* in a previous turn, is cleverly used to establish a link and continuity as well as to show disagreement. Her use of *interesting,* the exact opposite of the NES's *uninteresting* serves to indicate that the HKC is actually taking a contrary position despite her apparent strong agreement at the beginning. The HKC has also used hedging (*quite*), a negative politeness strategy, in her disagreement.

In lines 107–108, the NES is unhappy about the route for another reason, asking *[oh you're going that way through.* The HKC explains that the second part of the route, which is from Yuen Long heading towards Tsing Yi, is a nice walk. The NES disagrees with her, commenting that it means that the walkers will miss so much of Tai Tam Country Park. The NES's disagreement *[where will you you'll miss so much of Tai Tam Country Park* (lines 113–114) is directed at the HKC's view on the second part of the route.

In response to the NES's comment, the HKC gives a rebuttal, which is a disagreement. Her disagreement starts with *ahh,* followed by laughter: *well there is no comparison between the two I think* (lines 115–116). Note that 'well', as a discourse marker, bears the "conventional meaning that what follows is a dispreferred contribution (i.e. not quite what the hearer was hoping for)" (Grundy 1995: 208). In this utterance, the HKC expresses her view that the route of this particular charity walk can by no means be compared to the one that is implied by the NES (i.e. the one that would have the view of Tai Tam Country Park). Here, rather than explicitly and directly disagreeing with the NES, the HKC's disagreement is prefaced with a marker of dispreferred response, and is hedged, showing that she takes trouble to redress her FTA in order to preserve the NES's face. Her words *between the two* serve to show that she presumes that her colleague has shared knowledge with her about what 'the two' refers to.

It is interesting to note that right after her disagreement, the HKC changes the topic to commenting on how people in general feel about charity walks these days, and how she feels about last Sunday in particular (*but er (.) anyway I think er people are are are really upset with er so many Walk for Million these days (.) so last Sunday it was a very very er (pause) boring one*, lines 116–119) in order to indicate agreement with the NES's criticism. The HKC is changing topic from something that both of them disagree with to something that they agree with. This can be seen as a strategy of disagreement avoidance.

As the conversation unfolds, the NES extends support to and agreement with the HKC. He further criticizes the charity walk itself as a form of fund-raising activity, saying *I I always find that to be er rather sterile (.) [to be (.) just walking along the road and somebody (.) paying me ridiculous amounts of money per step taken or [per mile walked or per kilometre walked erm (.) I always feel that the energy [could be so much better harnessed to do something more positive* (lines 120–128).

In response, the HKC offers her disagreement *oh it is positive I mean by doing some sort of charity walk and (.) when you walk you feel like er somebody is sponsoring you and then somebody will be er benefited in the long run in due course* (lines 129–132). *Oh it is positive* is another instance of disagreement. It is prefaced by 'oh', which functions to "assess the news delivered" (Heritage 1984: 302) in the previous utterance. Further, the HKC has cleverly repeated the NES's word (*positive*), but has used it to contradict his utterance meaning. Her disagreement is quite explicit. The HKC's disagreement *oh it is positive* is followed by reasons and justifications. After the HKC has given reasons, the NES utters *yea* (line 133) but does not continue his turn. The HKC self-selects, still disagreeing with the NES's view. The disagreeing remark is still manifested in a positively worded positive declarative *it would be nice* (line 134) — another occurrence of a "token agreement", which refers to the propositional content of her prior turn. *It would be nice* uttered by the HKC is interpreted to mean 'it is nice', i.e. doing charity walks is nice.

After that, the HKC picks up on the criticism of the NES about the format of the walk, and changes her position from disagreeing with the NES's view to supporting it, by suggesting changing the format of the fund-raising activity *but er (.) I'll I'll rather they change the format these days because so many Walk for Million now* (lines 134–136). The propositional content shift takes effect instantly within the same utterance. This is another instance of face management strategy employed by the HKC to restore concern for the positive face of the NES colleague, immediately after having threatened it. She is careful in doing face management work, as reflected in the way she makes her point, through using hedging and mitigation devices (*but er (.) I'll I'll rather*).

In response to approval and agreement given by the HKC, the NES reiterates his earlier point about putting more focused effort into charity functions, followed by making some suggestions about alternative fund-raising activities that will produce more benefits, which echoes the HKC's earlier remark about benefits. The NES's *more benefit* (line 158), in a way, implies disagreement with the HKC's view about long-term benefits generated by charity walks.

During the NES's long turn, the HKC shows support. The HKC's initial back-channel responses are given to support the NES's utterance in the sense of signalling that the communication channel is open, and indicating her consent for the NES to carry on (*right yea*, line 151). Her *I see I see I see your point* (lines 145 and 147) shows her keenness in acknowledging the NES's view. She also uses a completion offer — *it's my effort* mm (line 149) — as the NES is expressing his views about better ways of raising funds. Completion offers are typically used to indicate supportiveness. Her back-channelling then develops into a kind of conceding that the NES's suggestion is a good idea, when she says *yea yea yea it would be a good idea actually* (lines 155 and 157). This concession ends with a concession marker 'actually'. Sinclair et al. (1995) examined the Bank of English Corpus and describes a total of five functions for 'actually' as used by native speakers. The five functions are (1) to indicate a situation exists or happened, (2) to emphasize the truth or correctness of something, (3) to correct or contradict someone, (4) to express an opinion that other people might not have expected from the speaker in a polite way, and (5) to introduce a new topic into the conversation. Lenk (1998) describes three functions of 'actually' in its discourse marker role: opinion marker, objective/correction marker, and topic shift marker. In the HKC's *yea yea yea it would be a good idea actually*, 'actually' is interpreted as a marker of opinion that other people might not have expected from the speaker in a polite way, particularly to mark her concession.

When the NES expresses his opinion that making his idea of fund-raising activity possible means that the administration would be phenomenally difficult (lines 160–161), the HKC disagrees with him, saying *but it depends on whether there are people interesting in doing all these* (lines 162–163). She, however, prefaces her disagreement with a token agreement (*it's true*, line 162). 'All these' is a cataphoric reference, referring forwards in the text, namely the alternative format of charity proposed by the NES as well as the associated administrative job. 'There are people' is a case of impersonalizing S and H. Using 'there are people', as opposed to, for example, 'but it depends on whether you are/I am/we are interested in doing all these' shows that the HKC does not want to impinge on the NES. The HKC then concludes by reiterating that the NES's suggestion is *a good idea actually* (line 167). The topic is finally closed in a jocular way, initiated by the HKC.

The sequential structure of each of the HKC's disagreements is shown below [(Agree) stands for agreement; (Disagree) stands for disagreement]:

- (Agree) *right exactly* (Agree/Disagree) *[and …* (Agree) *right [((laugh)) …* (Disagree) *but [if …* (Agree) *I totally agree* (Disagree) *and then after the walk I mean after the tunnel it it would it becomes quite interesting (.) because it will be [the Tsing Gu Bridge (.) and a lot of you know [to see* (lines 95–106)
- (Disagree) *ahh ((laugh)) well there is no comparison between the two I think* (Agree) *but er (.) anyway I think er people are are are really upset with er so many Walk for Million these days (.) so last Sunday it was a very very er (pause) boring one* (lines 115–119)
- (Disagree) *oh it is positive I mean by doing some sort of charity walk and (.) when you walk you feel like er somebody is sponsoring you and then somebody will be er benefited in the long run in due course* (lines 129–132)
- (Disagree) *it would be nice* (Agree) *but er (.) I'll I'll rather they change the format these days because so many Walk for Million now* (lines 134–136)
- (Agree) *it's true* (Disagree) *but it depends whether there are people interesting in doing all these (.) always is er you need somebody to do the back-up job behind (.) before things can be done (.) perfectly well* (lines 162–165)

The analysis of the sequential structures of the HKC's disagreements illuminates the HKC's recurrent effort in minimizing the face-threatening effect on her NES colleague, despite her disagreements with what he says most of the time. None of her five disagreements is bald-on-record, and all her disagreements are given with the use of redressive language. In many of her disagreements, after expressing disagreement, she very quickly shifts to agreeing. In her second disagreement, she even changes the topic altogether to resolve disagreement. The HKC has therefore been shown to be working consciously toward achieving alignment with the NES, and very quickly adjusts any deviation from his view. Conversely, both of the NES's disagreements are direct, bald on record, with few attempts to seek convergence.

In Extract 8, the male speakers were colleagues working for the Hong Kong Government. The recording was made in an Oliver's restaurant at lunchtime. The speakers are discussing the ingredients in the sandwich that the HKC is eating. There are disagreements made by both of the speakers.

(8) 001

b: male Hong Kong Chinese B: male Australian

12. b: what attract me to this is the er is the boiled egg
13. because I like boiled egg [very much
14. B: [yea
15. b: and if I only get (.) boiled egg sandwich it it would
16. be too plain (.) it won't satisfy me [so I would have
17. B: [well
18. well one thing good about Oliver's is that er you
19. know the the the the ingredients are very fresh
20. B: I see
21. b: isn't it
22. B: yea they must put fly stuff in (.) get stuff from
23. all over the world er where do they get this stuff
24. this stuff
25. b: I don't know from USA I suppose the lettuce (.) I
26. don't think it's local I think it's either from
27. Australia or from USA it's not I mean it's not
28. possible from Hong Kong or from China China you don't
29. have erm lettuce
30. B: you get local lettuce I buy local lettuce
31. b: yea local possible but I think the quality is not
32. that good
33. B: oh it's okay [I mean you pay in Seibu or erm Wellcome
34. b: [yea
35. you can buy local lettuce for about three dollars
36. b: oh you bought from (.) you bought from Seibu
37. B: mhmm
38. b: you find it very good
39. B: yea
40. b: yea
41. B: or from Wellcome
42. b: mm
43. B: three dollars
44. b: yea
45. B: we bought imported lettuce it's
46. b: yea
47. B: thirty dollars
48. b: three and thirty ((astonished))
49. B: yea

50. b: it's that much the difference [oh I don't re- I
51. B: [mhmm
52. didn't realize it
53. B: mm
54. b: well actually do we have er local lettuce do we
55. B: this is local I have [this
56. b: [no no the style is right the
57. style is very different this sort of lettuce is very
58. different from local lettuce local lettuce the er the
59. foliage is different isn't it
60. B: ah but there's a whole lot of imported lettuce as
61. well
62. b: is it
63. B: mm
64. b: yea
65. B: Seibu has a whole area with local vegetables
66. b: yea yea yea yea yea yea
67. B: it's cheap
68. b: it's cheap ((astonished)) oh your standard (.) you
69. know by Hong Kong standard Seibu's er goods (.) or it
70. well especially the er the the supermarket the price
71. there (.) are very expensive [by Hong Kong standard
72. B: [mm
73. B: mm
74. b: if you if you if you if you buy from the Park N' Shop
75. or Wellcome I think it it you you are well in
76. comparison you are only paying you know a portion of
77. that er [the price quoted
78. B: [but not for not the local vegetable
79. b: mm
80. B: Seibu's prices for local vegetable are the same as
81. Wellcome's
82. b: mm (.) oh yea
83. B: well every thing else is imported you see
84. b: yea
85. B: it's good though when you want something some olives
86. (.) some feta cheese
87. b: you bought food yourself
88. B: mhmm

The conversational topic is whether in Hong Kong there is local lettuce and the price of lettuce in different supermarkets. In response to the HKC's commendation on the fresh ingredients of the sandwich that he is eating, the NES suggests that Oliver's *must put fly stuff in (.) get stuff from all over the world* and asks the HKC *where do they get this stuff this stuff* (lines 22–24). The HKC's response is *I don't know from USA I suppose the lettuce (.) I don't think it's local I think it's either from Australia or from USA it's not I mean it's not possible from Hong Kong or from China China you don't have erm lettuce* (lines 25–29). His response shows that he accurately interprets the NES's *this stuff* to refer to *the lettuce* in the sandwich, and that he agrees to the NES's view that the stuff is flown in from overseas. Though the HKC suggests USA, the fact that his utterance is prefaced by *I don't know* shows that he is uncertain. 'I don't know' in this conversational environment serves as "a marker of uncertainty" (Tsui 1991b: 619–620) relating to the truth-value of the proposition 'from USA'. 'I suppose' may serve to indicate uncertainty with regard to the origin of 'the lettuce'. After a slight pause, the HKC reinforces his agreement with the NES, stating that the lettuce in the sandwich is not local *I don't think it's local I think it's either from Australia or from USA.* The HKC continues and provides reasoning for his agreement, saying *I mean it's not possible from Hong Kong or from China China* by giving a reason *you don't have erm lettuce.* In this utterance, the HKC supports the NES's view that *they must put fly stuff in* the sandwich.

The first disagreement in Extract 8 comes from the NES when he says *you get local lettuce I buy local lettuce* (line 30). His use of *you* (plural) echoes the HKC's *you don't have erm lettuce.* Pluralisation of the 'you' pronoun is a strategy used when a speaker is faced with opposing tensions, namely the desire to go on record on the one hand, and the desire to give the hearer an "out" by not singling out the addressee on the other (Brown and Levinson 1987). In other words, by employing the "plural" you in 'you get local lettuce', rather than saying, for instance, 'you (the HKC) are mistaken', the NES states his disagreement with the HKC, and at the same time shows concern for addressing the HKC's negative face. What is interesting about the NES's disagreement is the juxtaposition of 'you' and 'I' in *you get local lettuce* and *I buy local lettuce.* The former utterance is non-specific, while the latter is specific and certain. The latter is making a definitive statement that serves to support and strengthen the truth-value of the proposition of the former utterance. Hence, the NES's disagreement begins with a general truth (*you get local lettuce*), which is then substantiated by a personal, specific fact and an action verb (*I buy local lettuce*) in order to lend authority and to give credit to the general truth. It is interesting that in most cases, disagreements are usually followed by mitigation. In this case, the reverse is true.

The HKC responds to the NES's disagreement with a disagreement, which is prefaced by a qualified token agreement *yea* (*yea local possible but I think the quality is not that good*, lines 31–32), which functions to pretend to agree or to hide disagreement (Brown and Levinson, 1987: 113–114). After the token agreement (*yea*), the HKC hedges his agreement (*local possible*), and immediately announces a change with 'but'. He then offers his view about the inferior quality of local lettuce (i.e. giving reasons which is positive politeness) which can be interpreted as the HKC's saving his own face. He is effectively saying something like 'I don't think there is local lettuce and even if there is I think the quality is not as good as that of imported lettuce'. As a result, the face-threatening effect of the HKC's disagreement is mitigated. Due to hedging and giving reasons, the HKC's dispreferred response sounds less direct, and is potentially less clear, longer and more complex in structure, compared to the NES's disagreement (*yea you get local lettuce I buy local lettuce*). This gives the impression that the HKC finds it difficult and is not so willing to disagree. The HKC's assertion about local lettuce is hence softened and modified as a result of his employment of redressive language.

In the next turn, the NES insists in his view and disagrees with the HKC's negative statement — *but I think the quality is not that good* — with an opposing response — *oh it's okay* (line 33). This response is a softened disagreement. In this context, 'okay' implies that the NES finds the quality (of lettuce) is satisfactory or acceptable. He then goes on explaining why he thinks that the quality is *okay*, by saying *[I mean you pay in Seibu or erm Wellcome you can buy local lettuce for about three dollars* (lines 33–35) and *we bought imported lettuce it's thirty dollars* (lines 45 and 47). Compared to the high price of imported lettuce, the NES finds local lettuce *okay*. This is to address the HKC's assertion that the quality of local lettuce is not 'that' good.

After more than fifteen turns, the HKC re-introduces the topic of lettuce, saying *well actually do we have er local lettuce do we* (line 54), which can be seen as revisiting his previous objection to the NES's view that there is actually local lettuce in Hong Kong (*I don't think it's local*, lines 25–26), as well as revisiting his earlier partial agreement/partial disagreement (*yea local possible but I think the quality is not that good*, lines 31–32). The HKC's double question *do we have er local lettuce do we* (line 54) shows that he has not been totally convinced by the NES's earlier assertion: *you get local lettuce I buy local lettuce* (line 30). Neither is he convinced of and happy with his own concession to this assertion (*yea local possible*, line 31). His question, however, is asked in a hesitant manner, as evident in the double discourse markers *well* and *actually*, and *er* in the middle of the utterance to fill a pause. The two discourse markers *well* and *actually* have distinctive functions. "Well" bears the "conventional meaning that what follows is a dispreferred contribution (i.e. not quite what the hearer was hoping for)" (Grundy 1995: 208). 'Actually' can be interpreted as either a topic shift marker (Lenk 1998), or a discourse marker to correct or contradict someone (Sinclair et al. 1995); and in this case, himself. The addition of 'do we' to *do we have er local lettuce* could be interpreted as a repetition of his own question words for emphasis purposes. His interrogative is an indirect speech act, because it actually carries the illocutionary force of an assertion of disagreement, rather than seeking information. Hence the HKC's disagreement with the NES as a dispreferred response is heavily mitigated with redress action, and these are *well actually* (hedge) *do we have er local lettuce* (question; conventional indirectness) *do we* (question).

The response of the NES *this is local I have [this* (line 55) begins with a locutionary act bearing a positive verb, and yet its illocutionary force is one of disagreeing with the HKC. The NES is trying to use the lettuce in his sandwich as evidence to prove his assertion, and in turn disproves the HKC's assertion in a prior turn. Instead of explicitly stating what he is referring to, the NES uses 'this' as an exophoric reference. Therefore, the NES's disagreement with the HKC as a dispreferred response is mitigated by means of presupposing his knowledge about the ellipted nominal group. As both speakers are cooperatively involved in the discussion, the NES presumes shared understanding of the missing nominal group by the HKC. From the context of situation, nevertheless, the HKC does not seem to have any difficulty identifying the referent for 'this'. This is evident in the following utterance (lines 57–59), in which the HKC also uses *this sort of lettuce*, particularly comparing *the foliage* of this sort of lettuce to that of local lettuce.

In lines 56–59, the HKC cuts in on the NES's turn-at-talk to give his disagreement *[no no the style is well the style is very different this sort of lettuce is very different from local lettuce local lettuce the er the foliage is different isn't it.* In order to justify his disagreement, the HKC emphatically tries to come up with some sort of reason. First of all, he attributes the difference to *the style*, which is almost the most generic description that one can possibly think of. He then struggles to look for a specific description for the difference — *the foliage is different.* In order to involve the NES, the HKC gives reasons as to why he thinks what he thinks. By including the NES in his reasoning and assuming reflexivity (Brown and Levinson 1987), the HKC is leading the NES to see the reasonableness of his (the HKC's) FTA, i.e. disagreement.

Another instance of redressive language is the use of a tag question in his utterance *this sort of lettuce is very different from local lettuce local lettuce the er the foliage is different isn't it* (lines 57–59). A tag question functions to draw the hearer into the conversation (Brown and Levinson (1987). According to Brazil (1985), the use of tag questions is to solicit agreement, and is a commonly used means of establishing "common ground" with the addressee. Griffin (2000: 501) notes that the function of a tag question is to "soften the sting of potential disagreement and to invite participation in open, friendly dialogue."

What is immediately noticeable about the HKC's disagreement, as a dispreferred response, is that it is not a classic example of the typical dispreferred response discussed in the literature (Schegloff et al. 1977; Pomerantz 1978, 1984; Sacks 1978). Here the negation 'no no' (i.e. bald-on record) is right at the start of the response, rather than pushed back into the turn. It is, however, interesting to note that the HKC does not follow the negation with a head-on disagreement. Rather, he gives reasons by referring to the style and the foliage being different from those of local lettuce. Giving reasons to justify a disagreement serves the function of lessening the degree of imposition.

The last instance of disagreement comes from the NES when he says *but not for not the local vegetable Seibu's prices for local vegetable are the same as Wellcome's* (lines 78–81). Obviously, his disagreement is not structured in the way in which a typical dispreferred response is done, as it starts with a head-on negation, i.e. a bald-on-record disagreement.

To sum up, seven disagreements are found in Extract 8, four given by the NES and three by the HKC. Both speakers have used a bald-on-record disagreement once. Bald-on-record strategy, without any redress, is primarily used "whenever S wants to do the FTA with maximum efficiency *more than* he wants to satisfy H's face" (Brown and Levinson 1987: 95). Face is ignored or is irrelevant; and consequently, the face threat is not minimized. With respect to the use of mitigation devices, the HKC far exceeds the NES in the frequency of occurrence, indicating that the HKC is making a strenuous effort to minimize the face-threatening effect of his disagreements, and hence the HKC paying greater regard for the face of his NES interlocutor.

Given that there are seven disagreements exchanged in 38 turns, the two male speakers appear to be quite argumentative. They hold onto their beliefs, views and positions in relation to lettuce quite firmly. Neither of them backs off readily and easily. The HKC, in particular, persistently tries to prove that his assertion stands. He even re-opens the discussion about whether or not there is local lettuce, after the topic has changed direction and has moved on. Earlier on, the HKC opined that no local lettuce is sold in supermarkets in Hong Kong, and so it can be assumed that the HKC does not know what local lettuce looks like and how it differs from imported lettuce. Nevertheless, when the NES points out that the lettuce in his sandwich is local, the HKC objects by remarking that the foliage of the lettuce does not look like it is local. When the NES comments that Seibu's local vegetables are cheap, the HKC's immediate response is one of astonishment, disbelief and disagreement, followed by making culturally stereotypical assumptions about the NES's standard for prices of things in Hong Kong. However, at the same time that the HKC is expressing disagreements, he takes care to redress the face-threatening effects.

Actualized in the disagreement sequences is the level of meaning negotiation that is going on in the conversational interaction. As a result of producing a range of speech acts to perform a range of actions, the speakers manage to propose their own views, to refute the other's views, to clarify positions and to justify themselves. They work towards creating shared understanding of meanings regarding the topics on which they differ in their positions and opinions.

Discussion of disagreements in four extracts

An examination of the four most extended conversational extracts in the intercultural conversations that contain disagreements has produced sixteen disagreements in total, nine by HKC and seven by NES. HKC produce more disagreements than NES, and this concurs with the quantitative findings of the whole intercultural conversations. The most interesting finding is hence that HKC are not at all shy to disagree with NES. Compared to NES, they are certainly not less likely, if not more likely, to raise disagreement in order to present their different, or alternative views on issues or things. Despite disagreeing with NES more frequently, HKC tend to use a lot more redressive language for facework management. For HKC, disagreeing with the addressee involves a lot more facework and interpersonal management work, especially in order not to sound imposing.

Schiffrin (1984), in her earlier work in conflict talk, isolates a form of argument called "sociable argument", which she perceives to be prevalent among Jewish Americans. Sociable argument is considered "a co-operative enactment of conflict which actually demonstrates the solidarity of a relationship — simply because it displays the ability of that relationship to tolerate features of talk typically associated with conflict, e.g. disagreement, challenge, interruption, insult" (Schiffrin 1990: 256). John Sinclair (personal communication 1991; cited in Warren 1993) remarks, however, that in all arguments, participants are behaving co-operatively towards each other. The very fact that the participants in argument do not talk at cross purposes is another example of their co-operative behaviour. The HKC and NES speakers investigated in this study have supported the observations made by Schiffrin and Sinclair.

On the whole, it can be seen that, to a greater or lesser extent, both HKC and NES examined have made efforts to align themselves with their interlocutors in their disagreements. Alignment reveals the participants pursuing their goals co-operatively rather than individually, which is a requirement for a conversation to be coherent and to progress well. To do this, participants must carry out "aligning actions" (Stokes and Hewitt 1976). Stokes and Hewitt identify two forms of alignment. One is concerned with the resolving of problems arising from differences between a speaker's behaviour and cultural conventions. The second includes those activities by means of which participants successfully interact by constantly aligning their individual actions, and that is, the ways successive utterances are produced to "clarify and construct the orientation of both speaker and hearer" (Cheepen and Monaghan 1990: 14–15). HKC and NES have been shown to carry out both forms of alignment actions in their disagreements.

To varying degrees, HKC and NES are concerned with managing interpersonal relationships when they perform the act of disagreeing with the interlocutor. Managing interpersonal relationships involves politeness. Blum-Kulka (1987) defines politeness as "the interactional balance achieved between two needs: The need for pragmatic clarity and the need to avoid coerciveness". Negotiating common ground involves collaborative efforts on the part of all of the participants to arrive at mutual understanding of the meanings of utterances, both explicit and implied.

Nevertheless, the extent to which HKC and NES pay regard for the interlocutor's face is clearly different. There are three different ways of managing disagreements observed in this study: to disagree using a bald-on-record strategy, to push the disagreement deep into the turn, and to disagree upfront and then patch the disagreement up. NES are on the whole much more direct and blunt in their disagreements, observed in their relatively higher tendency to use bald-on-record disagreements. Regarding the use of disagreements with redressive language, HKC's disagreements are more likely to be realized in the form of a dispreferred response. In other words, NES are more likely than HKC to give a disagreement upfront, followed by redressive language.

The most important finding, drawn from the analysis of four lengthy conversational episodes, is that the HKC's disagreements as a dispreferred response are heavily redressed in order to mitigate the imposition of the disagreement (FTA) on NES, to disclaim an all-knowing and authoritative status, and to coerce and involve the interlocutor in the reasoning and in claiming common ground. Comparatively, the efforts made by NES in mitigating imposition are much less although the efforts to establish common ground with the HKC can be seen.

Conclusion

The results of the analysis of disagreements as a realization of preference organization have largely supported the preconceptions about intercultural differences between the Chinese and Westerners in managing conflict. HKC in this study have been shown to make a greater effort than NES in avoiding confrontation and in accommodating the interlocutor's face-want, rather than competing (Yuen 1992; Kirkbride et al. 1991). The conclusions are supported by the "independent and interdependent conceptions of the self" proposed by Markus and Kitayama (1991, 1994). Asian cultures are said to support the "interdependent conception of the self" more than Western cultures. The "interdependent self" is more likely to pay attention to the group when forming opinions and attitudes, to attach importance to preserving their own and others' "face", and emphasize harmony and cooperation in the ingroup. Western culture supports the "independent conception of the self" more than Asian cultures. The "independent self" is more likely to be willing to enter into confrontation and competition, be willing to express open criticism, and be disposed to express individual, unpredictable views.

What are clearly revealed in the employment of redressive measures and the organizational pattern of disagreements as a dispreferred response are the varying efforts HKC and NES make to align themselves with their interlocutors to manage interpersonal relationships and to negotiate common ground.

Chapter 5

Compliments and compliment responses

Analysis of compliments and compliment responses in the intercultural conversations

This chapter reports findings regarding paying and responding to compliments by HKC and NES, particularly compliment topics, types of compliment responses, and possible motivations for the usage and patterns identified. Two hypotheses were formulated. First, HKC and NES will give compliments on different aspects of the addressee as cultures vary in what constitutes acceptable or preferred compliment topics. Second, HKC will use more rejections and self-denigrating responses when being complimented on, and NES will use more acceptances and self-praise avoidance mechanisms.

Altogether seven compliments have been identified in all the intercultural conversations. Extracts 1 to 4 illustrate compliments given by NES, and Extracts 5–7 contain compliments produced by HKC. In the following, each occurrence of the speech acts of compliment and compliment response in the intercultural conversations will be examined, in terms of compliment topics and compliment response types.

Extract 1 shows an absence of a verbal response when the HKC woman is complimented by the Irish woman, who had been the English private tutor for her two daughters for more than eight months when the recording was made. Before the conversational excerpt starts, the speakers have been discussing the role of women in the family. The NES relates to the HKC that her relatives usually had large families, and that her father, being a member of the older generation and coming from a Catholic country, came from a family of fourteen. She recalls that she used to envy her relatives because large families were actually very happy in those days. She, however, *thought it must have been really hard for their mother because there was no privacy.* At this point, the HKC joins in and supports the NES's view that it might have been difficult for the mother in those days, as there was so much work in large families.

(1) 009
a: female Hong Kong Chinese A: female Irish
302. a: there is so much work to take care of fourteen
303. ((laugh))
304. A: that's right yes and nowadays we've we're becoming
305. more selfish aren't we [we we all like to have our
306. a: [uh huh
307. spare time to do our own things [you know to have a
308. a: [yes yes
309. quiet moment whereas in those days people were less
310. selfish I think [they were always giving everything
311. a: [uh huh uh huh
312. for the children [but now we want to have time for
313. ourselves [and time for the children
314. a: [yes yes
315. a: yes and especially for a working mother it's
316. particularly difficult to take care of a large family
317. you know like myself I am now er I am now also
318. studying for my PhD
319. A: oh very [good yea
320. a: [yea yea that's eh why I am so occupied fully
321. occupied every day [working from er er from morning
322. A: [yea
323. till really [midnight after midnight
324. A: [yea yea
325. [((laugh)) yes so I do my house I mean office work in
326. A: [((laugh)) studying
327. the morning and then when I come back I have to work
328. on my PhD [so erm so they say [that I am always in
329. A: [yea [yea
330. front of the er er er er TV screen but actually but
331. actually that's not TV screen that is a [computer
332. A: [computer
333. monitor
334. ((A and a laugh))
335. A: oh that's very admirable that is very good (.) tell
336. me do you think in Hong Kong erm today that both erm
337. husband and wife must work [do you think financially
338. a: [er
339. [it's a necessity

a: [it's
a: it's er it's not a must er there is still many family
where the (.) mother is still a full-time housewife
[but for er if the mother has got erm is well-
A: [yea
educated (.) then they will think that it would be a
waste
A: yea that's right yea

The NES compares women in the past, who were less selfish, with their counterparts nowadays. In her words, *nowadays we'll we're becoming more selfish aren't we [we we all like to have our spare time to do our own things [you know to have a quiet moment* (lines 304–309), and *we want to have time for ourselves [and time for the children* (lines 312–313). In response, the HKC says *yes and especially for a working mother it's particularly difficult to take care of a large family you know like myself I am now er I am now also studying for my PhD* (lines 315–318). The HKC identifies herself as 'a working mother' of the present time, and offers information to the NES that she is 'now also' studying for her PhD, on top of her job and her family.

The HKC continues to explain that she is fully occupied every day working from morning till after midnight, engaged in office work and her PhD study (*yea yea that's eh why I am so occupied fully occupied every day [working from er er from morning till really [midnight after midnight [((laugh)) yes so I do my house I mean office work in the morning and then when I come back I have to work on my PhD*, lines 320–328). In some ways, the HKC is quintessential of the modern woman, as depicted by the NES, in the sense that she is 'more selfish' as she has her own things (her job and her study) to do, apart from taking care of her family. However, in other ways, the HKC does not fit in the category of 'selfish' modern women as she does not spend her 'spare time' to have 'a quiet moment'. In fact, she has to work and study the whole day long day after day. It is interesting to note that the female HKC brings up the topic of her PhD study in the context of modern women being 'selfish', rather than bragging that it is an achievement to be doing a PhD in addition to having a job and looking after her family.

After hearing this, the NES says *oh that's very admirable that is very good* (line 335) in an appreciative tone to compliment the HKC on her hard work, ability and achievement. There is a slight pause after the compliment, and the NES changes to a new topic.

No compliment response is given by the HKC upon being complimented. The lack of a verbal response is not a response type documented in any of the frameworks discussed in the literature (Pomerantz 1978; Holmes 1988). It is not easy to account for the absence of a compliment response from the HKC. Absence of a response, however, cannot show whether the HKC agrees or disagrees with the proposition encoded in the compliment. There are, however, three possible explanations for the absence of a verbal response from the HKC. First, the HKC could have given a non-verbal response such as a smile or a nod to indicate acceptance of the compliment, or even a shake of her head to indicate rejection. This may be because she feels that the compliment is so profuse that she chooses not to give a verbal response to indicate modesty and humility, or she does not know what an appropriate response would be. The second reason is that the slight pause between the NES's compliment and her ensuing utterance is so short that there is no opportunity for the HKC to get a turn to produce a response. In other words, the HKC may not be quick enough to produce a response to the NES's compliment. The third and more likely reason is that the HKC is caught between responding according to the Chinese cultural norm, which is rejecting and self-denigration, and identifying with the cultural norm of the NES interlocutor, which is acceptance and downgrade.

In Extract 2, the participants were business friends and the conversation took place over lunch in a restaurant. The HKC has been telling the NES the plan of his company. His company plans to maintain the building project management and development arm of the business and to move beyond Hong Kong to explore development projects in China.

(2) 008
b: male Hong Kong Chinese B: male British
120. b: next year I still have to er search for some er
121. development projects in China erm because the erm
122. general the group will be on one side would be
123. concentrate on the erm on the retail property agency
124. business but on the other hand er er we we want we
125. still want to maintain er the er project management
126. and development building development business er in
127. the coming year we also concentrate we haven't we
128. haven't er worked on new projects since the er
129. Electric Road one six eight so after that er we have
130. to erm er more concrete to start on some business on
131. the project management
132. B: you know every single (.) I say this in an just as a
133. matter of comment not not a not a concern but every
134. single project that I have been I have got involved
135. in (.) to a certain extent has never materialised
136. with THO I mean like E Electric Road makes reminds me

137. there's another example you know how er I attend one
138. meeting or two meetings and come up with all these
139. management erm philosophies and then [the owner
140. b: [yes
141. doesn't want it [er for whatever reason I mean
142. b: [yes
143. there're different reasons very justified reasons
144. probably but every single [like Russell Street no
145. b: [yes say like er
146. nobody wants it I mean (.) I don't know (.) maybe one
147. b: Russell Street
148. day it's going to click er [but the problem at the
149. b: [but I would believe so er
150. moment
151. b: the reason is the erm (.) the developer that we
152. linked with is is not very long what (.) they're not
153. thinking long term er on the market
154. B: that's right
155. b: yea medium to small size developers
156. B: yes
157. b: so they want to have their money back as soon as
158. possible they are not like some kind of C_K_ with
159. a theme of philosophy to build up their name (.) they
160. are different kind of er says if we have a gimmick
161. that er we can say sell the property at a better
162. price or sell it quicker that they would be very
163. interested
164. B: yea
165. b: generally they are not very interested on er just er
166. rent out the house except for the Russell Street [the
167. B: [yea
168. the er the the sound view [which is su- supposed to a
169. B: [yea
170. bigger but then I think they are not that concerned
171. on their image (.) right so that's why they you see
172. that they are not they're not er putting up their
173. name (.) er so (.) consider so important for the
174. image
175. B: it's true yea (.) but it's good that you the company
176. your company is very service-orientated and (.) at

177.		least in the concept of service to the customer
178.		(pause)
179.	B:	it's gonna be (.) it's the way of the future I think
180.	b:	uh huh
181.		(pause)
182.	B:	I think if I didn't have a family
183.	b:	sorry
184.	B:	if I didn't have a family I would live (.) somewhere
185.		like this in the service apartments here in the
186.		Convention Plaza
187.	b:	very convenient here
188.	B:	yea
189.	b:	in fact the apartment er you know the er er many er
190.		company from China they [buy it

From line 132 onwards, the NES expresses his *concern* that he has not found that working with THO on some projects has been producing useful outcomes. THO is a developer with whom the HKC's company is 'linked'. The NES attributes the problem to some *management erm philosophies* (line 139) that THO and developers of a similar background and scale share. In lines 151–174, the HKC launches into a speech offering an account of the failure of those projects. The problem with those *medium to small size developers* (line 155) with which the HKC's company is linked is that they are *not thinking long term er on the market* (lines 152–153). These developers are more concerned about having *their money back as soon as possible* (lines 157–158), rather than building up their image.

The NES agrees with the reason offered by the HKC (*it's true yea*, line 175). After a slight pause, the NES shifts the topic to the HKC's company and makes some positive evaluative remarks about the company, beginning with *but* to preface views and remarks that are in contradiction to those expressed in previous utterances of the HKC. The NES's compliment is *it's good that you the company your company is very service-oriented and (.) at least in the concept of service to the customer* (lines 175–177). No response is given by the HKC. After a pause, the NES continues with his turn, saying *it's gonna be (.) it's the way of the future I think* (line 179). Following this, the HKC produces *uh huh* as a response (line 180).

The compliment topic is the 'customer-oriented' philosophy of the HKC's company, which is a quality of the company. The remark is approving and commendatory since being service-oriented to the customer is considered strength for a company that deals with building management projects.

Similar to Extract 1, there is no verbal response from the HKC in Extract 2 when he is complimented. However, absence of a verbal response, as shown in the transcription, cannot show whether the HKC agrees or disagrees with the proposition encoded in the compliment. Similar to Extract 1, it is possible that the HKC had made a nonverbal response to indicate acceptance or rejection of the compliment.

The NES's following utterance *it's gonna be (.) it's the way of the future I think* (line 179) states that the concept of providing service to the customer is the trend in business. This shows the NES making a generalization in order to reinforce and refocus his previous compliment, particularly to emphasize the approving aspect, that is, the organization being 'service-oriented'. In response to the NES's *it's gonna be (.) it's the way of the future I think*, the HKC utters *uh huh* (line 180). The HKC's *uh huh* functions as a "back-channel", which refers to "noises (which are not full words) and short verbal responses made by listeners which acknowledge the incoming talk and react to it, without wishing to take over the speaking turn" (Carter and McCarthy 1997: 12), and so is not considered a proper, expected second pair part to a first pair part and does not carry any semantic meaning.

With respect to the HKC's non-response to the NES's compliment (*it's good that you the company your company is very service-oriented and (.) at least in the concept of service to the customer*, lines 175–177), it is quite difficult to explain the reason or the underlying motive for the HKC's opting out. According to Chen (1993: 69) who compared PRC Chinese and American college students, the PRC Chinese tend to reject compliments on achievement, as achievement is perceived as "private to a person". It is plausible that the HKC in this extract does not perceive the compliment on his company as complimenting a possession of his, but rather the company he owns and runs as embodying some kind of personal achievements, or even personal qualities. This is because in previous exchanges, the HKC and the NES have been discussing other companies or developers in relation to their 'management philosophies' (line 139) or 'a theme of philosophy' (line 159), the formation and practice of which reflects the ideologies and vision of the people in the management. When the NES states that 'the concept of service to the customer' (line 177) is 'the way of the future' (line 179), he is likely to be suggesting that the customer-oriented philosophy of the HKC's company reflects that the HKC, being the owner of the company, is forward-looking and has the right kind of vision. Along this line of interpretation, it could be that, driven by a desire to act modestly, the HKC opts out of giving a verbal response to the compliment. The HKC's lack of a verbal response can be interpreted as a silent acceptance, rather than a silent disagreement, as he disapproves of the 'theme of philosophy' of those 'medium and small size developers' that is different from the philosophy of his own company.

Absence of a verbal response from the HKC is a marked feature in the conversation, even if he had given a non-verbal response. Compared to thanking or downgrading, lack of a response to the compliment is an outstanding difference from the Western practice. Plausible reasons include that the HKC had found the compliment too profuse, or that he was caught between the stereotypical expectations of Chinese and Western ways of dealing with the compliment in that particular context of situation, namely self-denigration or rejecting for the Chinese and thanking or downgrading for the West. The outcome of either possibility is the same; and that is, the HKC is at a loss as to what would constitute an appropriate response.

After a pause, in line 182 the NES initiates a topic change. He does not pursue his compliment paid to the HKC's company, or the propositional content embodied in his compliment.

Extract 3 was taken from a conversation in which the British male was the brother-in-law of the HKC female. His wife was the HKC woman's younger sister. This extract is interesting in that it shows a compliment, but the compliment is much more than a compliment. The likely reason for the complimenter to give the compliment, the compliment itself, and the compliment response are very interesting to examine.

(3)	004		
B:	male British		a: female Hong Kong Chinese
344.	B:	do you teach Maths	
345.	a:	Maths	
346.	B:	yea	
347.	a:	you can see (.) look at me	
348.		((B and a laugh))	
349.	B:	no isn't it right you have a good figure you're very	
350.		good on figures	
351.	a:	no of course not ((laugh))	
352.	B:	okay (.) there's a friend of mine do you remember E_	
353.	a:	I_	
354.	B:	[E_	

When being asked whether she teaches Maths (the HKC is an Art teacher in a secondary school), the HKC repeats 'Maths' in a surprised tone, indicating disbelief. When the NES confirms his first question, the HKC jokingly says *you can see (.) look at me* (line 347), followed by laughter. The NES laughs with her. The HKC's response suggests that she may have some kind of stereotypical assumption about how a Maths teacher should look, which is possibly one of unattractive appearance. At the same time, by inviting the NES to look at her to see for himself, she is assuming that the NES shares her assumption and judgment in terms of how a Maths teacher looks.

In response, in a teasing way, the NES says *no*, indicating disagreement with the HKC, followed by *isn't it right* (line 349) which seeks confirmation from the HKC.

After this, the NES makes a complimentary remark on the HKC's body shape — *you have a good figure*, and then puns *you're very good on figures* (lines 349–350). By playing on the word 'figure', the NES connects having *a good figure* with being *very good on figures*, the latter of which is a necessary quality of a Mathematics teacher. The NES upgrades the second mention of *good* to make it become *very good*. The compliment is performed explicitly, with the addressee (the HKC) directly mentioned (Yuan 1998). The preface *isn't it right* can be interpreted as the NES teasing the HKC about her view of the Maths teacher being unattractive, by saying the opposite is true in her case, and it logically follows that a woman with a good figure would be good at figures.

The response of the HKC to the "compliment" about her figure and ability in handling figures is a bald-on-record disagreement *no of course not* (line 351), followed by laughter. Disagreement belongs to "Self-praise Avoidance Mechanisms" (Pomerantz 1978). The NES responds with *okay*. After a moment of silence, the NES initiates a topic change.

In Extract 3, both the compliment and the compliment response are exchanged in a light-hearted way. Given a different context of situation, the response may have been very different. Instead of a direct disagreement, for instance, the HKC woman being "complimented on" could have gone along with the joke and made up some reasons to support her response, or she could have accepted the "compliment" in an equally humorous tone, or teased the complimenter back, and so on. What happens in this particular interaction is, however, an outright rejection of (a disagreement with) the "compliment" (Pomerantz 1978). The HKC's compliment response is a bald-on-record disagreement (Brown and Levinson 1987), which is different from the redressed response given by Holmes (1986):

A: You did a great job cleaning the house.
B: Well, I guess you haven't seen the kids' room.

Speaker B's disagreement is heavily hedged. There is no use of direct 'no', and counter evidence is offered to support the disagreement to make it convincing (Holmes 1986). None of these elements are, however, found in the compliment response of the HKC in Extract 3.

In a different context of conversation, an "outright rejection" without any redress action can be rude and face-threatening, as the compliment-recipient bluntly and baldly intimidates the complimenter's positive face. Rejecting the compliment may indicate rejecting the complimenter and his or her good intention. An explanation can be offered to account for the HKC's "outright rejection" of the compliment on her appearance and ability. In this context of situation, the reaction of the female HKC may have been due to the nature of the compliment topic, that is, her figure. Chen (1993) found that the Chinese tend to reject compliments on appearance, but tend to accept compliments on possessions, as "looks are more intimate and private to a person than achievement and possession" (Chen 1993: 69). Similarly, Ye (1995) found his Chinese informants more than twice as likely to opt out in scenarios related to appearance, compared to performance. A woman's 'figure', compared to her height, or her looks, is a more sensitive aspect of her appearance. 'Figure' is therefore a much more intimate and personal property of a woman's appearance. Commenting on a woman's 'figure' is a potentially great FTA. The HKC female may therefore feel so embarrassed by the "compliment" that she does not know how to react to it or what to say to react to it, apart from giving a direct disagreement and denial.

In Extract 4 below, the female NES was a pastor attached to a Protestant church in Hong Kong, of which the HKC was an active member. The speakers and other members usually had a chat after a Sunday service. Extract 4 came from a much longer recording made between the NES and the HKC after a Sunday service in a room in the church.

(4) 006
A: female American a: female Hong Kong Chinese
185. A: I will also at the meeting next week I want to review
186. well not review but go over the stories for the next
187. two months or maybe just one month so that everybody
188. understands er the points we're trying to make in the
189. [stories we can't tell the story and miss the point
190. a: [that's very important
191. [you know and so you know at the meeting I will at
192. a: [that's right that's right
193. least go over one month's worth of stories
194. [so everyone knows the applica[tion points we are
195. a: [that application [but that's that's
196. trying to make
197. a: your part to to find out [the the key er[er issues
198. A: [right [right
199. right how it fits into the whole and and I think you
200. do a very good job in the application for the round-
201. up and then you know today you also do a very good
202. job [reading the story
203. a: [I was surprised that they responded to that so
204. well they were you know
205. A: mhmm [that's right yea
206. a: [so

207.	a:	they they they they they they mem- they know the
208.		story [yea
209.	A:	[yes [they've heard
210.	a:	[they heard yea and they heard
211.	A:	yea
212.	a:	that's very good and then even you know the the key
213.		things to remember say Abraham for patience and then
214.		nations to [for for separation [that's good (.) er so
215.	A:	[yes yes
216.		maybe yea in our next meeting and then we so you you
217.		you jot it down [and for the teachers to do that
218.	A:	[yes I will have it ready mm
219.		so far it it's good and ano- and another part er is
220.		the songs you know seems you know we'll a lot of
221.		repetition of singing Father Abraham and the children
222.		got [bored

The compliment is given by the NES *I think you do a very good job in the application for the round-up and then you know today you also do a very good job [reading the story* (lines 199–202). The compliment response given by the HKC *is I was surprised that they responded to that so well they were you know (.) so (.) they they they they they they mem- they know the story [yea [they heard yea and they heard* (lines 203–210). In her response, the HKC has employed two strategies to deal with the compliment, namely "Self-praise Avoidance Mechanism: Praise Downwards: Agreement" and "Self-praise Avoidance Mechanism: Referent Shifts: Reassignment" (Pomerantz 1978).

The HKC expresses that she 'was surprised' that the story-reading session had gone so well. The use of 'surprised' implies that the propositions in the compliment were out of her expectation. As such, 'surprised' is used as an expression of modesty on her part. Among the Chinese, being modest as a manifestation of humility is regarded as ideal in daily communication (Gu 1990). Acting or speaking modestly means not to exaggerate their ability or accomplishments, so that they would not lose face if they are later discovered by others as idly boasting, or if something turns out differently (Brunner and You 1988). 'I was surprised' is therefore an attempt on the part of the HKC to minimize her ability or accomplishments reflected in the 'very good job' that she has performed. After responding with 'I was surprised', the HKC gives credit to the audience, saying *they responded to that so well.* She explicitly gives her opinion that 'they' (the people to whom she told the story) responded to the story so well, rather than, for example, 'I told the story so well'. This is a case of shifting reference to 'they' (the audience) and reassigning credit to 'they' (the audience). The HKC does not accept the compliment but shifts the credit to others.

Almost immediately after that, the HKC attempts, in a non-fluent way, to provide an explanation for her good performance in the story-reading session at Mass earlier that day, when she says *[so they they they they they they mem- they know the story [yea [they heard yea and they heard*. Her stuttering indicates that she is searching hard for the proper words to use. It may also indicate that she feels so flattered that she is lost for words. She wanted to use 'memorize' but changes halfway through to *know*, but stops to look for the right word. The NES offers the word *heard* (line 209), which is instantaneously taken up by the HKC, who says *they heard yea and they heard* (line 210).

The speakers in Extract 5 below were colleagues working in a centre in a university. The mission of this centre was to work collaboratively with academic staff to help improve the quality of teaching and learning in the university. Senior Officers in the centre were specialists in such areas as teaching and course development, student learning, educational technology, programme evaluation and web-based teaching. The NES was a Senior Officer responsible for educational technology. Similar to academic staff, Senior Officers working in this centre were active in research activities. The HKC belonged to a different rank of staff in the centre. Her job was mainly to provide audio-visual support to both the Senior Officers and academic staff in the university. For the HKC, the nature of her job did not require her to do research, and yet out of personal interest and professional development, she was involved in research projects. The NES and HKC were co-researchers in some projects related to educational technology.

In the extract the speakers are discussing an overseas conference. The HKC is more interested in visiting the country rather than presenting a paper because she has not been to that country before. The NES is not interested in the conference itself, but he offers to write a joint paper with the HKC. He suggests that if the HKC collects previous proceedings of the conference, he can come up with something. If the paper gets accepted, she can go there to present it. The practice has been that the centre in which they work sponsors staff to attend conferences.

(5) 007
B: male Australian a: female Hong Kong Chinese
89. B: that's why it would be good to get hold of all the
90. last year's conference proceedings
91. a: mhmm
92. B: that's what I would do and then you can get a flavour
93. of what the conference is all about
94. a: mhmm (.) I need to think seriously whether I really

95. want to go yea
96. B: yea well okay if you if you want to write a paper if
97. you decide you want to go and if you need to write a
98. paper to go if you want to write a paper if you want
99. to write a paper with me
100. a: yes
101. B: then all I ask you is to bring last year's conference
102. a: okay
103. B: we will sit down and we will come up with a paper
104. a: yea okay it's easy for you
105. B: guaranteed
106. a: guaranteed (.) good (.) guaranteed good quality
107. B: oh absolutely
108. a: ((laugh))
109. B: you wouldn't put your name to a poor quality one
110. would you
111. a: no
112. B: you knew that ((laugh))
113. a: okay so that's our office you just put a sign when
114. you see this one
115. B: I don't want that if if you come with with the
116. proceedings then we will have a look in fact I got
117. one on Friday I got this whole package on Friday
118. a: mhmm
119. B: I put it in the circular file
120. ((a and B laugh))

The background to Extract 5 can best be summed up in the NES's repetitive and quite convoluted turns in lines 96–99, 101 and 103 — *yea well okay if you if you want to write a paper if you decide you want to go and if you need to write a paper to go if you want to write a paper if you want to write a paper with me, then all I ask you is to bring last year's conference,* and *we will sit down and we will come up with a paper.*

The HKC says *yea okay* in response to his suggestion and request, followed by a compliment — *it's easy for you* (line 104). The NES responds with an explicit agreement (*guaranteed,* line 105). The HKC's reaction to the explicit agreement of the NES is to upgrade her compliment. In her upgrade, the HKC has effectively echoed the word used by the NES, on top of which she has added a positive adjective (*good*) to categorically say that the paper will be *guaranteed good quality.* The NES responds with a further upgrade *oh absolutely.* The HKC laughs at this point. Almost immediately, the NES asks a tag question (*you wouldn't put your name to a poor quality one would you*, lines 109–110) which is interpreted as returning a compliment. The HKC responds to this "return" by agreeing with him, saying *no*, which is then supported by the NES *you knew that* with laughter. Further analysis of this compliment-compliment response event is given below.

The HKC's compliment can be seen to have triggered a chain of upgrading action as well as a return compliment. The NES's compliment response *oh absolutely* is more than an agreement; it is an upgrade. As the participants have adopted a playful attitude in this context of situation, the NES's compliment response *oh absolutely* is therefore not likely to be perceived by the HKC as the NES being boastful and pompous, or lacking in modesty. In fact, after the playful and jovial *oh absolutely*, the NES adopts "return" as a compliment responding strategy by using a tag question (*you wouldn't put your name to a poor quality one would you*). The NES is saying that the HKC would care about the quality of the paper, and thus implying a high level of academic expectations or standard on the part of the HKC. "Return" is a sub-strategy of "Referent Shifts", which is a form of "Self-praise Avoidance Mechanism" (Pomerantz 1978). The object of compliment has effectively been shifted from his good quality work to the HKC's high levels of expectation.

The fact that the speakers are colleagues and have been working collaboratively on research suggests that the NES's response to the compliment is not likely to be taken at face value. In fact, this kind of response can only occur between people who know each other very well. Extract 5 hence illustrates the relevance and importance of such social parameters as power and social distance that determine what constitutes an appropriate compliment response. The extract also illustrates the importance of making sense of discourse within the immediate context of situation. First of all, it is clear from the context that *guaranteed (.) good (.) guarantee good quality* refers to the quality of the conference paper that the NES proposes to write with the HKC. Second, the interchange takes place in a light-hearted manner as both of the speakers sound playful, and the HKC actually laughs upon hearing the NES's compliment response. This is not to say that the complimenter is not serious about what she said. On the contrary, it is highly likely that the HKC really thinks that writing the paper is 'easy for' the NES, probably because the NES is an expert in the field and he is a native speaker of the language in which the paper is written. What is interesting about the HKC's compliment 'it's easy for you' is that it is actually substantiated by the compliment-recipient (the NS) who responds with an upgrade (*oh absolutely*). The "Self-praise Avoidance Mechanism: Referent Shifts: Return" (Pomerantz 1978) adopted by the NES as a compliment response strategy has demonstrated that the NES is concerned about addressing the positive face of the HKC (complimenter). This indicates that the participants paying concern for the "interests, needs and wants" of each other in the conversation (Brown and Levinson 1987: 103).

Apart from this, the response of the NES does reveal cultural differences. Though the NES is being playful and is deliberately flouting the maxim of modesty in responding to compliments, the fact that he positively evaluates himself (*guaranteed*, line 105; *oh absolutely*, line 107) says something about the cultural differences between the two speakers. In a way, his utterance *you wouldn't put your name to a poor quality one would you* (lines 109–110) is an oblique positive evaluation of himself, through the positive evaluation of the quality of the paper he writes.

In Extract 6 the participants were both working in the same university, but in different departments. The NES was an academic staff and the HKC an administrator. The HKC was a former student of the NES who had enrolled on a Postgraduate Diploma (PgD) programme offered by the NES's department. Due to the nature of the programme, which was part-time postgraduate, the NES had become quite friendly with the HKC. The HKC had recently invited the NES to attend her wedding, and asked the NES for lunch in a Chinese dim-sum restaurant to show him her wedding photos. Before the extract begins the HKC has asked the NES about his teaching duties this semester, and the NES is describing his teaching involvement in the PgD programme.

(6) 023
B: male British a: female Hong Kong Chinese
361. B: I've got a bit on that (.) and I'll be doing the PgD
362. a: mm how many subjects
363. B: mm (.) I think the first term I I don't have that
364. much teaching I just have the (.) the undergraduates
365. on er on our own English degree and the PgD I think
366. that's it (.) because now what I teach is in the
367. first semester on the PgD it's been reorganized with
368. the credit based [(.) so I I'll be teaching (.) well
369. a: [mhmm
370. and it'll be a pity not to teach on the PgD because
371. (.) I think everybody who teaches on the PgD (.) very
372. quickly it becomes their favourite programme
373. a: why
374. B: well I suppose (.) it's a mixture of things but one
375. of the reasons I think is the students (.) the
376. students are always (.) [great to teach well yea they
377. a: [more mature
378. are more mature they come from a variety of
379. backgrounds [so they've got a lot of experience which
380. a: [mm

381. they bring to class [so it's a it's much more a two
382. a: [mhmm
383. way process the students contribute a lot in terms of
384. their ideas and and so on it's very nice yea
385. a: do you know that mm our classes like you our class
386. like you very much your ranking
387. ((a and B laugh))
388. a: according to us is very high we like teaching we like
389. J_ to teach er I mean J_ L_ [and yea you two are the
390. B: [yea
391. most fa- favourite teachers
392. B: mm (.) well that's (.) that's kind of you to say that
393. (.) yea
394. a: we need S_ but for sometimes for sometimes we think
395. that she's too (.) too nervous mm or too too strict
396. I think we think

In lines 375–384, the NES praises the students on the PgD programme as a reason why he enjoys teaching on the programme. The HKC contributes to developing the topic by saying how the students perceive the NES as a teacher. What she says about the NES is positive, complimentary and flattering (*do you know that mm our classes like you our class like you very much your ranking [((a and B laugh))] according to us is very high*, lines 385–388). The compliment topic is the relevant qualities of the NES and his performance as a teacher of the PgD students.

After paying the compliment, she does not pause to receive a response from the NES. Rather, she continues and asks a rhetorical question, brings in another teacher J_ L_, and comments that both the NES and J_ L_ are their most favourite teachers (lines 389–391). The compliment is hence extended to another teacher (J_ L_) as well. In this case, the HKC supports her explicit compliment with a comparison. The utterance is a compliment from the NES's viewpoint, and is praise from J_ L_'s viewpoint (Holmes, 1988). Complimenting satisfies the addressee's expectations, while "praising" expresses a positive judgment for a referential/informative reason (Lewandowska-Tomaszczyk 1989).

The NES's compliment response is *mm (.) well that's (.) that's kind of you to say that* (line 392), which is an "acceptance". The response is, however, reformulated and hedged with mitigation, with the actual "acceptance" pushed into the turn. His acceptance *that's kind of you to say that* is prefaced with a hesitation marker *mm*, followed by a slight pause, and then *well*, which indicates that he is giving himself time to think about what to say next. As the acceptance is delayed or withheld until later in the turn, this compliment response has the features of a "dispreferred" structure (Pomerantz 1984). The dispreferred response is "the structurally unexpected next act" (Yule 1996: 79). The delayed acceptance indicates a degree of modesty on the part of the NES. However, compared to the previous extracts where the HKC participants give no verbal response at all, reject the compliment and use "Self-praise Avoidance", the NES in Extract 6 accepts the compliment despite the use of features typical of a "dispreferred response".

In Extract 7 below the participants were in-laws. They were in the NES's home having a chat before dinner. The NES is explaining to his sister-in-law some barter business on the Internet that he is thinking of starting up. Acting as a broker, he is planning to help people to advertise and exchange goods.

(7) 004
B: male British a: female Hong Kong Chinese

258. a: but (.) I think it's already had that kind of er
259. business (.) or I don't know I don't think there's
260. business in Hong Kong because it's free of charge
261. [because sometimes I read these er I I read these
262. B: [er
263. from the other magazines or newspaper etcetera it's
264. free of charge to exchange the things
265. B: er yea but you what I'll do is act as a broker [to
266. a: [mhmm
267. connect all the different firms together and I charge
268. them a [fee
269. a: [but (.) the people can do this through the
270. Internet can they
271. B: they can but there's nothing in Asia you can do it in
272. America
273. a: yea
274. B: you can do it in Europe but there's no company in
275. Asia no company in Hong Kong who does it 'cos I've
276. checked the Internet and there's no company in Hong
277. Kong that does this
278. a: no this kind of of business in in Asia in Hong Kong
279. B: no and that's amazing
280. a: oh you are the cl- clevelest the cleverest
281. B: cleverest genius
282. a: is it
283. B: ah well that may be
284. a: are you
285. B: I don't know I just it seems very I have checked

286. everything I cannot see any company that does
287. anything similar
288. a: have you talked (.) about this with your friends
289. B: yea and everyone I've spoken to people who're in
290. businesses who are in advertising agencies
291. a: yea
292. B: I haven't told every one 'cos I don't want every one
293. to know

The HKC queries him about the feasibility and viability of that kind of business in Hong Kong in lines 258–264, saying *but (.) I think it's already had that kind of er business (.) or I don't know I don't think there's business in Hong Kong because it's free of charge [because sometimes I read these er I I read these from the other magazines or newspaper etcetera it's free of charge to exchange the things.* In response the NES replies that he has done his research and is certain that *there's no company in Asia no company in Hong Kong who does this* (lines 274–275) business on the Internet.

The HKC then gives the NES a compliment by saying *oh you are the cl- cleverest the cleverest* (line 280), and the NES responds with an upgrade *cleverest genius.* This is challenged by the HKC who asks *is it* (line 282). The NES's response to this is a hedged one — *ah well that may be.* The HKC continues pushing the NES with another reduced question *are you* (line 284). The NES's response is getting increasingly tentative and hedged — *I don't know I just it seems very.* The NES does not finish this particular utterance, and he drifts to say *I have checked everything I cannot see any company that does anything similar* (lines 285–287). This is the NES trying to offer justification for his calling himself the 'cleverest genius'.

The HKC's explicit compliment is directed to the NES's ability or insights. The NES's compliment response is a sophisticated one. The first response is an "upgrade compliment" (*cleverest genius*). It is when the HKC asks *is it* that the NES becomes tentative (*ah well that may be*) which is "Self-praise Avoidance Mechanism: Praise Downgrades: (Implicit) Disagreement" (Pomerantz 1978). As discussed previously, the "praise downgrades" is performed by means of hedging, implicit disagreement, reformulation and justification, which function to mitigate the force of the compliment paid to him by the HKC. From *cleverest genius* to *ah well that may be* to *I don't know I just it seems very,* the NES has significantly and increasingly downgraded his first compliment response.

It is argued that in the course of the speech event, there is a change in the way the HKC and the NES perceive the compliment and response event, though in opposite directions. The compliment paid by the HKC (*oh you are the cl- cleverest the cleverest*) is a serious one, but the response from the NES (*cleverest genius*) is not serious but is playful. Hearing the response, the HKC changes to a playful mood and asks the NES challenging questions. When being challenged, the NES becomes embarrassed about himself, and then changes to a state of seriousness when giving the tentative and hedged response and drifts to justify calling himself the 'cleverest genius'.

Discussion of seven compliment-compliment response sequences

In the seven compliment-compliment response sequences, not every compliment is matched with a compliment response. In both Extracts 1 and 2, the compliment-recipients do not produce a response. Table 5.1 summarizes the compliment topics and compliment responses in Extracts 1–7.

Table 5.1. Compliment topics and compliment responses in seven extracts

Ext.	Speaker/ Adressee	Compliment Topics	Compliment Response Type
1	female NES/ female HKC	Hard work, ability, achievement at work and in studies	No opportunity, or not quick enough to produce a verbal response (possibly some kind of non-verbal response has been given)
2	male NES/ male HKC	Vision, ability, achievement reflected in company philosophy	No compliment response. Only back-channel *uh huh.*
3	male NES/ female HKC	Appearance: figure; ability on fugrues	Outright rejection: A bald-on-record disagreement
4	female NES/ female HKC	Performance in story-reading class in church	Self-praise Avoidance Mechanism: Downgrades: (Implicit) Agreement; Self-praise Avoidance Mechanism: Reference Shifts: Reassignment
5	female HKC/ male NES	Ability and predicted performance in writing conference paper	Acceptance (agreement) ↓ Further upgrade (following an upgrade compliment by HKC) ↓ Self-praise Avoidance Mechanism: Reference Shifts: Return
6	female HKC/ male NES	Implied teaching performance	Acceptance (agreement): containing features of a dispreferred response
7	female HKC/ male NES	Implied ability and insights related to running business on the Internet	Acceptance (agreement): An upgrade ↓ Self-praise Avoidance Mechanism: Praise Downgrade: (hedged) Agreement & avoid explicit disagreement with justification

Compliment topics

The intercultural conversations examined in the present study took place in various physical and social contexts of situation, and so the topics cover a wide range of subject contents, rather than being confined to a specific group of topics, unlike, for example, Wieland's (1995) study of dinner table conversations between French and American speakers of French, in which the topics for compliments are confined to food, apartment, language ability of the American speakers of French and personal appearance. The compliment topics given by NES in Extracts 1–4 are related to HKC's hard work, ability, or achievement (N=2), appearance: 'figure' (N=1) and performance (N=1). HKC's compliment topics in Extracts 5–7 are concerned with NES's ability, implied ability and predicted/implied performance (N=3). The findings lend some support to the literature regarding cultural differences in compliment topics.

Despite the very small number of instances of compliment topics, the findings seem to be largely similar to those of previous studies on compliments. With respect to favoured compliment topics among the Chinese, performance has been found to be the preferred compliment topic (Ye 1995), and this has been confirmed by HKC's compliment topics in this study. In Western culture, the most commonly evaluated aspects are concerned with appearance and/or possession or abilities and/or accomplishments (Manes and Wolfson 1981; Wolfson and Manes 1980; Manes 1983; Holmes 1988). In this study, NES speakers have paid compliments on HKC's ability, achievement, performance and appearance. The NES speaker in Extract 3 compliments the HKC on her figure.

What differs from previous studies is the wide range of contexts of conversation examined in this study. Most of the compliments examined are made in a serious way, but some of them are made in a playful manner intended to tease the addressee, for example, in the case of the NES teasing his sister-in-law about her figure and punning on the word 'figure'.

Compliment response types

The compliment response types given by HKC and NES have been classified by applying Pomerantz's (1978) taxonomy of compliment response types (Table 5.1). The compliment responses, or absence of verbal response, or even back-channel cues are interesting to analyze. In the case of HKC, their responses are more wide-ranging from absence of a verbal response to a back-channel signal to an (implicit) agreement to an outright rejection. Conversely, all of the NES's compliment responses are accepting the compliment, though the acceptances differ in linguistic realizations and implications.

Regarding the absence of verbal response in Extracts 1 and 2, this can be attributed to the naturally occurring conversations examined, which show what real people actually do, or do not do, verbally in real-life and real-time interaction. The fact that speakers take quick turns in the interaction means that a missed chance for a speaker to give a verbal response at a particular point may never be recovered. Another plausible reason is that Chinese is a high-context culture (Hall 1977). In high-context cultures, messages tend to be covert and implicit, meanings are internalized, and there is a great emphasis on nonverbal cues. In Extracts 1 and 2, nonverbal responses could very well have substituted a verbal response. The HKC in both extracts may have assumed that the sense of the non-response, which can be either silent acceptance or silent rejection, is taken for granted and shared by the interlocutor, and so there is no need to express it verbally. It is also likely that HKC, when being complimented, find themselves caught between the norms of behaviour of both Chinese and Western cultures. As the conversations were audio-recorded, the rich, fluid and informative nonverbal communication, such as facial expressions, is not available for examination. Nevertheless, no response or a minimal response is atypical of the Western cultural norm in terms of generally accepted compliment aspects that are considered to be positive by society.

Back-channelling is employed by the HKC in Extract 2. It is likely that he uses back-channelling to indicate that the message has been received (Tsui 1994). This study argues that back-channel cues should be treated as a warranted response to a compliment, especially in situations where either other possible compliment responses are not considered appropriate, or when the recipient of the compliment cannot decide quickly enough how to respond to the compliment. In such situations, back-channel signals may be preferred to a non-verbal response. Giving a back-channel response at least indicates interactive, supportive intention by the compliment-recipient.

Another interesting finding is that in two Extracts (5 and 7), the NES, as the compliment-recipient, have made more than one response, in the sense that they deal with the compliment with a series of different responses serving different purposes that are appropriate to the unfolding conversation. The response can change from non-seriously and playfully boasting to being modest and humble.

On the whole, the different compliment responding behaviours exhibited by HKC and NES appear to support previous research findings. The patterns observed can be explained by differences in the social norms between the Chinese and native speakers of English. Loh (1993), for example, points out that the proper response for HKC is to deny the compliment by means of disagreement, a downscaling of compliment, or a shifting of credit, and at the same time upgrading the complimenter. The Chinese social norm is such that the complimenter does not expect an agreement, and the compliment-recipient should appear modest, though not necessarily "think humbly of themselves" (Chen 1993: 67), as appearing humble and modest in compliment responding situations will help maintain and enhance one's face and image. As noted by Du (1986), in social interactions it is often best for the Chinese to appear respectful and modest as a manifestation of humility. In order to uphold the Chinese concept of politeness, the proper and polite way for the Chinese to respond to a compliment is to deny the compliment and to shift the credit either to the complimenter or others.

The NES in Extract 6 responds to the compliment with a delayed acceptance. This provides support to some research studies on Westerners' compliment responses which have found that Westerners are more likely to use the strategies of praise downgrade, acceptance with qualification, return, or even rejection (Pomerantz 1978; Herbert 1986, 1989). According to Pomerantz (1978: 81–82), when an individual receives a compliment, "the preferences to (*a*) agree with and/or accept compliments and (*b*) avoid self-praise stand in potential conflict". Herbert (1989) found a low frequency in "acceptance" among his American subjects due to American notions of equality and democratic idealism. In Extracts 5 and 7, acceptance is given by the NES speakers, but acceptance is given with an intention to be playful. The participants are teasing each other and having fun, and so some of the compliment responses have to be viewed and interpreted accordingly. In fact, in both cases, when the mood of the NES speakers changes from playfulness to seriousness, the NES change their strategy from "Acceptance" to "Self-praise avoidance mechanism: Reference shifts: Return" (Extract 5) and "Self-praise avoidance mechanism: Praise downgrades: Agreement and avoid explicit disagreement with justification" (Extract 7).

Conclusion

Sociolinguistic and pragmatic studies on complimenting have mainly focused on "fairly narrow linguistic contexts" and "compliment-response sequences consisting of two- or three-part exchanges" (Johnson 1992: 67), or employed instruments that elicit hypothetical and contrived data. In this study, individual speech acts of compliment and compliment response that occurred in naturally occurring conversations were investigated. The investigation has produced two major conclusions about the way HKC and NES manage the speech act of compliment response. First of all, different from HKC, NES are much more likely to accept the compliment, even though an acceptance is either delayed and hedged, or later on changed to praise downgrades and reference shift. HKC, however, do not use acceptance as a compliment response strategy. Second, different from NES, HKC are more likely to not give any verbal response when being complimented, and also in the case of one

HKC, a direct, blunt, outright rejection is given. With respect to managing the act of compliment response, differences can be seen to exist between HKC and NES.

The findings have confirmed some of the conventional wisdom relating to the relationships between socio-cultural variation and communicative behaviours. No doubt, there are socio-cultural factors and the process of socialization which influence what a speaker might choose to say in particular situations. Nevertheless, this study is of the view that there are context-specific factors that can exert influence on the choice of compliment response types. For instance, whether a speaker is serious or playful can inform the linguistic realizations of a compliment or a compliment response. In other words, whether a complimenter or a compliment-recipient has another level of meaning through particular linguistic realizations can determine how a compliment or a compliment response should be received. There is no one-to-one relationship between a compliment and how it should be responded to.

What is important is that the conversational participants co-ordinate what they mutually know in order to comprehend utterances (Gibbs 1987). Talk can be seen in terms of the action and interaction of the participants and a fundamental condition for talk is mutual understanding (van Dijk 1985). As observed by Taylor and Cameron (1987: 5), conversational participants almost invariably manage to meet accepted standards of relevance and politeness, resulting in talk which is both "co-operative and non-bizarre". Conversationalists are engaged in an ongoing negotiation of meaning which forms a "working agreement" (Goffman 1983: 10) on what constitutes mutual understanding in a particular conversation.

Chapter 6

Simultaneous talk

Introduction

Simultaneous talk in conversation is an important discourse organizational feature which reveals the ways in which conversationalists organize their turns relative to those of their interlocutors. Simultaneous talk in intercultural conversation can offer insights into the way speakers of different cultural orientations align their turns-at-talk in relation to those of others in a certain manner. This study investigates the nature of simultaneous talk and the functions of various forms of simultaneous talk; as well as the effects of social, cultural and contextual factors on the relative tendencies of HKC and NES both to initiate simultaneous talk and to yield the floor when simultaneous talk occurs.

A "Typology of Initiation of and Yielding to Simultaneous Talk" (see Figures 6.1– 6.3 below) was proposed by this study to capture and describe the major types of simultaneous speech of HKC and NES in their respective roles of Current Speaker (CS) and Initiator of Simultaneous Talk (IST). The Typology describes three types of simultaneous talk:

Type A: Simultaneous talk starting at a non-TRP of the Current Speaker's turn
Type B: Simultaneous talk starting at or near a TRP of the Current Speakers' turn
Type C: Simultaneous talk starting at turn beginning

Each type of ST was then further categorized to allow for yielding and unyielding verbal behaviours of HKC and NES, in their respective roles of CS and IST. The term "yield" is used in this study for both the CS and the IST. When a speaker yields, he or she stops talking and yields the turn to his or her interlocutor. Conversely, when a speaker does not yield, he or she holds on to the turn and continues speaking, but does not relinquish the turn.

Specifically, the Typology will be applied to:

1. compare the relative frequencies of occurrence of Type A simultaneous talk (non-TRP) and Type B simultaneous talk (at or near a TRP) initiated by HKC and NES respectively;
2. compare the relative tendencies for HKC and NES to yield, as well as not to yield, in situations of simultaneous talk when the "one-at-a-time" (Sacks,

1971) model of conversation is being violated (i.e. all of the three types of simultaneous talk in the Typology); and

3. explore data qualitatively with a view to accounting for the observed similarities and differences between HKC and NES when they produce simultaneous talk in conversation, as deduced from their acts of initiating simultaneous talk, yielding to initiation of simultaneous talk, and unyielding to initiation of simultaneous talk.

Stereotypical beliefs about the Chinese are that they are a collectivistic and hierarchical culture (Hofstede 1980, 1983, 1991). One would therefore expect that the Chinese would be similar to Murata's (1994) Japanese subjects, who defer more to the "territorial imperative". In other words, when engaging in social interaction, HKC are hypothesized to be vigilant and controlled in their verbal behaviours. They will show greater care about their interlocutor's negative-face and positive-face wants. They will be more mindful about not violating the speaker rights of their interlocutors. NES may dominate over HKC, as non-native speakers, by initiating simultaneous talk more frequently. Also, when HKC initiates simultaneous talk, NES will be less likely to relinquish their current turn.

Based on the cultural assumptions made about HKC and NES, it was therefore hypothesized that:

1. On the whole, HKC will initiate fewer instances of simultaneous talk than NES.
2. Compared to NES, HKC will be more likely to initiate simultaneous talk at or near a TRP (Type B) than at a non-TRP (Type A), as a non-TRP is not considered a rightful position for initiating ST.
3. Compared to NES, HKC will yield more readily, irrespective of the turn positions at which simultaneous talk is initiated, and irrespective of whether they are a CS or an IST.

Exemplifying typology of initiation of and yielding to simultaneous talk

In the following, each of the three types of simultaneous talk will be described and illustrated with excerpts drawn from the intercultural conversations. First of all, Type A simultaneous talk is described in Figure 6.1 below:

(A) Simultaneous talk starting at a non-TRP of CS's turn

```
(A1)   CS yields. IST does not yield.
       CS:     -----------[------------x
       IST:               [-------------------------------^
                          (non-TRP)
(A2)   IST yields. CS does not yield.
       CS:     -----------[----------------------------------^
       IST:               [-------------x
                          (non-TRP)
```

Figure 6.1. Typology of Initiation of and Yielding to Simultaneous Talk: Type A

The following excerpts illustrate (A1) and (A2) types of simultaneous talk. In both cases, simultaneous talk is introduced at a non-TRP of the Current Speaker's turn-at-talk. In (A1), the CS yields, but the IST does not. In (A2), it is the other way round.

```
(A1)   016
a:     female Hong Kong Chinese           B:  male British
165.   a:          you said your mother and your sister (.)
166.               [have come to
167.   B:   (A1)   [no just my mother yes my mother's come she's a
168.               [a
169.   a:   (A1)   [does she aware of the chicken disease in Hong
170.               Kong
171.   B:          oh she's read about it [yea yea
172.   a:                                 [yea yea what does she
173.               feel er it it
```

```
(A2)   004
a:     female Hong Kong Chinese           B:  male British
124    a:          but (.) did you earn
125.   B:          yep [I earn on warrant made just a profit not a
126.   a:   (A2)       [you made the profit
127.               big profit 'cos I only invested a small amount
128.               of money [but then I made profit (.) in New
129.   a:                   [mm
130.               Zealand on shares
```

Type B ST is described in Figure 6.2 as follows:

(B) Simultaneous talk starting at or near a TRP of CS's turn

```
(B1)   CS yields. IST does not yield.
       CS:     ----------[-----------x
       IST:              [------------------------------^
                     (at or near a TRP)
(B2)   IST yields. CS does not yield.
       CS:     ----------[-------------------------------^
       IST:              [------------x
                     (at or near a TRP)
```

Figure 6.2. Typology of Initiation of and Yielding to Simultaneous Talk: Type B

The following excerpts illustrate (B1) and (B2) type of simultaneous talk. In (B1), in line 53, the CS (HKC) yields to the simultaneous talk initiated by the NES.

```
(B1)    019
B:      male British                b:  male Hong Kong Chinese
51.     B:  so they are not giving me all in one go they're
52.         giving it to me (.) in installments
53.     b:  uh huh by [in
54.     B:  (B1)      [and that should go to me not to the
55.         company unless it goes to the company and
56.         the company pays [me
57.     b:                   [yea yea but that depends on
58.         the consideration of the new (.) new share
59.         issues
```

In (B2), the HKC initiates simultaneous talk (*yea because*, line 405) at a non-TRP of the NES's turn-at-talk. The HKC yields her turn before finishing it. She continues her unfinished utterance (lines 407–412) after the NES has completed his turn.

```
(B2)    023
a:      female Hong Kong Chinese              B:  male British
397.    a:  yea maybe pay for the extra if if [if the fare for
398.    B:                                    [right
399.        the wrong train is [higher than the original one
400.    B:                     [yea
401.        then you need to take another train to the place
402.        where you want to go to
403.    B:  so that's the complete opposite of Hong Kong then
404.        where you [with this would this Octopus card you can
405.    a:    (B2)    [yea because
406.        use it across different companies
```

```
407.    a:  because in Hong Kong for the MTR mm if you get on the
408.        opposite side then you can take back the train  [but
409.    B:                                                   [yea
410.        in Japan you can you cannot do so and in one station
411.        there are many many there maybe er four to five or
412.        even six to seven platforms
```

The last type of simultaneous talk, Type C, is described in Figure 6.3.

```
(C) Simultaneous talk starting at turn beginning
    (C1)  HKC yields. NES does not yield.
    *HKC: [-----------x
    NES:  [---------------------------------^
    (C2)  NES yields. HKC does not yield.
    *HKC: [---------------------------------^
    NES:  [----------x
```

* The schematic presentation does not indicate a particular sequence in which HKC and NES speak. The line by NES may very well be above that of HKC in the transcription. In fact, this category of simultaneous talk is that both HKC and NES start talking at the same time.

Figure 6.3. Typology of Initiation of and Yielding to Simultaneous Talk: Type C

The following conversational extracts illustrate (C1) and (C2) types of simultaneous talk. In (C1), both speakers start talking simultaneously at turn beginning position (lines 561 and 562). The female HKC yields her turn to the NES.

```
(C1)    015
B:      male British                 a:  female Hong Kong Chinese
558.    B:  I have to be thinking all the time about what to
559.        say and how to pronounce it
560.    a:  mhmm mm hm
561.    B:  erm (.) [whereas obviously in English I can talk
562.    a:     (C1) [but how
563.        without even thinking about it
564.    a:  mhmm mhmm (.) do you think if you stay in French
565.        for a long time in a French community for a longer
566.        time (.) it will help
567.    B:  definitely (.) in [fact most of my French speaking
568.    a:                    [mm
569.        ability has come from (.) long periods in France
570.        [you know (.) all my (.) education in English
571.    a:  [uh huh
572.        school to learn French
```

In (C2), the HKC is showing some old photos of her son in primary school. In response, the NES says *yea right* (line 22). After a slight pause, both speakers start to talk at the same time. The NES yields her turn. She probably tries to say that she must show the HKC some photos in return. The HKC does not yield but continues with her turn.

(C2)	022	
a:	female Hong Kong Chinese	A: female British
20.	a:	oh this is the first day we went to primary
21.		school
22.	A:	yea right (.) [I must show you
23.	a:	(C2) [and I can show you some picture
24.		about the last [day in primary school
25.	A:	[okay yea show me
26.	A:	yea right
27.	a:	oh this is a some sort of er information
28.		pamphlet about [his school but he hasn't
29.	A:	[oh yes yes
30.		opened it

Analysis of simultaneous talk in the intercultural conversations

All tokens of simultaneous talk identified in the 25 intercultural conversations were examined to find out the relative frequencies of occurrence of the three types of simultaneous talk initiated by HKC and NES respectively. For both Type A and Type B, HKC and NES were compared in terms of their relative readiness to initiate simultaneous talk. For all of the three types of simultaneous talk, HKC and NES were compared in terms of their relative readiness to yield or not to yield. Observed similarities and differences in the patterns will be accounted for, through deducing from the immediate intercultural context of situation.

Occurrence of simultaneous talk

A total of 974 instances of simultaneous talk were found in the 25 intercultural conversations. Each instance of simultaneous talk was coded and categorized, using the Typology devised by this study (Table 6.1).

Table 6.1. Breakdown of all instances of simultaneous talk into three types

Type A: At a non-TRP		**Type B: At or near a TRP**		**Type C: At turn beginning**		**Total**	
Tokens	%	Tokens	%	Tokens	%	Tokens	%
580	59.5	360	37	34	3.5	974	100

The most frequently occurring type of simultaneous talk has been found to be Type A (at a non-TRP) (59.5%), followed by Type B (at or near a TRP) (37%). Simultaneous talk starting at turn beginning (Type C) constitutes only 3.5% of the total. Its rare occurrence may be attributable to the nature of the data, i.e. dyadic conversations. This kind of simultaneous talk is likely to happen more frequently in multi-party conversations where more than one participant self-selects at the same moment.

For each of the three types of simultaneous talk, the frequencies of occurrence in initiation, yielding and unyielding by HKC and NES, in the role of CS and IST respectively, are presented in Table 6.2.

Table 6.2. Three types of simultaneous talk: Initiation, yielding and unyielding

Total tokens of ST	**Type A: At a non-TRP** 598	**Type B: At or near a TRP** 360	**Type C: At turn beginning** 34
	Tokens	Tokens	Tokens
HKC as CS	308	171	
HKC as IST	272	189	
HKC yielding	311	191	19
– as CS	182	93	
– as IST	129	98	
HKC unyielding	269	169	15
– as CS	126	78	
– as IST	143	91	
NES as CS	272	189	
NES as IST	308	171	
NES yielding	269	169	15
– as CS	143	91	
– as IST	126	78	
NES unyielding	311	191	19
– as CS	129	98	
– as IST	182	93	

Findings presented in Table 6.2 will be discussed in the following.

Initiation of simultaneous talk

Table 6.3 shows HKC compared to NES in terms of the initiation of Type A and Type B simultaneous talk. Type C is not considered, as the frequency of occurrence is the same for both NES and HKC.

Table 6.3. Instances of simultaneous talk initiated by HKC and NES: Type A vs. Type B

	Type A: **At a non-TRP** Tokens	**Type B:** **At or near a TRP** Tokens	**(A)+(B)(A)&(B) compared** Tokens	
HKC as IST	272	189	461	(A) >* (B) = 43.9%
NES as IST	308	71	479	(A) > (B) = 80.0%
Total	580	360	**940**	(A) > (B) = 61.1%

* The symbol ">" means 'more frequently than'.

Hypothesis 1 states that on the whole, HKC will initiate fewer instances of simultaneous talk than NES. This has been supported by the findings, although by a small percentage. HKC initiate 461 instances of simultaneous talk and NES 479 instances. HKC initiate 3.76% fewer instances of simultaneous talk than NES.

Hypothesis 2 states that compared to NES, HKC will be more likely to initiate simultaneous talk at or near a TRP (Type B) than otherwise (Type A), as a TRP is considered a rightful position for introducing simultaneous talk. The findings presented in Table 6.3 above, however, show that on the whole, both groups of speakers initiate greater instances of Type A than Type B simultaneous talk. For HKC, Type A exceeds Type B by 43.9%; for NES, Type A exceeds Type B by a much greater extent (80%). This suggests that although both HKC and NES are more likely to initiate Type A than Type B simultaneous talk, the difference in the instances of Type A and Type B simultaneous talk introduced by HKC is, however, not as great as that introduced by NES. Table 6.4 compares each of the two types of simultaneous talk.

Table 6.4. Initiation of Type A simultaneous talk and Type B simultaneous talk: HKC vs. NES

	Type A: At a non-TRP Tokens	**Type B: At or near a TRP** Tokens
HKC as IST	272	189
NES as IST	308	171
HKC & NES compared	NES > HKC = 13.2%	HKC > NES = 10.5%

For Type A, NES introduce 13.2% more instances than HKC; for Type B, HKC initiate 10.5% more instances than NES. These percentages hence confirm Hypothesis 2, demonstrating that HKC are indeed more likely than NES to introduce simultaneous talk at or near a TRP. The results suggest that in intercultural conversations, HKC are more aware of the turn-taking nature of conversation (Sacks et al. 1974). They are more mindful about turn organization in conversation, and thus introducing ST at the "rightful" position of the CS's turn-at-talk; in other words, cutting in on the CS's turn-at-talk at positions where speakers are normally entitled to take turns.

The turn-taking nature of conversation makes it essential for a participant to immediately get the turn-space at the next possible TRP in order to ensure his or her impending utterance being relevant to the ongoing talk. TRPs are projected as a turn unfolds, but not given in advance. HKC would need to monitor NES's talk to anticipate upcoming TRPs; and that is, to anticipate the first possible turn completion point within NES's utterance, and to then introduce a relevant utterance immediately. Further, HKC could not always be certain that an utterance is complete as speakers often add to what might appear to be completed turns. Such monitoring and self-selection (Sacks et al. 1974) is done "on-site" and in real time, i.e. as the current turn unfolds, and understandably requires a high level of skill in anticipating and recognizing TRPs. HKC have exhibited effective skilled performance in analyzing and understanding NES's utterance at the same time, and starting simultaneous talk effectively to achieve the intended functions. The result is interesting because one would have expected the opposite, based on the assumption that HKC, being non-native speakers of English, will not be as skillful as NES.

Nonetheless, until the functions of instances of simultaneous talk initiated by HKC, and by NES, are known, no conclusions can be drawn about the speakers' behaviours regarding initiation of simultaneous talk. As discussed in Chapter 2, simultaneous talk in conversation is more than indicative of conversational structure. It very often demonstrates complex interactional and conversational management strategies. Mey (2001: 277) points out that not only the rules that allow a speaker to "jump into" the ongoing conversation at a TRP vary from culture to culture, the notion of what constitutes a valid TRP can be different across cultures. The functions served by instances of simultaneous talk and the related strategies employed will be examined in the second part of this chapter.

Yielding to simultaneous talk

Hypothesis 3 maintains that compared to NES, HKC will yield more readily, irrespective of the turn positions at which ST is initiated, and irrespective of whether they are a CS or an IST. Table 6.5 compares HKC and NES in their relative tendencies to yield to initiation of the three types of simultaneous talk.

Table 6.5. Yielding to simultaneous talk: Type A, Type B and Type C

	Type A: **At a non-TRP** Tokens	**Type B:** **At or near a TRP** Tokens	**Type C:** **At turn beginning** Tokens	**Total** Tokens
HKC yielding	311	191	19	521
NES yielding	269	169	15	453
Total	580	360	34	974
HKC & NES compared	HKC > NES = 15.6%	HKC > NES = 13%	HKC > NES = 26.7%	HKC > NES = 15%

The findings presented in Table 6.5 show that overall, HKC are more likely than NES to yield to simultaneous talk initiated by the interlocutor. HKC yielded 521 times, while NES yielded 453 times, representing a difference of 15%. In fact, HKC yield more readily than NES in all of the three types of simultaneous talk: 15.6% for Type A, 13% for Type B, and 26.7% for Type C. The results support the first part of Hypothesis 3, which states that HKC, compared to NES, will yield more readily, irrespective of the turn positions at which simultaneous talk is initiated.

The results in Table 6.5 were further analyzed to test the second part of Hypothesis 3, namely whether HKC will be more likely than NES to yield, irrespective of whether they are in the role of a CS or an IST (Table 6.6). Only Type A and Type B were examined since for Type C, both HKC and NES, who start talking at the same time, are the CS.

Table 6.6. Yielding to simultaneous talk: CS vs. IST

	Type A: At a non-TRP		**Type B: At or near a TRP**	
	As CS	As IST	As CS	As IST
	Tokens	Tokens	Tokens	Tokens
HKC yielding	182	129	93	98
NES yielding	143	126	91	78
HKC & NES compared	HKC > NES = 27.3%	HKC > NES = 2.4%	HKC > NES = 2.2%	HKC > NES = 25.6%

Table 6.6 shows that HKC are more likely to yield than NES do, both as a CS and an IST, in both Type A and Type B simultaneous talk. However, the differences are very small (2.2–2.4%) when HKC initiate simultaneous talk at a non-TRP, and when they are a CS at or near a TRP. The difference is much bigger when HKC are a CS at a non-TRP (HKC>NES=27.3%), and when they are an IST at or near a TRP (HKC>NES=25.6%). In general, these findings support the second part of Hypothesis 3, as HKC are more likely to yield to initiation of simultaneous talk, both when they are a CS and an IST.

A closer examination of the differences underlines the phenomenon that compared to NES, HKC are more mindful about the turn-taking nature of conversation and observant of the turn-taking rules. HKC also behave in a much more cooperative manner. These phenomena are evident in two ways. First, when HKC are a CS, even when their NES interlocutors introduce simultaneous talk at a "non-rightful" position (non-TRP) of their turn-at-talk, HKC are 27.3% more likely to yield, compared to NES in a similar situation. Second, when HKC are an IST at or near a TRP of their NES's turn-at-talk, HKC are 25.6% more ready to yield, compared to their NES interlocutors in a similar situation. In other words, when HKC are introducing simultaneous talk at a "rightful" position, they are more conscious of the fact that they are violating the speaker's right of their NES interlocutors. On the whole, HKC, compared to NES, seem to be much more conscious of the cooperative nature of conversation, the success of which depends very much on the speakers' efforts to observe the turn-taking rules. Conversely, NES do not seem to be as mindful of the rules as HKC are in these respects.

So far, HKC have been compared to NES in yielding (Hypothesis 3) verbal behaviours. Below, each of the two groups of speakers will be examined individually (Tables 6.7 and 6.8). Only Type A and Type B simultaneous talk are studied.

As shown in Table 6.7, HKC are more likely to yield than otherwise at TRP (Type B), no matter whether they are a CS or an IST. Apart from that, HKC are a lot more yielding than unyielding (by 44.4%), even when NES initiate simultaneous talk at a non-TRP position (Type A). However, the findings show that HKC are more unyielding than yielding, when they initiate simultaneous talk at a non-TRP position, although the difference (10.9%) is not big. This particular finding seems to be at odds with the rest of the findings about HKC, which will be examined qualitatively in the second part of the chapter, where HKC will be compared with NES in terms of unyielding to simultaneous talk at a non-TRP position as an IST.

Table 6.7. HKC being yielding and unyielding to simultaneous talk: CS vs. IST

	Type A: At a non-TRP		**Type B: At or near a TRP**	
	Ac CS	As IST	As CS	As IST
	Tokens	Tokens	Tokens	Tokens
HKC yielding	182	129	93	98
HKC unyielding	129	143	78	91
Yielding & unyielding compared	yielding > unyielding = 44.4%	unyielding > yielding = 10.9%	yielding > unyielding = 19.27%	yielding > unyielding = 7.7%

Table 6.8 shows the NES's relative yielding and unyielding tendencies as far as simultaneous talk goes.

Table 6.8. NES being yielding and unyielding to simultaneous talk: CS vs. IST

	Type A: At a non-TRP		**Type B: At or near a TRP**	
	As CS	As IST	As CS	As IST
	Tokens	Tokens	Tokens	Tokens
NES yielding	143	126	91	78
NES unyielding	129	182	98	93
Yielding & unyielding compared	yielding > unyielding = 10.9%	unyielding > yielding = 44.5%	unyielding > yielding = 7.7%	unyielding > yielding = 19.2%

Similar to the preceding findings (Tables 6.5–6.6), NES tend to be more unyielding at TRP (Type B), no matter whether they are a CS or an IST. They are, nevertheless, a lot more unyielding when they themselves initiate simultaneous talk (by 44.5%), even at non-TRP positions. What differs from previous findings is that NES actually are inclined to yield, rather than not, when their HKC interlocutors cut in on their current turn-at-talk. The difference is 10.9%, which is not great.

As revealed in Tables 6.7 and 6.8, HKC and NES are similar in that at a non-TRP location (Type A), both are more ready to relinquish their turn when being interrupted, but less ready to do so when they themselves cut in on their interlocutors' current turn. The extent, however, differs between HKC and NES. Resistance is still less on the part of HKC. Nevertheless, HKC and NES are different when simultaneous talk occurs at or near a TRP (Type B). At the rightful position of turn-taking, HKC tend to be more yielding than unyielding, irrespective of whether they are a CS or an IST. Conversely, NES are more unyielding than yielding, both in the roles of a CS and an IST.

Proposed turn-taking patterns in HKC-NSE conversations

Below the major results of the quantitative data analysis are summarized. Accordingly, a set of ten turn-taking patterns specific to simultaneous talk in the HKC-NSE conversations is proposed. Compared to NES, HKC initiate 10.5% more simultaneous talk at or near a TRP (Type B) (Table 6.4). ST beginning at this position shows the speaker's orientation to the rules of the turn-taking system (Sacks et al. 1974). This indicates that HKC tend to observe the turn-taking rules more often than NES. Conversely, NES, who initiate 13.2% more simultaneous talk at a non-TRP (Type A), tend to deviate from the turn-taking rules more frequently than HKC do (Table 6.4). Hence, the first of the ten proposed turn-taking patterns specific to the intercultural conversations examined in this study is as follows:

Pattern 1 HKC are more likely than NES to observe and conform to the normative turn-taking rules, as observed in their initiation of simultaneous talk.

Sacks et al. (1974) suggest that interruptions can be repaired if one of the speakers stops in order to prevent violating the rule of one-at-a-time in conversation. HKC in this study are in general, irrespective of whether they are a CS or an IST, more likely than NES to stop and yield the floor (Table 6.5). In other words, HKC seem to be more conscious of turn-taking violations, and the need for repairing simultaneous talk. They appear to show a greater concern for orienting towards the turn-allocation rules, both in terms of "local turn-by-turn organization" (Sacks et al. 1974) and in terms of overall organizational structure in conversation (Schegloff and Sacks 1973), as evident in HKC's relatively greater readiness to yield to simultaneous talk.

Pattern 2 HKC are more likely than NES to observe and conform to the normative turn-taking rules, as observed in their yielding to initiation of simultaneous talk.

For both Type A and Type B simultaneous talk, the more yielding CS and IST are HKC (see Table 6.6). These findings have been transformed to turn-taking patterns 3 and 4.

Pattern 3 HKC are more likely than NES to be yielding to initiation of simultaneous talk.

Pattern 4 HKC are much more likely than NES to be yielding both as a CS at non-TRP positions and as an IST at or near TRP positions.

For both Type A and Type B, the more unyielding CS and IST are NES (see Tables 6.7 and 6.8). These findings have been transformed to turn-taking patterns 5 and 6.

Pattern 5 NES are more likely than HKC to be unyielding to initiation of simultaneous talk.

Pattern 6 NES are much more likely than HKC to be unyielding both as an IST at non-TRP positions and as a CS at or near TRP positions.

When the relative tendencies of yielding and unyielding verbal behaviours of HKC and NES are compared, the most noteworthy patterns are as follows.

Pattern 7 At a non-TRP, HKC as a CS are more yielding than not, and as an IST are more unyielding than not.

Pattern 8 At or near a TRP, HKC are more yielding than not, both as a CS and an IST.
Pattern 9 At a non-TRP, NES as a CS are more yielding than not, and as an IST are more unyielding than not.
Pattern 10 At or near a TRP, NES are more unyielding than not, both as a CS and an IST.

Discussion of simultaneous talk in six extracts

Below six extracts in the intercultural conversations with instances of simultaneous talk will be analyzed to offer a description of the patterns of turn-taking and the functions of simultaneous talk. Specifically, the analysis focuses on first, whether Type A simultaneous talk (non-TRP) is uncooperative and Type B simultaneous talk (TRP) cooperative and second, whether, and in what ways, HKC are more cooperative than NES, as suggested by the quantitative findings.

The participants in Extract 1 were colleagues working in the Civil Service. They were having lunch in an Oliver's restaurant when the recording was made. When the excerpt begins, the HKC initiates a topic about his experience of employing Filipino maids.

(1) 001
b: male Hong Kong Chinese B: male Australian
555. b: so I I I my experience with er with with er maids is
556. that er it really depends on your luck whether you
557. are fortunate enough to er [to get a good one
558. B: [get a good one
559. B: 'cos they occupy a position of trust I mean you leave
560. them in your house
561 b: they do oh yes yes yes yes (.) so so they have they
562. [have to be reliable
563. B: [they can steal everything or what
564. b: they can steal anything actually actually I I think
565. they are very important so that's why (.) er that's
why if you are lucky enough to have a good maid then
566. you are re- really er blessed in a way because er
567. especially in my case I leave my two kids with my
568. maid and you know life is much more you know
569. [precious than the money so we we in a way we we are
570. B: [um yes

572.   entrusting [the most precious the most valuable
573. B: [the most valuable
574.   things (.) er in our life to to to a maid so er
575.   [(inaudible)
576. B: [that's why A_ said she paid more 'cos the maid was
577.   so good
578. b: oh yes [yes yes

In Extract 1, there are three instances of simultaneous talk (lines 557 and 558, 562 and 563, 572 and 573), all of which are initiated by the NES speaker at a non-TRP. The first one is initiated in line 558 — the NES's *[get a good one* and the HKC's *[to get a good one* (line 557) are almost uttered simultaneously. The HKC stops and the NES self-selects to offer a reason for the importance of getting a good maid (*'cos they occupy a position of trust I mean you leave them in your house,* lines 559–560). It should, however, be pointed out that the NES's *get a good one* is actually a "completion offer", the function of which is to complete the HKC's previous turn (*so I I I my experience with er with with er maids is that er it really depends on your luck whether you are fortunate enough to er to,* lines 555–557). Both the completion offer and the reason given show a high degree of attentiveness and collaboration on the part of the NES. As suggested by Jefferson (1973), hearers can very often predict when an utterance of the current speaker is complete, and they almost invariably possess the ability to self-select to add to what might appear to be completed utterances of the current speaker. Jefferson (1973) illustrates this ability with three instances. First, a listener is able to add to a previous speaker's otherwise completed utterance without a pause. Second, a listener comes in just at the right time with his or her own idea of how the utterance should be completed. Third, a listener is able to predict the ending of a sentence and tries to say the same thing at the same time. In this extract, the NES's *get a good one* illustrates the third instance of "self-selection" (Jefferson 1973).

The second instance of simultaneous talk is also initiated by the NES at a non-TRP (*they can steal everything or what,* line 563). The HKC, agreeing with the reason offered by the NES, says *they do,* but then for a moment he seems to be at a loss for words or a reason to support his statement, saying *oh yes yes yes yes (.) so so they have they.* At this point, the NES introduces simultaneous talk to continue where he left off in line 560, by giving an exaggerated exemplification (*they can steal everything or what,* line 563). This instance of simultaneous talk appears to be competitive, rather than cooperative, talk. At the same time, the HKC is saying *(they) have to be reliable* (line 562).

The third instance of simultaneous talk is the NES's *the most valuable* (line 573), which again occurs at a non-TRP. Similar to the first instance of simultaneous talk, this represents the NES's attempt to self-select and complete the HKC's utterance (Jefferson 1973). This time, the NES stops after saying *the most valuable*, and the HKC continues his utterance. In fact, the HKC's *the most precious* occurs simultaneously with the NES's *the most valuable*. The meanings of the two phrases are close enough to show that the NES has been listening attentively, making logical prediction about how the conversation is liable to unfold, and collaboratively contributing an utterance that is of immediate relevance to the HKC's ongoing turn. Note that the HKC includes and repeats the NES's *the most valuable* verbatim in his turn, without breaking his step. It can be seen from this example that the NES is behaving co-operatively towards the HKC but is not seeking to stop the HKC's flow or to take over the HKC's turn in the conversation. Similarly, the HKC does not perceive the NES's contribution as a hostile take-over. Instead, the HKC shows his acceptance of what the NES says to his own discourse.

To sum up, the first and the third instances of simultaneous talk initiated by the NES are cooperative as they are completion offers. The second one, also initiated by the NES, is more like competitive talk. In none of these instances does the HKC relinquish his turn. However, there is no sign of any speaker being uncooperative or dominant.

Extract 2 shows simultaneous talk initiated by the HKC at a non-TRP. The participants were colleagues working in the in-house training unit of an organization. The HKC is describing her experience of dealing with Malaysians in business.

(2)	013	
a:	female Hong Kong Chinese	B: male American
256.	a:	the Malaysians are totally different even though
257.		they're so so close even though they're
258.		neighbours ((laugh)) (.) the the Malaysians are (.)
259.		much bright (.) and mm more serious [about business
260.	B:	[mm
261.	B:	why do you think that is are they just hungrier for
262.		the business
263.	a:	mhmm mm
264.		(pause)
265.	a:	because they're always on time or even ahead of time
266.		it's also (.) it's
267.	B:	which is also [a headache
268.	a:	[er which is also also a headache
269.		(pause)

In line 265, the HKC says *because they're always on time or even ahead of time it's also (.) it's*, and then she seems to be at a loss for words. The NES cuts in on her turn, bailing her out (*which is also*, line 267), which is an instance of self-selection to help the HKC out of the difficult situation of searching for words. In the middle of the NES's turn-at-talk (non-TRP), the HKC initiates simultaneous talk. Her *[er which is also also a headache* (line 268) actually repeats and echoes the NES's completion offer (*a headache*, line 267). Both participants get to finish their turns. The HKC's simultaneous talk is apparently one of collaborative, rather than uncooperative and intrusive. It acknowledges speaker B's utterance completion in line 267, rather than a case of not respecting a TRP in the sense of usurping the current speaker's turn. In fact, the HKC's simultaneous talk follows on from the previous turn of the NES who cuts in on her turn in order to bail her out.

Similar to the two instances of cooperative simultaneous talk introduced by the NES in Extract 1, the simultaneous talk introduced by the HKC in Extract 2 demonstrates that she is attentive and able to make quick reactions to what is being said in the unfolding conversation. Neither initiating simultaneous talk at the CS's turn-at-talk nor being unyielding is perceived as intrusive by either of the participants.

According to Zimmerman and West (1975), interrupting can result in usurping the floor from the current speaker, and is hence considered uncooperative. Extract 3 below, which was taken from the same conversation as Extract 2, shows the HKC (Initiator of Simultaneous Talk) successfully usurping the floor from the NES (Current Speaker). However, the usurping of the floor is perceived as cooperative by both paritipants. Also, similar to those in Extracts 1 and 2, the instance of simultaneous speech in Extract 3 is initiated at a non-TRP position and is unyielding in the sense that the HKC completes the turn whereas the NES relinquishes the floor.

Before Extract 3 begins, the speakers have been comparing the duration of official Christmas holidays in Hong Kong, the U.K., the States and France. The HKC tells the NES that she had worked in a French company in Hong Kong before.

(3)	013		
a:	female Hong Kong Chinese		B: male American
136.	a:	I work for er I work for a French boss for some years	
137.		ago and the French are mm (.) in in some ways quite	
138.		similar to the Chinese	
139.	B:	really how's so	
140.	a:	mm we're conservative (.) [the Chinese the old	
141.	B:	[mm	
142.		Chinese	
143.	B:	you mean like how they [approach business or what	
144.	a:	[the way they they do	
145.		business yes right	
146.	B:	mm mhmm	

The female HKC is comparing her previous *French boss* with the *old Chinese* (lines 136–142). In response, the NES says *you mean like how they* (line 143), implying that he would like the HKC to clarify something she has just said. The HKC interprets these opening words uttered by the NES to mean 'like ways in which the Chinese do something'. Without waiting for the NES to finish his utterance, the HKC initiates an instance of simultaneous talk, at a non-TRP of the NES's turn-at-talk, to say what she thinks his question is going to be (*the way they they do business*), as well as to answer the question (*yes right*) (lines 144–145). Simultaneously, the NES says *approach business or what* (line 143).

In Extract 4 below, four instances of ST are observed, two of which are introduced at a non-TRP, and two at a TRP position. Three instances of simultaneous talk are introduced by the HKC, and one by the NES. The participants went to the same church and had become friends. Their conversation took place in a common room in the church. The topic has been the puppet performance to be staged in the church.

(4) 002
a: female Hong Kong Chinese B: male British
111. B: at the moment because of people's (.) commitments
112. everything else hopefully if we have two more we've
113. only got three more hours of rehearsal we should be
114. okay ((B is laughing when saying the last few words))
115. a: so on the fifteenth we'll stay er er longer here (.)
116. er in the afternoon
117. B: we'll come back after lunch in the [afternoon and
118. a: [so how about
119. B: have a bit of rehearsal
120. a: how about the stage
121. B: we will see parts of that next week B_ and I are
122. making the stage up and finishing the puppets
123. a: mhmm okay
124. B: so we will see that [next week
125. a: [so I tell you what because you
126. know because I forgot the the performance on the
127. twenty second and I I promised to go to mainland
128. China [on on on ((laugh)) let me finish the story
129. B: [what
130. B: okay [sorry
131. a: [and I I I you know T_ and F_ they've been to

132. China for the the er er missionary [for short term so
133. B: [yea
134. they invite me to go on the from the twenty first to
135. er twenty sixth for four days and I say yes ((laugh))
136. and then I forgot this er er this performance and
137. later on you know I found out you know there is a
138. clash of time so so I called them up and say okay
139. maybe I'll come on the twenty third that's for after
140. the performance in on the twenty second so I think it
141. is the right thing to do you know that I I made the
142. commitment to come and then even I I wanted to go to
143. China and (.) you know (.) I've I've been thinking of
144. finding a replacement for me but I say M_ will kill
145. me ((laugh))
146. B: I think you're right yes ((laugh))

When the extract begins, the two speakers are talking bout the rehearsal. In line 115, the HKC asks whether they will stay on in the afternoon on the fifteenth for rehearsal. In response, the NES gives an affirmative answer (*we'll come back after lunch in the*, line 117). At this point, the HKC initiates simultaneous talk at a non-TRP to ask a question about the stage that is going to be set up in the church for a puppet show. The NES gives an answer (*we will see parts of that next week B_ and I are making the stage up and finishing the puppets*, lines 121–122), which is acknowledged by the HKC. Then the NES tries to continue with the topic by repeating the words in his prior utterance (*so we will see that*, line 124). Without waiting for the NES to finish his utterance, the HKC initiates simultaneous talk, also at a non-TRP of the NES's turn, to complete her story related to the puppet show. Her story is that she had forgotten about the performance that was to be staged on the twenty-second in Hong Kong, but had promised to go to mainland China. On hearing this, the NES initiates simultaneous talk — *what* (line 129) — at what could be a TRP, that has caused the HKC to stop to say to the NES explicitly *let me finish the story* (line 128).

The NES's one-word simultaneous talk (*what*) is an expression of surprise. It is usually considered legitimate to utter the word at any point as an indication of the instantaneous reaction of the NES, which can be seen as an expression of high involvement style. The NES's 'what' is not an attempt to bring the HKC's story to an end. In fact, the HKC does not perceive the instance of simultaneous talk as threatening, dominating, uncooperative, or intrusive in any way. She simply takes it in her stride by reacting with laughter, and her *let me finish the story* is uttered in a light-hearted manner. Then the NES actually apologizes for his simultaneous talk (*okay [sorry*, line 130). The fourth instance of ST occurs in line 131, introduced by the HKC at a TRP position. She cuts in the NES's turn when she says *okay [sorry* (line 130) in order to continue with her story-telling. The NES yields to the HKC, who is unyielding in her story-telling.

Extract 4 shows a story, told by the HKC in conversation that is produced through routine conversational processes. First of all, she initiates simultaneous talk in order to tell a story. Second, she is given an extended turn by her NES interlocutor to produce the story. As noted by Nofsinger (1991: 155–156), "in order to tell a coherent story longer than one turn unit (longer, say, than one sentence) the teller needs cooperation from the recipients in order to take an extended turn." Eggins and Slade (1997: 227) also point out that in story-telling in conversation, one speaker (the story-teller) usually dominates for a sustained period of time. Therefore, it seems legitimate that the HKC is being unyielding in the simultaneous talk she introduces.

Extract 5 demonstrates a case of the HKC, as a CS, being unyielding to the initiation of simultaneous talk at a TRP by the NES. The participants were colleagues working in a hospital. The HKC was a nurse and the NES an anaesthetist. The conversation took place in the car of the HKC, who was giving the NES a lift home. The HKC has been telling the NES that in the week before some experts were sent from another hospital to assess the standards of the hospital in which both the HKC and the NES were working. Part of the assessment programme was to see the computers.

(5) 014
a: female Hong Kong Chinese A: female Scottish
23. a: and the computer programme the whole programme is er
24. (.) is written by erm [Mr C_ and that is none of
25. A: [Mr C_ yes I know that
26. her erm (.) her contribution[s okay but er on that
27. A: [no
28. Friday evening er Friday afternoon she talk with
29. sisters and ask sister how to manage to assess
30. the data all the things (.) and Mr T_ is around and
31. he know about it very well and (.) he have the
32. conflict with er with her [before (.) so this time
33. A: [mm
34. she he don't want her to get everything (.) [so he
35. A: [yea
36. overwrite it lock up he didn't do anything wrong he

37.   just lock it up [that's all he put in the erm the
38. A: [I understand
39.   secret code [and he didn't he [didn't do nothing
40. A: [yeah   [he didn't
41.   other than tha [t and on Saturday morning (.) mm Dr
42. A: [yeah
43.   C_ come up er she at the time she want to show off
44.   she can't turn it on [and she is so mad about
45. A: [oh no ((laugh))
46.   tha[t and she is she know what's going on (.) and on
47. A: [oh (.) right
48.   Monday (.) er when we all come back because before
49.   we didn't know about that (pause) [because on Monday
50. A: [no because it's
51.   everyone's guessing [and we have the (.) nearly same
52. A: Saturday morning [uh huh
53.   ideas but we don't want to let her er Dr C_ disclose
54.   it erm [she's just asking is there somebody's
55. A: [I see
56.   overwriting it or locking it and we say no we are
57.   ignorant about computer we know nothing
58.   abou[t computers because we just want don't want to
59. A: [yea
60.   let her [knows what's going on
61. A: [yea
62. A: I see

The HKC is narrating to her NES colleague what she heard about Dr C_ the previous Saturday in the hospital. Her narration then moves from Saturday to Monday, saying *because before we didn't* (the HKC and other colleagues) *know about that* (i.e. about what had happened to Dr C_), lines 48–49. She pauses, and then both the HKC and the NES start talking at the same time. The HKC's *[because on Monday everyone's guessing* (line 49) is spoken simultaneously as the NES's *[no because it's Saturday morning* (line 50). The NES yields right away and the HKC continues with her turn. The NES thought that the HKC had a slip when she said 'on Monday' and tries to correct her, and she is being cooperative. Her utterance is a way of indicating interest and comprehension and is very much part of the co-operative nature of conversation.

The HKC does not yield but carries on with her turn. This unyielding behaviour is probably due to the fact that she is telling a story to which she is privy, or of which she is the "primary knower" (Berry 1981). "Primary knower" is a notion proposed by Berry (1987) to describe an interlocutor who has the missing information in an exchange initiated by a question. Hence, the fact that the HKC does not yield has to do with the knowledge of the story which only she herself has but the NES does not have, rather than the HKC being uncooperative or aggressive. Besides, the NES's utterance *[no because it's Saturday morning* (lines 50–52) is a comment which does not require a response from the HKC. There is no evidence to suggest that the NES is in the least bothered with her own yielding or the HKC's unyielding behaviour. In fact, the NES attentively listens to the HKC telling the story, and participates in constructing the story together (not shown in the extract).

Extract 6 below is quintessential of the organization of turn-taking in conversation. There are eleven instances of ST. The participants were friends. They were in the home of the NES, and the conversation took place in the evening before dinner. The speakers are discussing the leasing contract that the NES has signed and the rental of the flat.

(6) 017
a: female Hong Kong Chinese B: male American
120. a: mm (.) but how long (.) you think you'll er leave er
121. Tuen Mun (.) at least one year (.) be[cause you abide
122. B: [perhaps
123. by the contract
124. B: perhaps one year
125. a: mm
126. B: yea (.) erm it's (.) always (.) uncertain of course
127. but
128. a: uncer[tain but you have to finish contract at least
129. B: [that's
130. one year one [year is optional is it [the second year
131. B: [one [mm
132. was er is optional (.) but the first year is binding
133. B: well now (.) now (.) I'm not under a working contract
134. with my comapny
135. a: no I mean er (.) the last (.) la[st year
136. B: [oh the last year (.)
137. well it's two months' notice
138. a: two months' notice
139. B: yes
140. a: oh I see (.) but [you can terminate the contract
141. B: [but it's

```
142.        anytime
143.   B:   it's a year's contract (.) er extended to be two
144.        years
145.   a:   yea
146.   B:   er (.) but at the moment for one year is two months'
147.        notice period
148.   a:   oh but you can you can leave any time within the
149.        first year (.) by er giving  [er two
150.   B:                                [by giving two months'
151.        notice that's  [right
152.   a:                  [well then that's very [flexible
153.   B:                                         [erm er (.)
154.        conversely the landlord can give me two months'
155.        [notice
156.   a:   [can do the same thing
157.   B:   yea
158.   a:   but do you have to pay er a higher rent because of
159.        this fle- flexibility
160.   B:   no
161.   a:   no
162.   B:   no the rent is er
163.   a:   reasonable  [market price
164.   B:               [it's competitive marketed market price
165.        market  [and this is I mean as far as I know it's
166.   a:           [um how much
167.        the [standard form  [for any any rental
168.   a:       [er             [yea
169.   a:   oh I see but I suppose in the first year mm you can't
170.        break the contract either party (.)no it's [not the
171.   B:                                              [well (.)
172.        case
173.   B:   I I could but I'd forfeit my er [my deposit
174.   a:                                   [deposit
175.        presumably
176.   a:   oh I see how much commission you have to pay for
177.        renting [monthly
```

Table 6.9 summarizes the functional analysis of each of the eleven instances of simultaneous talk in Extract 6.

Table 6.9. Functional analysis of instances of simultaneous talk in Extract 6

Line no.	**Position**	**IST (yielding or otherwise)**	**Function of ST (whether the interlocutor yields or not)**
136-137	non-TRP	NES –unyielding	*[oh the last year (.) well it's two months' notice* - Completion offer: The NES repeats the HKC's words, completes her phrase, and provides information required, showing the NES making correct prediction about the content of the HKC's utterance. The completion offer is followed by a response. - The HKC finishes her phrase (*last year*) and yields her turn.
141	non-TRP	NES – yielding	*[but it's* - An unfinished turn. The NES wants to offer additional information to what he has just said about the lease contract with M_ K_. - The HKC does not yield her turn.
143-144	TRP	NES – unyielding	*[it's a year's contract (.) er extended to be two years* - Immediately after yielding, the NES re-introduces simultaneous talk, the function of which is to offer more information about the lease contract. - The HKC yields her turn.
150-151	non-TRP	NES – unyielding	*[by giving two months' notice that's [right* - The NES completes the HKC's utterance, indicating that the NES is able to make correct prediction about the content of the HKC's utterance. This is a feature of cooperativeness and support. - The HKC yields.
152	non-TRP	HKC – unyielding	*[well then that's very [flexible* - The HKC gives a comment on what the NES is saying about the 'two-month notice'. - The NES yields his turn.
153-155	non-TRP	NES – unyielding	*[erm er (.) conversely the landlord can give me two months' [notice* - The NES continues his own prior turn and provides further information on the topic. - The HKC yields her turn.
156	non-TRP	HKC – unyielding	*[can do the same thing* - The HKC initiates simultaneous talk to paraphrase 'two months' notice'. - The NES yields his turn.
164-167	non-TRP	NES – unyielding	*[it's competitive marketed market price market [and this is I mean as far as I know it's the [standard form [for any any rental* - In the prior turn, the HKC offers 'reasonable' for the rent of the NES's flat. The NES initiates simultaneous talk to provide an alternative description of the rent ('competitive'). After this, the NES continues his turn. He has included the term 'market price' just said by the HKC in his turn. - The HKC yields her turn.

Table 6.9. Continued

Line no.	Position	IST (yielding or otherwise)	Function of ST (whether the interlocutor yields or not)
166	TRP	HKC – yielding	*[um how much* - The HKC asks a question to obtain information (*um how much*), after hearing the NES's *it's competitive market price market.* - The NES does not yield his turn. He does not directly answer the HKC's half-finished question by saying what the rental is. He describes the rental as 'the standard form for any any rental'.
171 and 173	non-TRP	NES – unyielding	*[well (.) I I could but I'd forfeit my er [my deposit presumably* - The NES initiates simultaneous talk to respond to the HKC's comment - 'I suppose in the first year um you can't break the contract either party'. - The HKC yields her turn.
174	non-TRP	HKC – yielding	*[deposit* - The HKC's simultaneous talk ('deposit') is a completion offer, functioning to complete the NES's utterance. The NES actually utters the same word simultaneously. - The NES does not yield and continues with his utterance.

The cultural attribute of HKC is other-orientation, as opposed to self-orientation specific to NES. Analysis of the situated discourse in Extract 6 aims to show whether or not the HKC is inclined to be other-oriented and the NES self-oriented, as manifested in yielding, or not, to self-initiated simultaneous talk; and, if so, in what ways.

There are eleven instances of ST, four initiated by the HKC and seven by the NES. All eleven instances of ST have been found to be supportive and cooperative as they enable the participants to make sense of the coherence of the ongoing utterances and produce more meaningful utterances, even though all but two of the instances of simultaneous talk are initiated at a non-TRP position of the current speaker's turn-at-talk. Most of the instances of simultaneous talk perform such cooperative and supportive functions as utterance completion, providing additional information, commenting on the previous utterance, and asking a question for confirmation of understanding, all of which are supporting and developing the topic at hand. Such instances of simultaneous talk are co-operative as they enable the speakers to make sense of the coherence of the ongoing utterances and produce more meaningful utterances. The CS may or may not yield; the IST may or may not yield. Nevertheless, the general flow of the conversation is smooth. The speakers are intensely engaged in the interaction, by performing a range of appropriate and timely acts of speaking. There is no sign of either of the speakers being the least bothered by the initiation of simultaneous talk at any point.

Having said that, there is a difference between the HKC and the NES. For the two instances of the HKC being unyielding, at a non-TRP position, she gives comments on the NES's prior utterance and paraphrases the NES's prior utterance, both of which are oriented towards the NES friend. However, there are more instances of unyielding for the NES where he is pursuing his own topic of talk, on lines 153–155 and 164–167. When the HKC asks *mm how much* (line 166), the NES does not yield to his interlocutor's half-finished question but pushes on with his own turn.

Both speakers in Extract 6 appear to be adherents of the "high involvement" style described by Tannen (1989). They frequently begin speaking while the other speaker is already speaking. They adopt strategies that place a higher priority on the need for positive face to show involvement. They converse at a fast pace. For them, speaking together at the same time may serve to "grease the conversational wheels" (Tannen 1994: 63), rather than to obstruct or to dominate the other speaker. In fact, the conversation continues over to the dinner table, although that part of the interaction was not recorded.

Analysis of the immediate context of the situated discourse has shown that ST often takes place, initiated by the HKC and the NES participants as a high-involvement device for maintaining social relationships, and for organizing their conversational turns in a co-ordinated, fast-paced fashion. This is a product of the immediate context; and the frequency of ST is participant-specific, rather than a cultural attribute. It needs to be pointed out that such factors as the social relationships between the participants, the nature and proposition of the topic at hand, and gender may have contributed to the conversational style of both participants, particularly the HKC.

Conclusion

The "Typology of Initiating of and Yielding to Simultaneous Talk" was devised to show the various points in the CS's contribution when he or she is most vulnerable to initiation of simultaneous talk. The Typology has been shown to be a useful framework for investigating and describing different aspects of simultaneous talk, namely initiation of, yielding to, and unyielding to simultaneous talk initiated at different positions in the current speaker's turn-at-talk. The analysis has provided insights into the turn-taking, turn-yielding and turn-holding behaviours of HKC and NES speakers in the 25 intercultural conversations examined in this study.

On the whole, compared to NES, HKC appear to be more oriented to the "one-at-a-time" model expounded by American conversation analysts. This is demonstrated both in their turn-taking and turn-yielding behaviours. Levinson (1983: 300–301) observes that the turn-taking system is locally managed and provides an "intrinsic motivation to both listen and process what is being said" in order to monitor for upcoming TRP. Therefore, HKC in this study can be said to be more mindful of monitoring an utterance of their NES interlocutors from its beginning, and seeing what is likely to constitute a point of completion. When the point of completion occurs, HKC may take a turn. Simultaneous talk occurs when the NES current speaker has decided to continue. Regarding turn-yielding, HKC are more likely than NES to readily remedy the problem of simultaneous talk by yielding the floor. In fact, all of the four hypotheses have been confirmed, which lends support to the perspective that HKC are more observant of the organizational rules in conversation.

Quantitative findings relating to the general interactional, turn-taking patterns of the two groups of speakers need to be substantiated by examining conversational episodes as they occur in their immediate contexts of situation. Qualitative, content analysis of six extracts has demonstrated active participation on the part of both HKC and NES in developing the ongoing conversation and building rapport. Simultaneous talk has been found to be employed by both HKC and NES as a device for maintaining social relationship between speakers, and for organizing their conversational turns in a co-ordinated fashion.

There is, nevertheless, evidence to suggest that HKC are more cooperative than NES. Compared to NES, HKC initiate fewer instances of simultaneous talk and they more readily yield to initiation of simultaneous talk. The most noteworthy finding is that HKC are more unyielding as an IST at a non-TRP (Table 6.7), which, as discussed, is considered an anomaly. Qualitative findings have illuminated this phenomenon. In the few cases examined in this chapter, HKC's unyielding behaviour tends to be oriented to the interlocutor, or such unyielding behaviour occurs due to the fact that HKC has knowledge of the topical content, and so has the speaker right to take an extended turn. Therefore the findings lend support to the view about the main functions of communication in Chinese societies (Yum 1988). Communication is defined as "an infinite interpretive process where all parties are searching to develop and maintain a social relationship" (Jandt 1998: 34).

The result has also shown that the range of diverse evaluative or value-laden terminology employed in the literature on simultaneous talk is by and large not very helpful, and even confusing and misleading at times, in describing the phenomena and functions of simultaneous talk found in conversation. This study has clearly rejected the claims that simultaneous talk starting at a non-TRP (Type A) is uncooperative, and that simultaneous talk starting at or near a TRP (Type B) is cooperative (Schiffrin 1986). Equally, no evidence of NES exercising power and control has been observed in the instances of simultaneous talk examined so far. No speakers have shown any signs of being offended or intruded upon when the interlocutor initiates simultaneous talk. In fact, the results show that similar to Type B, all of the functions of Type A simultaneous talk represent various ways in which the speaker contributes to developing the topical framework, organizing the turn-by-turn real time interaction, negotiating common ground and managing interpersonal relationships. All of these are intertwined with one another and work interdependently towards creating shared understanding and meaning, collaboration, and support between the HKC and NES participants.

Having said that, by and large, cultural differences are manifested in the way HKC and NES are oriented to observing the turn-taking rules, in the way they initiate simultaneous talk, yield to simultaneous talk and, in particular, the way they are unyielding to the initiation of simultaneous talk.

Chapter 7

Discourse topic management

Introduction

Discourse topic management in this study refers to the ways in which conversational participants contribute towards the topic subject contents and the direction and organization of the topical framework, both informed by and reflecting the context of situation and the goals for interaction. In order to gain insights into discourse topic management, three essential elements were examined, namely strategies for topic introduction, orientation of topic subject contents and management of culturally sensitive topics.

Through comparing the number of topical strategies initiated by HKC and NES, the study aims to find out whether topic control or domination by any one cultural group exists; in other words, whether equality of speaker rights in discourse topic management is manifested. Three hypotheses were formulated. The first hypothesis was that HKC, compared to NES, will initiate and use fewer strategies for topic introduction. Employment of topical strategies of change, shift, drift, digression and resumption indicates different forms of topic introduction. These five topical strategies adopted by HKC and NES will reveal the ways in which these speakers determine and direct the ongoing conversation in their interest. The second hypothesis was that HKC are more likely to introduce and organize topics in an interdependent manner; conversely, NES are inclined to introduce and organize topics independently. In other words, compared to NES, HKC are more concerned about initiating topics that are semantically or propositionally connected to the previous one; and specifically, HKC are more likely to initiate topic shifts, drifts and resumptions; but less likely to initiate topic changes and digressions. The third hypothesis concerned resumption to the old topic, and that is, HKC are more likely to resume to the old topic that was initiated by their interlocutors rather than to that initiated by themselves.

Regarding orientation of topic subject contents, two hypotheses were formulated:

1. HKC will initiate topics in descending order of frequency as follows: Addressee-oriented, Speaker and Addressee-oriented and Speaker-oriented.

2. NES will initiate topics in descending order of frequency as follows: Speaker-oriented, Speaker and Addressee-oriented and Addressee-oriented.

When conversationalists are involved in the exchange of culturally sensitive or socially taboo topics, they very often adopt a range of conversational strategies to express and organize ideational messages, and to temper the face needs of both the speaker and the addressee so as to manage interpersonal relationships. In this study, the strategies used by HKC and NES to manage the organizational and interpersonal aspects of culturally sensitive topics were compared, in order to examine:

1. the ways in which speakers invoke cultural knowledge and cultural identity in presenting and negotiating ideational messages related to cultural stereotypes and prejudice in discourse,
2. the strategies employed by HKC and NES to express and organize ideologies related to cultural stereotypes and prejudice in discourse, and
3. the strategies employed by HKC to temper the face needs of both the speaker and the addressee so as to manage interpersonal relationships.

Topical strategies

Exemplifying topical strategies

Each of the five topical strategies (Stenström 1994: 151–160) will now be exemplified in turn. First, Extract 1 shows topic change, which is defined as abandoning the current topic in favour of a new, unrelated topic. The old topic is never returned to in the conversation. The participants were friends and the conversation took place in a common room in a church. Before the extract begins, the topic has been the NES's recent trip to Florida.

(1) 002
a: female Hong Kong Chinese   B: male British
40. a: oh so have you accomplished er the the work you you
41. need to to finish
42. B: more than I needed to do I saw what people I had to
43. see and did and did more besides that
44. a: have you seen the er former pastor of this church er
45. Pastor M_ do you know them
46. B: I know I know of [him yes
47. a: [Mr and Mrs M_
48. B: but where are they (.) [in Florida
49. a: [they were in Florida they

50. retire and settle in Florida
51. B: no I haven't seen them
52. a: but yea but oh you just went there for a week
53. B: three days
54. a: three days (.) oh in Florida three days is [enough
55. B: [three
56. days in Orlando
57. a: oh Orlando yea they were in Orlando [particular for
58. B: [oh
59. yea so so today is really ((laugh))
60. B: jetlagged [for me
61. a: [jetlagged yea aha
62. a: so have you found a replacement for for the maid that
63. you you mentioned earlier that the one who didn't er
64. er doing you know take care of the childrens well
65. B: sort of [(.) yes and no
66. a: [uh huh
67. a: why
68. B: because we we thought somebody was coming but maybe
69. they won't now [so we have to find yet another
70. a: [oh
71. replacement
72. a: but she's still working there helping er er er
73. B: no
74. a: I_
75. B: no
76. a: she's gone

The NES has just returned from a trip to America. The topic is changed by the HKC from what the NES did and whom he visited when he was in America to whether the NES has found a replacement for his maid at home in Hong Kong (lines 62–64).

Topic shift is "moving from one topic to a related topic or from one aspect of the current topic to another" (Stenström 1994: 156) and is linguistically marked. Extract 2 below shows a topic shift. The speakers were in-laws having a conversation in the home of the NES.

(2) 004
a: female Hong Kong Chinese B: male British
458. a: you know but er as time it's going when she grows
459. grows up time by time er now she's getting more

460. interested in it [and last time she brought a letter
461. B: [right
462. back to school to apply
463. a: the scholarship
464. B: oh yea what happened
465. a: a music scholarship and later on about I think after
466. one or two months she has to sit for the examination
467. for the scholarship
468. B: you must be very proud
469. a: I hope she can she can gain it but never mind if she
470. can not [since she has (.) tried her best
471. B: [what
472. yes that's the most important part what about the
473. violin does she manage to play the violin
474. a: violin yea even she he she likes violin more than
475. playing piano

In lines 458–470, the topic framework is that the HKC's daughter needs to work hard to get a music (piano) scholarship. In line 472, the NES initiates a topic shift, when he says *what about the violin does she manage to play the violin.* The content is shifted to the HKC's daughter's ability to play the violin. This is a topic shift for two reasons: (1) the topic subject content is still about the musical abilities and performance of the girl, and so falls within the current topic framework, and (2) the topic movement is signalled by a framing expression *what about the violin* to effect a distinct movement to a related aspect of the current topic framework. This topic shift is supported by the HKC whose contribution fits closely to the preceding utterance by the NES.

Extract 3 shows the strategy of topic drift. Topic drift differs from topic shift in that it is almost imperceptible, and hence blurs borders between topics (Stenström 1994: 157). The participants are colleagues working in different departments in a university. Their conversation took place in a restaurant in the university.

(3) 025
a: female Hong Kong Chinese B: male British
2. a: so you like Chinese food
3. B: yes [oh yes I'd much prefer to be up here than I
4. a: [((laugh))
5. would downstairs
6. (pause)
7. a: er better than a[nd I (inaudible)

8. B: [well upstairs yes [yes
9. a: [mhmm nothing much
10. B: it always takes so long to get served up there
11. a: oh yes ((laugh))
12. B: and when it comes it's er ju- ju- er just awful
13. a: yea I I took a a quick meal last time and it came
14. only at one fifteen
15. B: I know yes [yes it makes you wonder what the slow
16. a: [((laugh)) forty five minutes [to ((laugh))
17. meal would look like [yea oh it's
18. a: take a quick meal
19. dreadful dreadful

In lines 3–9, the topic subject content is Chinese food served in the restaurant upstairs. In line 10, the NES initiates a topic drift to the service in the restaurant downstairs. This is a topic drift for two reasons: (1) the topic subject content is related to the current topic framework, and (2) the topic is changed in an imperceptible manner; the drift is not linguistically marked.

Topic digression represents a temporary move away from the current topic, and topic resumption "involves ending the digression and going back to the old topic" (Stenström 1994: 158–160). Extract 4 illustrates both topic digression and topic resumption, performed by different speakers. The participants were civil servants and were having lunch at an Oliver's restaurant. Before the extract starts, the HKC has said to the NES that he is living in government quarters.

(4) 001
B: male British b: male Hong Kong Chinese
605. B: what form do government quarters take are they like
606. blocks of apartments or [apartments just randomly
607. b: [well a lot of different
608. chosen
609. b: forms er usually they are government owned (.)
610. government owned
611. B: the whole block or just er part of that
612. b: well the whole own block (.) the own site the whole
613. site actually you know er for example my er flat is
614. is is is on Conduit Road
615. B: Connaught Road
616. b: Conduit Road Conduit not Connaught Connaught Road is
617. [in in the harbour Conduit Road is Mid-level

618. B: [yea
619. B: right
620. b: and
621. B: where near Robinson Road
622. b: yeah up er the the road above Robinson Road is the
623. Conduit Road
624. B: because is Park Road comes up to [Robinson Road
625. b: [comes up to
626. Robinson Road and then further up is the Conduit Road
627. B: okay I haven't been up there yet
628. b: no you haven't yet er and there that site is wholly
629. owned by the government [and on that site we have six
630. B: [right
631. blocks altogether they are all government quarters
632. B: right
633. b: some government quarters are are are are are are a
634. few blocks within a big [yeah yeah
635. B: [yes
636. bigger site where you have er you know er other
637. blocks which belong to the private
638. B: (inaudible) of apartment
639. b: developers
640. B: right ((cough))

Extract 4 starts with the NES asking about the form of the Hong Kong government quarters for its civil servants, with the HKC giving him information. The HKC then mentions the block of government quarters on Conduit Road in which he lives. An instance of digression is initiated in line 615, when the NES has misheard 'Connaught Road' for 'Conduit Road'. The HKC then addresses the NES's mishearing and question. After that, in line 628 the old topic is resumed by the HKC.

Analysis of topical strategies in the intercultural conversations

The 25 intercultural conversations were examined for a quantitative analysis of the five strategies of topic introduction initiated by HKC and NES. HKC and NES have been found to initiate a similar number of topical strategies; HKC initiate 335 and NES initiate 338 topical strategies. The findings do not show that NES control and dominate the HKC in introducing topics into the conversation. In fact, equal speaker rights between HKC and NES have been observed. Hypothesis 1 is therefore not supported.

Table 7.1. Comparison of topical strategies: HKC and NES

	Hong Kong Chinese		Native Speakers	
	Tokens	%	Tokens	%
Change	68	20.3	45	13.3
Shift	95	28.4	116	34.3
Drift	116	34.6	120	35.5
Digression	16	4.7	21	6.2
Resumption	40	12.0	36	10.7
Total	335	100.0	338	100.0

The conversations were further examined to compare different kinds of topical strategies employed by HKC and NES. For each group of speakers, the relative distribution of the five types of topical strategies is presented in Table 7.1.

When frequencies of occurrence were compared, HKC and NES are similar in the initiation of topic drifts, topic digressions and topic resumptions. They differ in topic changes and topic shifts. HKC initiated a greater proportion of topic changes than NES (HKC: 20.3% and NES: 13.3%), and NES initiated a greater proportion of topic shifts than HKC (NES: 34.3% and HKC: 28.4%). Therefore, on the whole, stereotypical assumptions about cultural influences on employment of topical strategies do not appear to be supported. The hypothesis that HKC will initiate more instances of topic shift and topic resumption than NES is not supported. Equally, the hypothesis that the HKC will initiate fewer topic changes is not substantiated.

In this study, both topic shifts and topic drifts are regarded as forms of interdependent topic organization, as opposed to topic changes which represent changing the propositional content of the topic altogether, with the two topics independent of each other. In terms of topic shifts and drifts combined, HKC initiated 211 of them (63% of all topical strategies) and NES 236 (69.8% of all topical strategies). Conversely, in terms of topic changes, HKC (20.3%) are more likely than NES (13.3%) to introduce topic changes. Consequently, the hypothesis that HKC will have a greater tendency to introduce topics in an interdependent way, and NES in an independent way, is not supported. Instead, it suggests that HKC do not mind breaking the internal relatedness and coherence of a topic as much as predicted. Given the findings, the overriding hypothesis, which states that compared to NES, HKC will be more in favour of consecutive topics being propositionally related to each other, is not confirmed. This phenomenon might be explained in terms of the conversational skills of HKC. Topic development which involves the exploitation of propositional relationships within the discourse can be more difficult to achieve than topic development that does not. Thus, HKC might find it more demanding on their conversational skills to develop a topic in an interdependent fashion, compared to NES.

Another finding is that there is a preference for topic drifts over topic shifts among HKC speakers. In this study, both topic shifts and topic drifts are regarded as forms of interdependent topic organization, though topic drifts is more so. This is because topic drifts, done without being marked linguistically, represent an almost imperceptible move to a related aspect of the current topic, and so the degree of connection, or interdependence, between related topics is higher. When the relative proportion of topic shifts and topic drifts used by HKC are compared, HKC seem to favour introducing a related topic, or a related aspect of the current topic, in an imperceptible manner (i.e. topic drift), rather than in a distinct manner (i.e. topic shift). Topic drifts make up 34.6% of HKC's employment of topical strategies, and topic shifts 28.4%. This preference could have been motivated by a desire to develop a topical framework, which comprises different related aspects, coherently and interdependently, and not to appear to be breaking the connection between related aspects of the topic. Unlike HKC, NES are equally likely to use topic shifts (34.3%) and topic drifts (35.5%) when moving to a related topic, or to a related aspect or phase of the current topic. In other words, NES do not seem to mind as much as HKC do about whether or not to make the transition within the current topical framework a smooth one, or an imperceptible one.

HKC and NES were also compared in their topic resumption behaviour. The number of instances of occurrence of topic resumption is similar for both groups of speakers. Nevertheless, the hypothesis was that HKC will be more likely to resume the old or current topic that was initiated by their interlocutor rather than by themselves, after a topic shift, digression, or a change has occurred. This is because of the belief that HKC care more about their interlocutors and try to involve them in the conversation, and so are keener to return to their interlocutors' topic after a temporary move away from it. Conversely, NES, who tend to be more individualistic and care more about their own topics, are more likely to resume the old topic that was initiated by themselves rather than by the addressee (Table 7.2).

The results reveal that contrary to the hypothesis, HKC are more likely to resume topics that were initiated by themselves (75%) than by the NES interlocutor (25%), whereas NES are more inclined to resume topics that were initiated by the HKC (41.7%) than by themselves (58.3%). The findings, therefore, appear to show

Table 7.2. Comparison of topic resumption strategies: HKC and NES

	Hong Kong Chinese		Native Speakers	
	Tokens	%	Tokens	%
Resume speaker-initiated old topic	30	75	21	58.3
Resume addressee-initiated old topic	10	25	15	41.7
Total	40	100	36	100.0

that in terms of topic resumption strategies, it is HKC and not NES who show to be more concerned with their own topic agenda, and so less concerned with the interdependent organization of topic.

Topic content orientations

Exemplifying topic content orientations

Below, the three categories of topic orientations are defined and illustrated with examples drawn from the intercultural conversations.

1. "Speaker and Addressee-oriented" topic is about, involves, or is oriented to all of the conversational participants; and in the case of a dyadic conversation, both of the participants. The speakers in Extract 5 were colleagues in a university, working in different departments. The NES was a member of the academic staff and the HKC was a member of the administrative staff. After a long pause, the HKC initiates a topic change, the content of which involves both of the speakers, namely rumours that the two departments will merge into one.

   (5) 023
   a: female Hong Kong Chinese B: male British
   759. (long pause)
   760. a: have you heard that your department and our
   761. department will merge into one department
   762. B: er we've heard we we've heard that from a
   763. number of sources then we heard that it's not
   764. a high priority that other departments will
   765. merge before (.) we do if we ever do so what
   766. have you heard

2. "Speaker-oriented" topic is about, involves, or is oriented to the speaker of the utterance. The speakers in Extract 6 were friends. The HKC is talking about two academic papers that she has written, and all the utterances made by her are classified as Speaker-oriented.

   (6) 024
   a: female Hong Kong Chinese B: male British
   125. a: but maybe because (.) I don't know (.) and I think
   126. my second essay is (.) even better than that one
   127. (.) I think
   128. B: the second one (.) which one the
   129. a: the one about language and identity (.) no

130. B: I thought that one was about language and identity
131. a: no that one is about mm (.) we're (.) born alone
132. we what alone we die alone and get something like
133. that

3. "Addressee-oriented" topic is about, involves, or is related to the addressee in the conversation. The same example in Extract 7 illustrates this category. All utterances made by the NES are classified as Addressee-oriented topic as they are concerned with the HKC interlocutor, namely the second paper about language and identity that the HKC wrote.

(7) 024
a: female Hong Kong Chinese B: male British
125. a: but maybe because (.) I don't know (.) and I
126. think my second essay is (.) even better than
127. that one (.) I think
128. B: the second one (.) which one the
129. a: the one about language and identity (.) no
130. B: I thought that one was about language and
131. identity
132. a: no that one is about mm we're (.) born alone we
133. what alone we die alone and get something like
134. that

Analysis of topic content orientations in the intercultural conversations

The frequencies of occurrence of the three orientations of topic subject contents introduced by HKC and NES in the intercultural conversations are given in Table 7.3.

The findings have largely confirmed the two hypotheses. First, as hypothesized, HKC are more likely to initiate topics that involve the interlocutor (Addressee-oriented) rather than themselves (Speaker-oriented). In fact, HKC initiate 55.6% of Addressee-oriented topics, but only 32.8% of Speaker-oriented topics, representing

Table 7.3. Comparison of topic content orientations: HKC and NES

	Hong Kong Chinese		Native Speakers	
	Tokens	%	Tokens	%
Speaker and Addressee-oriented	22	11.6	7	4.5
Speaker-oriented	62	32.8	75	48.4
Addressee-oriented	105	55.6	73	47.1
Total	189	100.0	155	100.0

a difference of 22.8%. Also as hypothesized, NES are less likely than HKC to introduce topics that are oriented to the interlocutor (Addressee-oriented). NES initiate a similar proportion of Speaker-oriented topics (48.4%) and Addressee-oriented topics (47.1%). Second, as hypothesized, HKC do initiate a greater proportion of Speaker and Addressee-oriented topics than NES. HKC initiate 11.6% and NES only 4.5%, representing a difference of 7.1%. The result shows that compared to NES, HKC are more concerned about all the participants in the immediate context of situation as far as introducing topic contents is concerned. Third, contrary to the hypothesis, for both HKC and NES, Speaker and Addressee-oriented topics constitute only a small proportion of their topic content orientations. It is 11.6% for HKC and only 4.5% for NES. Therefore, the hypotheses that HKC will initiate more Speaker and Addressee-oriented topics than Speaker-oriented topics, and that NES will initiate more Speaker and Addressee-oriented topics than Addressee-oriented topics are not supported. However, HKC do initiate a higher proportion of Speaker and Addressee-oriented topics (11.6%) than NES (4.5%), indicating that HKC are more concerned than NES with introducing topic content that involves both themselves (the Speaker) and their interlocutors (the Addressee).

The findings can be attributed to the way the Chinese (HKC in this study) conceive "self". Both the notions of the Chinese self and the interdependent self define the way a Chinese person deals with surrounding relations. The Chinese self involves multiple layers of relations with others, and needs to be recognized, defined and completed by others. The development of the Chinese self hinges on the self's orientation to others' needs, wishes, and expectations (King and Bond 1985; Gao 1996). Besides, being group-oriented and collectivistic, in Hofstede's (1976, 1977) sense, the Chinese put the interests, needs and expectations of the group before those of their own. The findings presented here have provided evidence which supports these conceptions and the accompanying preferred cultural values.

Discussion of culturally sensitive topic management in seven extracts

An examination of the intercultural conversations has produced seven extracts with topical subject contents relating to issues and ideologies such as cultural identities, stereotypes and prejudice. In these extracts, HKC and NES are engaged in interaction in informal social settings. In some cases, they are talking about ethnic or racial groups that neither of them belongs to. In other cases, their talk is concerned with the racial or ethnic group of which one of them is a member. Since the participants are friends and colleagues and, in a small number of cases, relatives, they should at least have some knowledge and understanding of each other's backgrounds, it is therefore not too strange that topics such as race and ethnicity would emerge in their conversation.

The following discusses the seven extracts (Extracts 8–14) one by one. In Extract 8, the speakers were former classmates on a postgraduate programme and currently colleagues in a university in Hong Kong. The male British NES was an academic staff member and the female HKC was an administrative staff member. The conversation was recorded in a restaurant on campus. The speakers have been talking about the HKC's current job as an executive officer in the university.

(8) 025
a: female Hong Kong Chinese B: male British

314.	a:	I wish I could be here earlier two to three years
315.		earlier ((laugh)) makes my life so happy ((laugh))
316.		[well you don't know my days two or three years ago
317.	B:	[well
318.		working at that (.) factory
319.	B:	ah well
320.	a:	yeah the boss's really mad
321.	B:	yes
322.	a:	mm
323.	B:	was he he was the owner of the company as well was he
324.		or was it
325.	a:	er he and his wife
326.	B:	ah
327.	a:	traditional Chinese type
328.	B:	oh dear dear that [could be difficult to work in
329.	a:	[mm
330.	a:	really difficult
331.	B:	unless you are among the family in which case er you
332.		know
333.	a:	((laugh)) I am not luckily or (.) luck unlucky
334.	B:	when those businesses grow beyond the family they can
335.		be enormously difficult er you know
336.	a:	right
337.	B:	I keep telling my students we I teach organizational
338.		communication (.) using all of these very idealistic
339.		American materials based on very liberal [business
340.	a:	[mm
341.		practices and [er open practices and [er open
342.	a:	[mm

343.		friendly bosses and so on shall I say well (.) this
344.		this would be very nice but when you get out into the
345.		real world you may be working for somebody who really
346.		doesn't give a damn about you
347.	a:	right it's a whole different culture
348.	B:	all they care about is profit [production you know
349.	a:	[mm
350.		[don't really care about er relationships [and er
351.	a:	[mm [mhmm
352.		things like that [so er
353.	a:	[those are the people I think most
354.		of our students have to face
355.	B:	well probably at least at the beginning er of their
356.		careers (pause) er yes can be a shock to them and
357.		it's a shock to me when I learn about how businesses
358.		are run here how how everything is run the school I
359.		was in how that was run [by the one person
360.	a:	[mm

In Extract 8 that invokes cultural identity and compares different ethnic and racial groups, the speakers employ a range of strategies to manage the topic. The analysis below focuses on how the HKC and the NES present the culturally sensitive contents and ideas, and how they initiate, structure and close topics. The HKC initiates the topic when she starts complaining about her former *mad* boss (line 320). The NES gives a minimal response *yes* (line 321) but since the HKC does not further her topic, he asks a question, that is, whether the boss owns the company, which supports further development of the topic. The HKC develops the topic by supplying information about the wife, and then labelling the husband and wife as *traditional Chinese type* (line 327). The NES suggests that she must have experienced working in a difficult situation, to which she agrees. As will be discussed in Chapter 8 about indirectness, the NES's response demonstrates that he has shared understanding about what constitutes the traditional Chinese type of company owners, and so he is able to infer correctly from the HKC's indirect utterance. On lines 328–336, the two speakers collaboratively develop the talk by making general statements about traditional Chinese type of owners.

Then the NES shifts the topic to *very idealistic American materials* that he has used in teaching: materials that paint a rosy picture about business practices and bosses (lines 338–344). After that, he gives his opinion that what is described in those materials is contradictory to that found in the *real world* (line 345) in Hong Kong. It is interesting to see the movement to a non-ethnic specific evaluative comment from a discourse about ethnicity and race. The HKC agrees with the NES's assertion and supports it by adding *it's a whole different culture* (line 347). The NES then supplements the HKC's notion of 'culture' by supplying specifics and features, saying *all they care about is profit production you know don't really care about er relationships and er things like that so er* (lines 348–352), to each of which the HKC responds favourably. The HKC responds by saying *those are the people I think most of our students have to face* (lines 353–354). From the HKC's *it's a whole different culture*, the talk that typifies ethnicity and race and the associated cultural values has effectively changed to one about a non-ethnic specific 'culture', which consists of people 'in the real world' who subscribe to the characteristics and practices listed by the NES.

The HKC contributes to developing the talk by linking *the people* in *the real world* with students whom the NES has just mentioned, saying *those are the people I think most of our students have to face* (lines 353–354). This particular utterance shows that when the HKC completes her interlocutor's utterance, she at the same time draws a conclusion by connecting a few things together, namely those people who belong to *a whole different culture* (line 347) and *our students* (line 354) who have to face it. After this, the NES shifts the topic to his previous work experience in a school.

Analysis of Extract 8 shows the participants in the conversational interaction exchanging and sharing concrete personal experiences, beliefs (correct or incorrect), opinions, attitudes and emotions related to groups of people belonging to different races and cultures. The speakers are found to express and validate a few ideological assumptions. First, factories or companies whose owners belong to the traditional Chinese type and whose businesses grow beyond the family could be enormously difficult to work in for outgroup people who are not part of the family. Second, open friendly bosses and liberal business practices as portrayed in much idealized American materials are more like illusions than reality. Third, in *the real world*, which is *a whole different culture*, which the NES's Hong Kong students are going to enter, all bosses care about are *profit* and *production* but not *relationships and things like that*. Hence, a contrast exists between what university students in Hong Kong learn from idealized American books and what they will face and experience in reality upon graduation. Finally, the reality in Hong Kong is more on a par with traditional Chinese practices than with what is depicted in certain American materials.

A few utterances show invocation of cultural identity, and especially when the HKC is presenting her perception of her identity. She expresses a negative view towards being a member of the traditional Chinese type of family and she does it in a clever and playful way by using a pair of antonyms — *lucky* and *unlucky* (line 333). Specifically, she indicates her unfavourable view towards the traditional Chinese by saying that it is lucky she is not part of the traditional Chinese family (*I am not (.) luckily or (.) luck*), but immediately after that, she uses *unlucky* to imply that since she is not part of the family, she was not happy working for that Chinese boss.

Concern for interpersonal relationships, mainly manifested in facework, is clearly evident, too. The fact that the speakers jointly construct criticism against the traditional Chinese type of bosses and companies is potentially face-threatening for them. Such open criticism of an ethnic (from the HKC's perspective) or a racial group (from the NES's perspective) could threaten the positive face of both of the speakers. The positive face of the HKC may be threatened, as it is her ethnic Chinese group who are being criticized. At the same time, the positive face of the NES speaker could be threatened, as his HKC interlocutor may dislike him as a racist, consequent to his open racial attack on the Chinese.

Nevertheless, there is no evidence that either of the speakers feel any face loss. Such a phenomenon could be explained in terms of the extent to which the HKC identifies herself with the ethnic group being discussed. It is interesting to note that for the HKC, her identity is not a matter of Chinese or non-Chinese. The fact that she says *traditional* Chinese type presupposes that there is the *non-traditional* Chinese type. By saying this, the HKC is effectively distancing herself from the *traditional* type of Chinese whom she is criticizing, and at the same time, has identified with the *non-traditional* Chinese group.

Also, coming out quite prominently from the analysis is the collaborative efforts the speakers make to express, develop and negotiate these ideological assumptions, as well as the smooth interactional pattern between the speakers when they take turns putting forward their views, positions and attitudes. The speakers collaboratively contribute to constructing and developing the topical framework.

There is other evidence that supports the observation that the speakers are concerned about interpersonal relationships. First, the HKC upgrades *difficult* (line 328) uttered by the NES to *really difficult* (line 330), which indicates support lent to her interlocutor. Second, each of the three times when being appealed for feedback (the NES saying *you know*), the HKC provides appropriate responses (lines 333, 336 and 351). Her back-channels mm and *mhm* (lines 340, 342, 349 and 351) indicate continued support for her interlocutor's opinions and beliefs.

The NES contributes to the topic framework by offering and presenting his position in relation to the boss of the *traditional Chinese type* and that portrayed in American materials (line 337 onwards). He also employs a range of strategies to manage interaction as well as interpersonal relationships. In his utterance on lines 337–346, he shifts the topic away from dwelling further on the Chinese. He presents a contrasting view regarding *very liberal American business practices* and *open friendly bosses* described in *very idealistic American materials*, but then by giving his views about what is happening in *the real world* in Hong Kong, he is effectively saying that those bosses are similar to the traditional Chinese in terms of what they really care about in business. This topic shift can be seen as illustrating that the NES is aware of the identity of his HKC friend in relation to that of the members of the racial group that are being criticized. In addition, by relating Western business ideologies and practices to those of the Chinese, the NES is paying concern to his HKC's face. Typically, it is a face-saving strategy to put oneself in the same category as the other party in self-denigration (see, for example, Pomerantz 1984; Tsui 1994). Finally, moving from a high-risk topic (the ethnic group of which the HKC is a member) to a safe topic (Americans of which neither the HKC nor the NES is a member), the NES has made a move to ease off potential discomfort and embarrassment inherent in this kind of topic.

To sum up, in Extract 8 the strategies employed by the NES to create shared meanings with the HKC include topic management (topic shift, development and termination), using turn-final mild "appealer" *you know*, and making comparative statements about ethnic and racial stereotypes. He shows sensitivity towards the topical content by bringing in criticism of Americans, and then adopts a face-saving strategy by distancing himself from the criticized group and shifting the topic from American culture to the general work culture in the business world. Similar to the NES, the HKC also uses a wide range of strategies in constructing and re-constructing her ideologies of ethnicity, namely topic management (topic initiation and development), repetition, upgrade ('really difficult'), utterance completion, antonyms ('lucky' and 'unlucky'), responding to appeals for feedback and backchannelling.

In Extract 9, the Irish woman was the private English tutor for the daughters of the HKC woman. The recording was made in the HKC's home. In the conversation, the speakers exchange their ideological assumptions, views and beliefs about the relative statuses between women and men in various ethnic and racial groups, and the changes in the roles of and attitudes towards women and men in these groups over time. They also discuss reasons for these changes.

(9) 009
A: female Irish a: female Hong Kong Chinese
359. A: how do you think er nowadays do you think men in Hong
360. Kong are taking more of an active role in raising the
361. family than before like maybe in your parents' time
362. it was mainly your mother that took the active role
363. [do you think fathers now are taking much more of an
364. a: [yes
365. active role
366. a: er for those er families er (.) yes which I know

[I think the the fathers are playing a more er active
A: [yea
role in the in the household responsibilities [and er
A: [yea
(.) I I think this change of attitude is brought
about by the economic er the yea the structure [it's
A: [yea
because the women are playing erm are taking more
role in the financial er parts [and so they have
A: [yea yea
er more say in the house [and they can then direct
A: [mm
their husband to take more responsibility of the of
the household [yea house household business
A: [yea
A: responsibilities
a: yea responsibilities but in the past the the concept
is really the man is the er responsible for the
financial side and so they are already working so (.)
so hard outside and so it is fair for them to be
the king er when they come back er er home and just
lie down and relax and enjoy [so they they don't feel
A: [mm
guilty if they just er they just do that (.) and the
the wife will er will think it is really their duty
to serve their [husbands yes but nowadays is so
A: [husbands yes
different the [the wives are also working like a dog
A: yea
outside [((laugh)) and so the when when when we come
A: [that's yea
back er we should share out [our duties mm hm yea
A: [that's right yea [that's right yea
A: it's quite interesting actually to see how quickly in
just in one generation how it's [just changed almost
a: [yea
whereas it's totally equal [yea
a: [yea er not totally but
nearly ((laugh))
A: nearly equal yea but it's been a big erm a big change

for men I think it's been quite hard hard in some
cases [for them to accept this change [and some of
a: [yes [uh huh uh huh
them are still quite traditional or old-fashioned I
think [so they like to still think that the woman
a: [yes yes yes
should stay at home [like I was talking to some erm
a: [yea
(.) students of mine who were Japanese [and they were
a: [uh huh
[telling me that they
a: [oh (.) Japanese are more er [traditional
A: [traditional yes it's
very very traditional they're they're holding on
very much to their traditional values
a: yes
A: but once once a woman gets married that she almost
has to leave her (.) job [and stay at home [even
a: [yea yea yea [yea
though she has no children
a: yea yea so so I am always glad that er I am er born
in Hong Kong [which I think Hong Kong is a place er
A: [yea
where woman er enjoy er quite high status
A: that's right they do actually yea and it's it's
almost equal and you know it's the same as the
Americans very international Hong Kong [the I I find
a: [mm mm mm yes
I am glad er that I am a Chinese and born in Hong
Kong ((laugh))
A: so what do you think in Japan I mean for one of the
most powerful industrial nations in the world they
still have erm (.) a very er old-fashioned idea of
woman's role [it seems [quite strange [doesn't it
a: [yea [uh huh [yea yea very
A: yea
a: and contradicting and er and er I am always wondering
since they have wasted half of their manpower
A: that's right yes
a: and er but still they they they get so advanced in

447. their technology [and that's something amazing
448. A: [yea
449. A: yea it is amazing
450. a: and which I don't understand ((laugh))
451. A: yea maybe that's er maybe something to do with the
452. way that erm the power structure [you know they try
453. a: [yea
454. to keep the men erm (.) encourage the man to stay in
455. the same position [all the way through in their
456. a: [mm
457. career [they encourage the men to continue er to
458. a: [mm
459. work and (.) they don't seem to trust the women [they
460. a: [mm
461. feel the woman is who has married er almost has erm
462. her responsibilities are split [and she is not as
463. a: [mm
464. loyal to her job [so they they encourage the man to
465. a: [mm
466. keep on his job and he is the main breadwinner
467. [whereas I don't know if it will ever change I mean
468. a: [mm
469. we're they're very erm they are very determined to
470. keep these values [I think yea
471. a: [yea yea I don't know ((laugh)) so
472. the er I I I've only got daughters I don't have [sons
473. A: [sons
474. so I I would like the that'll ((laugh)) become more
475. equal
476. A: you like Hong Kong attitude ((laugh))
477. a: ((laugh)) yea yea so daughters er so girls you know
478. work harder so that's er when you grow up you can
479. play a part too [((laugh)) you know they'll play a
480. A: [play a big part
481. part in the in the [society
482. A: [yea yea it's very important very
483. very important I think [that they continue their
484. a: [yea
485. education [and become a part of erm the working
486. a: [yes yes

487. environment [I think it is very sad when erm you
488. a: [yes
489. have you know like in places like China you know they
490. have and also in most erm countries that are not very
491. well developed [the woman has to stay at home and
492. a: [mm
493. very much erm keep the household together and she has
494. she doesn't get a chance they don't give her a chance
495. to get an education and have a choice (.) whereas men
496. all through the generations always had choices [but
497. a: [yes
498. now it seems like women are just getting the
499. opportunity [to have an equal say [over their destiny

The analysis below examines the types of strategies and devices employed by the speakers to collaboratively develop and manage this discourse. The extract starts with the NES initiating a new topic in which she asks the HKC about her views on the relative roles of husband and wife in the family in Hong Kong nowadays which are different from those of the older generation. In response, the HKC indicates agreement *I think the the fathers are playing a more er active role in the in the household responsibilities* (lines 367–369). The HKC then supports the topic by offering an explication and by characterizing the different roles nowadays — *and er (.) I I think this change of change of attitude is brought about by the economic er the yea the structure [it's because the woman are playing erm are taking more role in the financial er parts [and so they have er more say in the house [and they can then direct their husband to take more responsibility of the of the household [yea house household business* (lines 369–380).

After this, the HKC has a long turn, which constitutes presentation of the ideological assumptions that she has regarding the relative roles, statuses and responsibilities of Hong Kong men/husbands and Hong Kong Chinese women/wives in the past and nowadays, before and after the change in attitudes (lines 383–398) — *in the past the the concept is really the man is the er responsible for the financial side and so they are already working so (.) so hard outside and so it is fair for them to be the king er when they come back er er home and just lie down and relax and enjoy [so they they don't feel guilty if they just er they just do that (.) and the the wife will er will think it is really their duty to serve their [husbands yes but nowadays is so different the [the wives are also working like a dog outside [((laugh)) and so the when when when we come back er we should share our [our duties mm hm yea.* The HKC is both describing some phenomena and negatively evaluating them. This is revealed in her choice of words. She uses metaphors *the king* (line 387) to describe the status enjoyed by the husband at home in the past, and describes the wife's role as *serving their husbands.* She also uses *a dog* (line 394) to describe the working life led by the wife nowadays. These words imply a contrast in the view and perception that she has, or that she thinks people have, about gender status in the past and present. Further, her descriptions imply that in the past, there was a huge, unjust and disapproved status difference between the working husband and the housewife, while today, women play two roles and lead a tough life both at work and at home.

In lines 400–421, the speakers express and negotiate their own beliefs about the extent of changes or differences in the roles played by men and women. The NES thinks that the current generation is totally different from the previous one — *it's quite interesting actually to see how quickly in just in one generation how it's [just changed almost whereas it's totally equal [yea* (lines 400–403). The HKC disagrees *yea er not totally but nearly* (lines 404–405). The NES agrees with the HKC and says *nearly equal yea*, but with the reservation *but it's been a big erm change for men*, implying that generally men have changed so that they are equal to women, but then softens her position by quoting exceptional cases *I think it's been quite hard in some cases [for them to accept this change [and some of them are still quite traditional or old-fashioned I think* (lines 407–411).

The NES uses *still quite traditional or old-fashioned* to characterize those Hong Kong men who find it difficult to change their attitudes towards the role and status of women. In the same utterance, she uses a drift to move to a related topic about Japanese men, but she is interrupted by the HKC who offers an utterance completion. The HKC repeats the word *traditional* but adds *more* to intensify the extent to which Japanese men are traditional, as opposed to Hong Kong men. Apart from this, the completion offer indicates that the HKC does not have difficulty inferring the meaning of the NES's utterance. The NES interrupts the HKC and keeps using *traditional*, and this time uses *very* twice to intensify or to upgrade, to describe the values upheld by Japanese *[traditional yes it's very very traditional they're they're holding on very much to their traditional values* (lines 419–421). This upgrade is used to intensify the negative evaluation of Japanese attitudes toward their values.

The repetition of the word *traditional*, which depicts a quality, by the two speakers across a few turns indicates the NES and the HKC jointly constructing and presenting a discourse related to how one racial group compares with another. Effectively, they use the same word to link up two racial groups to indicate sameness between the groups, and even intensify the degree of a quality characteristic of one group by using qualifying adverbs (*more, very*). Another instance of actualization of an interactional pattern is interruptions. The speakers interrupt each other, resulting in the current speaker yielding her turn, and yet the interruption can be considered co-operative, as it is used to complete the current speaker's utterance and to provide supportive information to develop the current topic.

Invocation of identities of gender and ethnicity is observed too. In line 404, the HKC identifies herself as a woman born in Hong Kong, for which she feels grateful. She also provides a reason for her view *yea yea so so I am always glad that er I am born in Hong Kong [which I think Hong Kong is a place er where woman er enjoy er quite high status.* The NES agrees with her and drifts the topic to comparing Hong Kong with America, saying that they are the same in terms of women's status *that's right they do actually yea and it's it's almost equal and you know it's the same as the Americans very international Hong Kong [the I I find* (lines 431–433). By saying this, the NES is making a positive evaluation of the HKC addressee's identity.

The HKC interrupts the NES to indicate agreement, reiterating her identity. This time round, however, she identifies herself as Chinese and born in Hong Kong *[mm mm mm yes I am glad er that I am a Chinese and born in Hong Kong ((laugh))* (lines 434–436). The implication generated is that she is glad that she is Chinese and born in Hong Kong, and not Japanese. Her NES interlocutor is able to infer the meaning, which is evident from her shifting the topic back to the strange situation in Japan.

Managing interpersonal relationships by the women is evident. In the case of the HKC, for example, she uses *contradicting* (line 443) to supplement *strange* by the NES (line 440). She emphasizes her agreement with and support for the NES's view regarding Japanese by means of exaggeration *I am always wondering* (line 443). She crystallizes and contextualizes what the NES says about *a very er old-fashioned idea of woman's role* (lines 439–440) to become *they have wasted half of their manpower* (line 444). She paraphrases the NES's *in Japan I mean for one of the most powerful industrial nations in the world* (lines 437–438) to become *they get so advanced in their technology* (lines 446–447).

In the case of the NES, she employs involvement strategies. She closes her utterance with a tag question *it seems [(.) quite strange doesn't it* (line 440), spoken with a falling tone. This is a Type 3 tag question, based on its syntactic structure (Quirk et al. 1985: 811). The tag question spoken with a falling tone, nevertheless, indicates a communicative choice made by the speaker, namely that the speaker is certain of the assumption and the addressee is invited to agree with her (Tsui 1994: 70). As expected, the HKC responds with *[yea yea* (line 441) to indicate agreement. Another instance of involvement strategy is echoing the HKC's words. In response to the HKC closing the utterance with an evaluative statement *that's something amazing* (line 447), the NES repeats the HKC's words *yea it is amazing* (line 449).

An interactional pattern is also observed in the relative roles taken by the NES and the HKC in lines 451–470. The NES takes a long turn to present her view about the inequality between men and women in Japan, which is attributable to *the power structure* (line 452). The HKC plays a supportive role and gives back-channel responses throughout. The NES closes her turn by means of an evaluative remark *I don't know if it will ever change I mean we're they're very erm they are very determined to keep these values I think yea* (lines 467–470). In response, the HKC says *yea yea I don't know*, followed by laughter (line 471). In lines 451–470, the NES is making most of the contribution to the proposition, while the HKC is playing a supportive role.

After the brief laughter, the HKC brings the propositional content of the racial talk away from the Japanese to herself. The topic invokes identity issues. The HKC identifies herself as having daughters, but not sons, and says that *I would like the that'll ((laugh)) become more equal* (line 474–475), implying that she can identify with and sympathize with the treatment extended to Japanese women, and so hoping that the situation in Japan will change in favour of women. Near equality in status is what the HKC is implying, and the NES picks up on this, saying *you like Hong Kong attitude ((laugh))* (line 476). The HKC responds affirmatively, and starts to mention her daughters, but stops to talk in a general sense about girls in Hong Kong, saying *so daughters er so girls you know work harder so that's er when you grow up you can play a part too [((laugh)) you know they'll play a part in the in the [society* (lines 477–481).

Support, which is part of the interpersonal relationship, is extended to the HKC when the NES develops the topic by means of basically paraphrasing the HKC's utterance *[yea yea it's very important very very important I think [that they continue their education [and become a part of erm the working environment* (lines 482–487).

Another instance of this interactional pattern is observed in lines 487–499. In the same utterance, the NES moves to a related topic by drifting the topic; and that is, in China and other countries that are developing, women have just started to get better opportunities in education and work. The HKC contributes to topic development only in the sense of giving supportive back-channels. From there, the topic is then changed by the HKC (not shown).

To sum up, the speakers in Extract 9 are involved in a topic framework that is concerned with the roles and statuses of women, as opposed to those of men, across several ethnic and racial groups. The analysis has shown a great deal of negotiation taking place in the discourse. The speakers present, exchange, discuss, develop and mull over various ideas, assumptions, beliefs, values and attitudes relating to the topic at hand. Also, through sequencing topics, the speakers jointly develop a series of logically connected topics, and this is represented diagrammatically as follows:

> Hong Kong (past) and Hong Kong (now) → Japan (now) →
> Hong Kong (now) → Hong Kong (now) and America (now) →
> Hong Kong (now) → Japan (now) → Hong Kong (future) →
> Hong Kong (now) → China and other countries (now)

Hong Kong, with which the HKC woman identifies, is the theme running through the conversational excerpt. As the conversation develops, the speakers discuss the past, the present and the future of Hong Kong. Acting as the focal point of reference, Hong Kong is discussed in relation to other countries, namely Japan, America, China and other countries and their cultural values and beliefs.

In terms of interactional pattern, the two female speakers assume a variety of roles at different stages of the discourse. At times, their contribution to the talk is shared and equal in terms of content and turn-taking. At other times, the NES is the primary speaker, while the HKC plays a supportive role. Their goals of interaction, nevertheless, are common, and have been realized in several ways. First, the speakers share and exchange common ground in that both are being positive about women's status in Hong Kong and critical about the status of Japanese women and mainland Chinese women. Specifically, they share and exchange their personal and social knowledge and experiences related to propositions that can easily invoke basic human rights, gender discrimination, prejudice and injustice, involving various ethnic and racial groups, one of which the HKC identifies with. Second, each of the speakers presents herself as both an individual and a social being, embodying a set of values, assumptions and beliefs with regard to the topic being constructed and negotiated. Third, the speakers may gain mutual and better understanding from the interaction that involves sharing and exchanging views, beliefs, and even emotions relating to the topic. Finally, and probably more importantly, as a result of socializing personal experiences and self-presentation of views and beliefs, the speakers may feel a greater sense of camaraderie.

The analysis of Extract 9 has demonstrated the process and strategies of managing sensitive discourse topics in discursive interaction between speakers from different cultural backgrounds. The nature of the topic is highly likely to invoke cultural knowledge, attitudes, ideologies; and, most importantly of all, cultural identities specific to individual participants. The HKC and NES participants have effectively employed devices and strategies to collaboratively manage not only the ideological, but also interpersonal, aspects of the topic. Invocation of cultural identity and membership is also apparent in the interaction.

Compared to Extract 8, the topical subject matter in Extract 9 is much less culturally sensitive and face-threatening for both speakers. In Extract 9, the HKC and the NES collaboratively criticize Japanese men as being 'traditional' and then upgrade the criticism to 'very very traditional', with the NES expressing pessimism about the Japanese attitude toward their traditional values (*they are very determined to keep these values*, lines 469–470). The HKC woman in Extract 9 is blunt and direct in criticizing the 'traditional' Japanese cultural values and practices, and is explicit about being proud of her social identity (*I am always glad that er I am er born in Hong Kong*, lines 427–428; *I am glad er that I am a Chinese and born in Hong Kong* ((laugh)), lines 435–436). In Extract 8, however, the HKC and especially the NES have been shown to be paying greater concern managing the topic. With the

NES introducing a shift from criticizing the 'traditional' Chinese to Americans and then to the general business world, the HKC endorses and develops the NES's topic in order to dissociate herself from the 'traditional' Chinese group being criticized.

Extract 10 below shows the two business friends communicating and negotiating beliefs and attitudes along the line of ethnic and racial stereotypical assumptions and practice, namely the relation between man and animals in general, and that between man and dogs in particular, both within and outside the speakers' respective racial and ethnic groups. More specifically, they are comparing the eating habits of Hong Kong Chinese, mainland Chinese and Americans, as well as the views of these groups towards animals.

(10) 020
b: male Hong Kong Chinese B: male American
82: b: do you do you like to eat the inside body I mean the
83: animal inside body do you get the meaning
84: B: do I eat meat
85: b: meat yea not inside body just like er brain er the
86: the heart er
87: B: oh no I don't eat that [you eat that
88: b: [((laugh))
89: b: yea because I'm Chinese sorry I'm Chinese I will eat
90: this (.) all animals who is the with four foot
91: sounds good we'll eat just like dog er cat er
92: B: you eat the dog
93: b: no no no but
94: B: you don't eat dog
95: b: yea
96: B: but when you will when you will go to China you will
97: see something (.) food stall you'll (.) you'll (.)
98: eat the dog
99: B: yea
100: b: ((Cantonese))
101: B: they sell dogs there
102: b: yea
103: B: it's hanging
104: b: yea hanging the dog
105: B: oh my god
106: b: yea
107: B: [you don't eat that
108: b: [it's it's terrible [oh I don't know no no it's

109:	B:	[oh my
110:		terrible [you'll see ((Cantonese))
111:	B:	[wow
112:	B:	do they sell that in Hong Kong
113:	b:	no it's illegal
114:	B:	that's illegal yeah it's crazy
115:	b:	it's very terrible
116:	B:	oh my god
117:	b:	yea
118:	B:	they eat anything over there
119:	b:	yeap (.) anything
120:	B:	oh my god
121:		(pause)
122:	B:	you have to be careful (.) they could call it beef
123:		and and put dog in your food (.) right (.) over in
124:		China
125:	b:	mm
126:	B:	if you ordered [er
127:	b:	[yea be careful
128:	B:	beef
129:	b:	[yea
130:	B:	[it could it could be somebody's cat
131:	b:	well mix up er
132:	B:	they can mix it up with some [cat and [dog and some
133:	b:	[yea [yea
134:		noodles and call it er pork call it [chick
135:	b:	[you must you
136:		must ah V_ you must ask V_ don't eat don't eat that
137:		things
138:		((B and b laugh))
139:	b:	maybe er V_ make a joke joking with you give you the
140:		(first dish) just like that
141:	B:	that that that is nasty let me tell you (.) if that
142:		ever happened in the United States someone could get
143:		killed for that
144:	b:	it's very
145:	B:	for serving dogs someone would get really killed (.)
146:		that's like er in America dog is man's best friend
147:	b:	mm
148:	B:	[you don't kill it for for food

149: b: [I think so I think so
150: B: that's that just downright crazy [(.) crazy people
151: b: [mm
152: across the border ((laugh))
153: b: mm mm I think so
154: B: yea ((laugh))
155: b: mm

The HKC starts the topic, when he asks his American business friend whether he eats the insides of the animal, to which the NES disaffirms, saying *oh no I don't eat that* (line 87). In return, the NES asks the HKC whether he does (*you eat that*, line 87). The HKC gives an affirmative answer, followed by a reason *yea because I'm Chinese*, followed by an apology for being Chinese *sorry I am Chinese I will eat this (.) all animals who is the with four foot sounds good we'll eat just like dog er cat er* (lines 89–91). Giving a reason is a positive politeness strategy to involve the hearer as a participant in the conversation, which is a sign of interpersonal relationship management. What is more, the response represents the HKC identifying himself with the Chinese and the associated stereotypical eating habits, i.e. the Chinese eat the insides of animals, and is hence a case of invocation of identity. Following that, in a half-joking and half-boasting manner, the HKC continues, giving his opinion that the Chinese, as a racial group, eat all animals with four feet, and giving dogs and cats as examples. Hearing that, the NES asks in a surprised tone for clarification and confirmation, saying *you eat the dog* (line 92).

Invocation of cultural identity is at work in the turns that follow. In relation to eating dog, the HKC, however, clearly distances himself from the ethnic mainland Chinese by means of a number of discourse strategies. He uses strong denying *no no no* (line 93), saying that he does not eat dog. He agrees with the American's view towards the habit of dog-eating in mainland China by repeating the negative evaluation *[it's it's terrible [oh I don't know no no it's terrible* (lines 108–110). When the NES asks whether dog is sold in Hong Kong, the HKC denies that and provides an explanation *no it's illegal* (line 113) to sell dogs in Hong Kong, implying that selling dog is not illegal in China and confirms the NES's allegation that mainlanders *eat anything* in China (line 118). The HKC clearly distinguishes between Hong Kong and mainland China. In Hong Kong it is illegal to eat dogs but in mainland China you can find food stalls selling dogs, with dogs hung up. At the same time, he is distinguishing the mainland Chinese who eat dog and cat from Hong Kong Chinese who do not. By doing that, he is categorically dissociating himself, a Hong Kong Chinese man, from mainland Chinese.

The verbal exchanges that follow illustrate the collaboration process undertaken by the speakers to manage the topic. The NES shifts the topic, and jokes about what might happen to somebody eating out in mainland China *you have to be careful (.) they could call it beef and and put dog in your food (.) right (.) over in China if you ordered [er* (lines 122–126). The HKC shows full support to his NES interlocutor by collaboratively developing the topic, agreeing that people need to *be careful* (line 127). Each of the speakers contributes to creating the story about the terrible kinds of food that somebody eating out in mainland China might possibly be given to eat by means of quick overlapping talk, building on the previous utterance to increase the absurdity in the jointly constructed proposition of the talk. When the NES suggests that beef *could be somebody's cat* (line 130), the HKC interrupts and makes the NES's story even more horrible, saying *well mix up er* (mixing up beef, dog and cat) (line 131). Building on that and making the story even more vividly disgusting, hideous and ghastly, the NES adds more details *they can mix it up with some [cat and [dog and some noodles and call it er (.) pork call it chick* (lines 132 and 134). The HKC supports the topic by giving backchannel responses (line 133), and collaboratively develops it by suggesting *you must ah V_ you must ask V_ don't eat don't eat that things* (lines 135–137).

The two speakers have a good laugh at the topic. Then the American man shifts to a related topic. After an evaluation *that is nasty* (line 141), he follows up by saying that Americans regard the dog as *man's best friend*, and that killing a dog is a very serious offence. Here the American man is contributing to the racial and ethnic discourse by comparing the behaviours and practices of various racial groups. He then expresses his aversion to the mainland Chinese, saying *you don't kill it for for food that's that just downright crazy [(.) crazy people across the border* (lines 148–152), to which the HKC agrees and which the HKC supports with *mm I think so* (line 153). Then the speakers are ready to close the topic, as each of them says *yea* and laughs but neither contributes further to the topic. The topic is finally changed by the NES.

Compared to the previous extracts, the participants in Extract 10 appear to hold stronger and more critical ideological positions regarding ethnic and racial stereotypes and prejudice. Neither of them, however, seems to feel intimidated by or uncomfortable about constructing the racist discourse. In fact, they seem to be enjoying this joint construction of prejudiced talk. They develop it, appearing to derive a lot of fun out of doing so.

A change in the stance of the HKC has been observed when the conversation unfolds. In line 89, he apologizes for being Chinese, but as the topic develops, he starts to differentiate between mainland Chinese and Hong Kong Chinese. After the HKC man has explicitly "announced" that he is different from people in mainland China, and made it clear that Hong Kong is different from mainland China in terms of eating habits and practices, he can be seen to be as unrestrained as the NES in cracking racist jokes about China and the mainland Chinese. Indeed, by exaggerating the offensiveness and formidability of these habits and practices, the HKC is trying to distance himself more from his fellow countrymen born and living in mainland China, and thus disclaiming membership from the grotesque group of mainland Chinese who feed on such animals as cat and dog.

Extract 11 is another excerpt that demonstrates disclaiming of membership of a cultural group by the HKC. It begins with the HKC comparing Hong Kong and Japan regarding the seriousness of illegal immigrants and over-stayers in the cities/countries. His view is that it is much more serious in Japan than in Hong Kong because first, Japan is much bigger and so implying that it is much more difficult to discover illegal immigrants and over-stayers; and second, Japan does not legally require citizens to carry their identity cards with them when they go out, and so it is much more difficult to identify people who are not granted permission to stay in the country (lines 450–465).

(11) 001
b: male Hong Kong Chinese B: male Australian
450. b: there is no check unlike Hong Kong [where you you
451. B: [mm
452. you you have this er I mean you know Hong Kong
453. residents we are required to er carry our identity
454. card and we and the policemen can stop us and ask to
455. check our identity card
456. B: mm
457. b: so but in Japan you don't (.) you don't have this
458. sort of requirement [and Japan is such a big
459. B: [oh
460. country Hong Kong is such a small place [and big
461. B: [yea
462. country and even in Hong Kong we have many illegal
463. immigrants [over-stayers and I mean er not to
464. B: [yes
465. mention not to to mention Japan
466. B: they're pretty obvious aren't they
467. b: who
468. B: you can usually pick a mainlander (.) here
469. b: er [well
470. B: [they have bad hair cuts [they wear bad suits
471. b: [yea yea yea
472. they wear blue suits with white socks or
473. [socks don't match they have terrible shoes

474. b: [yes yes yes yes yes yes yes yes
475. b: yea but but mind you they're they're very clever now
476. they they know how to dress them up er they they
477. they would usually be dressed in a most fashionable
478. way er that it is difficult to distinguish them from
479. you know Hong Kong people
480. B: mhmm
481. b: so the fourth one (.) let me see the er the fourth
482. one I've used well that first maid ran away and then
483. I have to er get one from Hong Kong immediately
484. during my annual leave back to Hong Kong
485. B: alright

In response to the HKC's *even in Hong Kong we have many illegal immigrants [over-stayers and I mean er [not to mention not to to mention Japan* (lines 462–465), the NES asks a confirmatory question tag *they're pretty obvious aren't they* (line 466). The HKC is puzzled as to who 'they' refer to, and so asks *who* (line 467). Then the NES paraphrases his previous utterance to make the "who" clear and to add the "where" — *you can usually pick a mainlander (.) here* (line 468). The NES goes on characterizing what, in his mind, a mainlander in Hong Kong looks like, or dresses like, as realized in his presentation of ideas — *[they have bad hair cuts [they wear bad suits they wear blue suits with white socks or [socks don't match they have terrible shoes* (lines 470–473). On hearing this, the HKC gives a stream of supportive, affirmative response *[yes yes yes yes yes yes yes yes* (line 474).

In lines 475–479, the HKC indicates his cultural knowledge, assumptions and attitudes regarding the mainland Chinese living in Hong Kong, which he shares with his NES interlocutor. He seemingly corrects the NES's stereotypical assumptions about the appearance of these mainlanders, saying *yea but but mind you they're they're very clever now they they know how to dress them up er they they they would usually be dressed in a most fashionable way er that it is difficult to distinguish them from you know Hong Kong people.* Nevertheless, judging from the linguistic context, when the HKC uses *clever* to describe mainlanders in Hong Kong, he is not using this word in a positively evaluative or an appreciative way. Use of this word is similar, in certain ways, to *devious* uttered by the NES in Extract 13, line 143 in this chapter to describe the Filipino maid. To respond to the HKC's implied criticism of those mainlanders who dress themselves up to look like Hong Kong people, the NES gives a minimal response. Neither of the speakers dwells on the current topic, which simply dies off when the HKC imperceptibly moves to a related topic by means of drifting the topic.

Extract 11 shows two speakers openly criticizing and making fun of another ethnic (from the HKC's point of view) or racial (from the NES's point of view) group, in the course of which each of them presents their ideological positions, assumptions and opinions concerning the topic. They are involved in the negotiation of common ground. They jointly manage the interaction pattern of the discourse. The NES's stereotypical assumptions about mainlanders in Hong Kong are evident in the contemptuous and disdainful way in which he depicts their hairstyles and clothing and the way they dress. The HKC contributes to this discriminatory talk by agreeing with the NES's assumptions, followed by offering additional information about this group to show support for the NES's prejudiced view against mainlanders.

Several implications can be made from the HKC's utterance which reflect his ideological assumptions concerning the mainland Chinese: (1) it is *clever* for the mainland Chinese to dress themselves like Hong Kong people, (2) Hong Kong people are dressed *in a most fashioned way*, which is a drastic opposite to the way mainland Chinese usually dress, (3) the intention for these mainland Chinese is that their identity and illegal status will not be easily exposed and discovered, and (4) mainland Chinese are distinct from Hong Kong people, despite the fact that both are Chinese. These assumptions demonstrate the HKC dissociating himself, or Hong Kong Chinese, from mainland Chinese. This is again an issue of membership and cultural identity, which permeates all of the excerpts that have been described so far.

The racial topic is initiated by the NES (*they're pretty obvious aren't they*, line 466) and supported by the HKC. Regarding managing interpersonal relationships, neither of the speakers seems to feel that engaging in this discriminatory talk is an FTA. The speakers jointly construct a mockery of the appearance of the mainland Chinese, a group of which neither of the conversationalists is a member. They exchange their mocking remarks frankly. The HKC gives an update on the behaviour of mainlanders in Hong Kong. A sense of camaraderie is observed in this prejudiced discourse.

In Extract 12, the British man was the brother-in-law of the HKC woman. He married the younger sister of the HKC. They are discussing some kind of 'barter' business the NES is interested in starting up.

(12) 004
B: male British a: female Hong Kong Chinese
164. a: how how is it going now
165. B: er it's onto stage two stage s[tage one yea stage
166. a: [stage two
167. one was contacting the company in America
168. a: mhmm
169. B: and they sent me by DHL all the information
170. a: yea

171. B: and then stage two [is the
172. a: [you mean you mean you want to
173. get the information or to learn about this from erm
174. from America from that company
175. B: yea learn yea er to learn from the American company
176. [cos they are very stupid in America cos I asked
177. a: [yea
178. them I'd like to set up a company [similar to yours
179. a: [mhmm
180. in [Asia and should I send you all the details
181. a: [mhmm
182. a: and then they are so generous [to tell you all
183. B: [yea yea they're very
184. very stupid (inaudible) oh they sent me all the
185. information ((laugh)) oh okay so I just copied
186. [and I did the same thing here
187. a: [uh huh
188. a: is it a lot of information
189. B: yes it's a big folder
190. a: wow
191. B: and they sent it by DHL [they sent it in two days cos
192. a: [mm
193. they want to work with [people here
194. a: [and free of charge to send
195. you to send you all these
196. B: oh yea
197. a: and free of charge wow
198. B: and by courier by courier they sent it (.) so I don't
199. know why I think because they realise here is a big
200. market [and no one is in it so they wanted to work
201. a: [mm
202. with me
203. a: yea yea yea
204. B: they're a big company in America erm (.) and I said
205. okay right I
…
218. B: yea I've found one person already er
219. a: because of the capital [or
220. B: [don't need capital

221. a: no
222. B: just cost of the (.) only [I need the
223. a: [or human resource
224. B: human resource because he (.) he has his own business
225. and he can work from his office
226. a: yea
227. B: I can't do this cos I have my own job so I need
228. somebody who has their own office space and telephone
229. so when I contact people I can tell them to contact
230. him
231. a: yea
232. B: and not me until it's really successful then I can
233. leave my job but
234. a: but why doesn't he do it himself
235. B: er he could do but I'm (.) sort of helping him cos I
236. have all the information for the moment [(inaudible)
237. a: [she can he
238. can also get the infor [mation
239. B: [exactly I trust him that he
240. would not do it I think [he will need I think (.)
241. a: [why
242. he's he's an American
243. ((B and a laugh))
244. B: er I think he will he'll want someone it's hard to
245. start a business just on your own so we both need it
246. also I have lots of contacts in this barter business
247. lots of advertising contact so I can help him I know
248. more people than he does so he needs me and people
249. cos I know all the people I need him cos he's got
250. the office and we use erm maybe use your your
251. brother's company
252. a: what what kind of company
253. B: shell company
254. (pause)

…

281. a: have you talked (.) about this with your friends
282. B: yea and everyone I've spoken to people who're in
283. businesses who are in advertising agencies
284. a: yea

285. B: I haven't told every one "cos I don't want every one
286. to know
287. a: yes
288. B: er but oh I there's no company like that and no
289. nobody can think of it anyway that does this
290. a: but what's their opinion would would they think that
291. it can earn money
292. B: yea because you can earn money by being the central
293. person the broker you charge so much for being the
294. broker you charge the commission for selling the
295. goods for exchanging
296. a: because er Chinese er most probably are quite
297. stubborn and cannot accept new things or new ideas it
298. is quite difficult for Chinese to do this especially
299. in business
300. B: but if you go to a Chinese person and say hey look
301. you've got a computer which you've not sold [and it's
302. a: [yea
303. you are not doing anything with it (.) I can give you
304. something for it (.) won't cost you anything [or very
305. a: [mm
306. little a few hundred dollars (.) okay if he can't
307. sell it then he's happy to get rid of it

The ideological assumptions of the two speakers regarding Americans and the Chinese in the business world are revealed in the conversational episode. The NES believes that people in companies in America are very stupid, and he supports his racist, prejudiced belief by giving a specific illustration. In contrast, the HKC considers what the NES describes as stupidity to be generosity. Her view toward the Chinese is that they are quite stubborn and resistant to new things and new ideas. As a member of the Chinese race, the HKC's negative opinion of the Chinese constitutes self-denigration. In response and as a face-saving strategy, the NES, however, expresses opposing views about the Chinese.

When Extract 12 opens, the HKC enquires about the barter business that the NES mentioned the last time they met. The NES describes stage one of his barter business, which is learning from an American company that is involved in the barter business. He prefaces his narrative with a racist remark *cos they are very stupid in America* (line 176). Then he describes what he requested from the American company—*I'd like to set up a company similar to yours in Asia and should I send you all the details* (lines 178 and 180). In response, the HKC says *and then they are so generous to tell you all* (line 182). The NES reiterates his prejudiced perception regarding Americans (*yea yea they're very very stupid,* lines 183–184), laughs and describes the stupid things the American company has done, namely that the Americans responded very quickly and sent off to him a big folder of information about their company by courier (DHL) that arrived in two days. Interestingly, the HKC attributes these behaviours of the American company to generosity rather than stupidity, remarking *and free of charge to send you to send you all these* (lines 194–195). It is interesting that after the HKC has described Americans as generous, the NES upgrades 'very stupid' to 'very very stupid'. The NES is so abrasive, probably because the group he is criticizing is unrelated to either himself or his HKC interlocutor. The HKC, however, does not join the NES in ridiculing Americans.

In response to the HKC's question about whether the American company sends all the information free of charge, the NES reiterates that the company sends the information by courier, implying that the postage must be costly, which confirms, and actually adds weight to, his remark about the stupidity of the American company. By doing so, the NES brings up and negotiates his interpretation of the behaviour of that particular American company.

Later on in the conversation, the NES describes the second stage of his barter business which involves finding business partners. He says that he has already found one person. Then the HKC asks *but why doesn't he do it himself* (line 234) and suggests that *she can he can also get the information* (lines 237–238) that the NES provides him. In response, the NES makes fun of Americans, when he explains why he trusts that the American man would not hijack his information and do the barter business by himself (i.e. without collaborating with the NES), by saying that *he's an American* (line 242). Both the NES and HKC laugh at the humorous implication of the remark, whereby the NES is implying that the American man being discussed is either stupidly honest or stupid and lacking initiative. From there, the NES generalizes that all Americans are like that. After cracking the racist joke, the NES switches to a serious tone, giving the reason for thinking that that man is the right partner for him.

The HKC makes a comparison between Americans and the Chinese. When she hears that there is no similar business in Asia or in Hong Kong, and when she asks how his friends have reacted to the idea of the new barter business (*but what's their opinion would would they think that it can earn money,* lines 290–291). She justifies herself by presenting her ideological assumptions about the Chinese. She organizes the utterances by first expressing her beliefs regarding the Chinese in general, i.e. they are quite stubborn and cannot accept new things or new ideas, and then applying the generalization to a specific situation, i.e. the stubborn Chinese will find bartering, a new idea to them, difficult to accept *because er Chinese er most probably are quite stubborn and cannot accept new things or new ideas it is quite difficult for Chinese to do this especially in business* (lines 296–299).

Facework, and in this case, to temper the FTA directed at her own positive face, takes place. When the HKC expresses her views towards the Chinese, she hedges her ideological assumptions about the stubborn characteristic of the Chinese with hesitations *er* and modality *most probably*. The purpose of these negative politeness strategies is to mitigate her denigrating remark against the Chinese (Brown and Levinson 1987), as she is literally criticizing her own fellow countrymen; in other words, an act of self-denigration. This utterance also shows that the topical contents being discussed invoke issues and thoughts related to cultural identity. It is interesting that the female HKC manages the topic of criticizing Americans and the topic of criticizing the Chinese differently. While she does not join the NES in ridiculing Americans, she actually introduces the criticism of the Chinese. The HKC woman in this extract has, therefore, shown herself to be self-critical.

Facework is also evident when the NES expresses disagreement with her. He starts describing how a Chinese person may react to an offer that helps him or her to get rid of an obsolete possession, and even from which he or she will make some money, implying that the Chinese are actually clever and shrewd in business, contrary to the HKC's portrayal. The NES's contradiction of the HKC's perception of the Chinese can actually be seen as a face-saving, rather than a face-threatening, strategy.

The HKC and the NES perform a range of strategies to manage conversation whose topical framework is inherently sensitive socially and culturally. These strategies include offering views that are either similar or divergent to those of the other, agreeing and disagreeing, shifting between serious and jocular exchanges, use of conversational implicature, use of negative politeness strategies, and shared laughter. Through the interaction, the speakers have socialized personal experiences, presented their ideological information, persuaded each other into adopting certain positions or beliefs, obtained amusement and solicited camaraderie.

Extracts 13 and 14 below are taken from the same recording. The speakers were colleagues working for the Hong Kong Government. Extract 13 is interesting in two ways. On the surface at least, it exemplifies the extreme of racial discourse — racial discrimination, in that the HKC man explicitly accuses the native English speaker of being racist.

(13) 001
b: male Hong Kong Chinese B: male Australian
108. b: so that's why most of the time it would be you and
109. J_ at home [and they well they they when when when
110. B: [mm
111. both of you were out are out for work and they came

112. they come home [they
113. B: [mm (.) so we get on well but it's
114. good it's working quite well
115. b: mm mm
116. (pause)
117. B: except the maid's really (.) I have a lot of
118. difficulty coming to grips with the maid
119. b: what maid Filipino maid [or Chinese maid
120. B: [mm
121. B: Filipino
122. b: why (.) you have discrimination against her
123. B: we're not used to having servants
124. b: oh I see
125. (pause)
126. B: and I think she's been (.) with er (.) with him for
127. a long time being his maid for a long time
128. b: oh I see (.) how long your friend has been in Hong
129. Kong
130. B: eighteen years
131. b: eighteen years oh well he must be an old Hong Kong
132. hand
133. B: mm
134. b: he he used he has been using that maid for eighteen
135. years no
136. B: no no no about six six years
137. b: I see (.) well probably that maid knows er more
138. about Hong Kong than you do isn't it
139. B: oh yea [I think
140. b: [and what sort what sort of problem you
141. encounter (.) you don't know how to communicate with
142. her ((laugh))
143. B: I think she is very devious (.) sort of you know
144. b: mm what do you mean [oh I see well I think she may
145. B: [well
146. be may be she have some some bad feeling about you
147. know having to serve er one more couple isn't it
148. B: yea
149. b: yea that's the problem I think (.) I mean she used
150. to [play with him is that I pay part of the money
151. B: [but the arrangement I've got
152. that I pay is for her

Extract 13 shows that the HKC is very direct in his question, addressed to his Australian interlocutor, relating to racial prejudice. The NES complains that he has *a lot of difficulty coming to grips with the (Filipino) maid* (lines 117–118). In response, the HKC very bluntly and directly asks *why (.) you have discrimination against her* (spoken in a rising tone) (line 122), which can be regarded a serious FTA in terms of lessening the Australian NES man's positive face. It is noticeable that no redressive language of any kind is used by the HKC; instead the FTA is performed on record baldly (Strategy 1 to deal with an FTA, Brown and Levinson 1987). The NES, however, does not seem to be upset by the choice of wording and the directness in the HKC's challenge, and responds by giving a reason — *we're not used to having servants* (line 123), which the HKC acknowledges by plainly saying *oh I see.* Here the NES is denying discrimination against Filipinos and toning down his criticism as merely *not used to having servants.* The significance of these exchanges, particularly the NES's response to the HKC's bald-on-record allegation will be discussed later on.

The HKC further develops the ideological talk by asking the NES *what sort of problem you encounter (.) you don't know how to communicate with her ((laugh))* (lines 140–142). Then, the NES directly and bluntly criticizes the maid by giving a negative evaluation of her *I think she is very devious (.) sort of you know* (line 143). This is followed by the HKC pursuing the topic and actually suggesting a reason to account for the ill feelings that the NES has for the maid. With the HKC's contribution to the topic framework, the reason that the NES is not used to having servants has turned out to be not the real reason for him to have found it difficult to come to grips with the maid. The true picture is that the difficulty was actually due to an unsatisfactory arrangement whereby the NES and his wife are sharing the maid with their friend.

The conversational management strategies employed by the speakers in this racist talk are different. The fact that the HKC has used the bald-on-record linguistic strategy and that the NES does not seem to feel that his face has been threatened could possibly be due to the attitudes of the speakers towards prejudiced discourse in this particular informal social communicative context. The HKC may not have estimated a high face loss on the part of the NES as a result of hearing his abrupt, blunt and direct remark. In fact, in earlier parts of the conversation (not shown), the NES has criticized the work performance and attitude of this maid, which is supported and developed by the HKC. Common ground has already been established between the speakers. It is possible that both speakers share a negative attitude towards Filipino maids and so they consider it appropriate to be so direct and open about their opinions and attitudes. As the topic, being jointly and co-operatively developed, is agreeable to both speakers, the HKC feels more able to be provocative in his comment. The HKC's bald-on-record "allegation" that the NES is a racist is not perceived by the NES to be a seriously intended attack on himself, but instead the utterance is dismissed by the NES as non-serious.

The most interesting part is the change in the NES's reasoning and justification from line 123 to line 143. In response to the HKC's non-serious "accusation" of being racist, the NES gives a neutral reason, *we're not used to having servants*, implicitly rejecting the "allegation" directed at him. After a pause, in line 126, the NES begins to offer a reason, i.e. this maid has been working for his friend, with whom the NES and his wife are living, for a long time. Mentioning the maid, the NES is implying that the problem comes from the maid. The topic is then shifted by the HKC. In line 140, the topic is resumed when the HKC asks what sort of problem the NES encounters with the maid, and then asks in a joking way whether it is because the NES does not know how to communicate with her. When being provoked, the NES becomes very direct and open in his criticism, offering his view that the maid is *very devious* (line 143). Despite the fact that the criticism is hedged with *I think*, it is nonetheless quite open and blunt revealing that the NES is not shy to make negative remarks about the maid, who is the object of their "racist" and "discriminatory" talk. The fact that the HKC offers justification to account for the NES's "racist" remark is evidence of the collaborative effort in managing interpersonal relationships in this discursive interaction.

The HKC in Extract 13 is being direct, which is quite different from those in previous extracts that have been examined. Here the HKC confronts the NES with direct questions like *you have discrimination against her, you don't know how to communicate with her*, and *she may have some bad feeling about you know having to serve er one more couple isn't it*. All of these questions potentially threaten the NES's face, and hence indicate that the HKC does not sympathize with the NES and does not attempt to save his face. The HKC is also very direct in his comments about the maid knowing about more Hong Kong more than the NES does. It is, however, important to point out that the conversation is conducted in a light-hearted atmosphere, rather than serious and solemn. The HKC's directness and bluntness is rarely found in other extracts.

The communicative goals of the talk include amusement, camaraderie and socializing personal experiences. In fact, as the conversation unfolds, the NES's personal experiences and attitudes towards this particular maid have become shared meanings and experiences, based on which further talk and opinions are created. Later on in the same conversation (not shown), the HKC describes at length his experiences with four Filipino maids[1] that he has employed. Some experiences are unpleasant. It becomes clear later that both the HKC and the NES see maids as inherently 'devious'.

Extract 14 shows the same Hong Kong Chinese man and Australian man exchanging ideological views concerning three racial groups: the Hong Kong Chinese, expatriates who are usually native speakers of English, and Filipino women who work as maids for the first two groups.

(14) 001
b: male Hong Kong Chinese B: male Australian
334. b: [I think I think she's spoiled I
335. er well the fact is that (.) well at at the present
336. moment the about hund- er er hundred thousand
337. Filipino maids are working in Hong Kong [and most of
338. B: [hundred
339. the fifty it said in the paper
340. b: well yea maybe hundred and fifty so hundred and
341. fifty thousand Filipino maids are working in Hong
342. Kong and I believe most of them are getting the
343. minimum pay only three thousand seven hundred fifty
344. and er in fact er the Chinese community the
345. Chinese employers are saying that the expatriate er
346. employers are spoiling the er Filipino maids because
347. our standards are very different because we we well
348. the Chinese the Hong Kong Chinese they are very er
349. you know they know how to calculate the the sums add
350. the sums up so they most of them the great majority
351. of them are paying the minimum salary to the maids
352. (.) and the expatriates as far as I know er you know
353. A_ A_ S_ A_ S_ is paying her maid five thousand five
354. hundred [it's amazing I actually I criticise er her
355. B: [yea
356. I complain actually I lodge a complaint with her and
357. say er and and ask her to stop mm you know paying so
358. much to her maid because it would er [you know
359. B: [((cough))
360. disturb the er the the the the market situation
361. ((laugh))
362. B: yea ((laugh))
363. b: isn't it I mean I mean if you are paying five
364. thousand five hundred compared with three thousand
365. seven hundred fifty with the er great majority of
366. course you knowmost of the erm actually if you if
367. you if you ask the er Filipino maids to choose
368. obviously they would er opt for the er expatriate

369. employers because relatively speaking expatriate
370. employers are more generous (.) more generous
371. B: and less demanding
372. b: and less demanding yes that's true I mean they as
373. you well perhaps because you are quite used to doing
374. your how house chores house chores [by yourselves
375. B: [yea
376. because you told me you I mean you don't have any
377. maids in Australia and er so you're quite used to er
378. doing all the work yourself [er so er I suppose er
379. B: [mm
380. even if you even when you are in Hong Kong you oh
381. since you are used to doing the work yourself you
382. you would er as a matter of habit you know do the
383. work yourself [and leave er your know some of the
384. B: [yea
385. you know more time-consuming ones to your your maids
386. [and so they are I think relatively [they are
387. B: [mm [so I think she
388. is on a very very good position
389. b: yes I think so

The participants discuss two racial groups (i.e. Hong Kong Chinese and the Anglo-Saxon expatriates residing in Hong Kong), to which each participant can identify himself with. The conversation begins with the HKC opining that the NES's Filipino maid, whom the NES has criticized as 'devious', is 'spoiled' because she is over-paid. The HKC then compares Chinese and expatriate employers in terms of the salary they pay to their Filipino maids. He remarks that Chinese employers have very different standards (line 347) compared to expatriate employers in that the majority of Chinese employers are paying the minimum salary to their maids, whereas expatriates are *spoiling the er Filipino maids* (line 346) by paying a lot more over and above the minimum salary. He then provides justification for this; and that is, the Hong Kong Chinese *know how to calculate the the sums add the sums up so they most of them the great majority of them are paying the minimum salary to the maids* (lines 349–351). The minimum salary is Hong Kong dollars 3,750. The HKC speaker supports his own criticism of expatriate employers by quoting a specific complaint that he has lodged against a female expatriate colleague A_ S_ who pays $5,500 to her maid (lines 353–354), complaining that A_ S_ should stop paying so much to her maid as she disturbs *the er the the the the market situation ((laugh))* (lines 360–361). The HKC goes on remarking that *relatively speaking expatriate employers are more generous (.) more generous* (lines 369–370) than Chinese employers. In reaction, the Australian speaker says *and less demanding* (line 371), making a comparison between these expatriate employers and their Chinese counterparts, and thus generating an implication that functions to criticize Chinese employers and praise expatriate employers.

The stereotypical views invoked are that when it comes to hiring Filipino maids, Chinese employers are less generous and more demanding, whereas expatriate employers are more generous and less demanding. Given what has been said, the stereotypical image of the Chinese employer, with which the HKC naturally identifies himself, is one of shrewdness. The HKC is hence being self-critical but, at the same time, he defends Chinese employers being *more demanding*. When comparing Chinese and expatriate employers, he implies that Chinese employers know better how to handle finances, and expatriate employers are not as good in that regard. Hence in a systematic manner, the HKC presents his ideological assumptions and beliefs.

The HKC has adopted a number of interpersonal relationship management strategies to diffuse any potential face-threat that may be derived from the NES's assertion that Chinese employers are 'more demanding' on their helpers. He first indicates agreement by means of a repetition, repeating the words of his NES interlocutor *and less demanding yes that's true* (line 372), probably because he feels unable to disagree because in the earlier part of their conversation he was party to leading to such conclusions. However, after agreeing, what he continues to say in the rest of his utterance shows that he is making attempts to compensate for the face loss, through justifying his criticism regarding expatriate employers, basically that expatriates are used to doing housework by themselves, and so they will do some work at home and only give the more time-consuming work to their maids, implying that the Hong Kong Chinese give all, or most of the housework, to their maids and hence are more demanding (lines 372–385). Note that the HKC's lengthy turn is marked by a great deal of verbal fillers, hesitations, reformulations, hedging and "appealers" (*you know*), which indicate a strenuous process of thinking and reasoning on the part of the HKC.

The HKC uses politeness strategies to mitigate the face-threatening act (FTA) when he is faced with the situation where he feels that his face is lost twice (on being criticized as both *less generous* and *more demanding*). The main strategy he employs is Strategy 2 (Brown and Levinson 1987: 135), i.e. dealing with the FTA on record, but with redressive action in the form of positive politeness. First of all, the HKC tries and gives reasons for the criticism; he actually quotes the reason that the NES has given him before in relation to the NES being used to doing housework by himself. He uses *you know* three times, as an attempt to create the impression that he and his interlocutor share common ground. When giving reasons, the HKC also gives his personal opinion, realized by *I suppose* and *I think* (Stenström 1994: 90). By doing so, he is trying to include and involve both himself and his interlocutor in his reasoning. The NES's completion of the HKC's utterance *so I think she is on a very very good position* (lines 387–388) indicates that the NES agrees with and supports the view of the HKC. Finally, the HKC is being voluble, which is a strategy of "involvement" (Scollon and Scollon 1995: 40–41) although he is far from fluent in his utterance.

To sum up, regarding strategies employed to deal with culturally sensitive topics, the speakers in this extract are quite different. In terms of the amount of talk, the NES does not say much, which contrasts greatly with the HKC. The HKC is being voluble, which is considered to be an involvement strategy (Scollon and Scollon 1995). It is the HKC who introduces criticism against expatriate employers, claiming that they have spoilt the maids by being *more generous*. When confronted, the NES, tactfully, suggests that expatriate employers are *less demanding*, and hence turns the criticism around to level at Chinese employers being more demanding but less generous. The HKC must have felt the face-threatening criticism directed at the group of Chinese employers, of which he is a member. This is reflected in his long-winded, heavily hedged justification of expatriate employers being less demanding, using the NES as illustration. It is interesting that the HKC attributes the *less demanding* quality of the NES to social and environmental reasons, rather than ethnic ones. This is a strategy to save the HKC's own face, as a Chinese employer of Filipino maid. Overall, the HKC has employed mainly positive politeness strategies, or involvement strategies, to diffuse face loss. Positive strategies include giving reasons, presupposing and asserting common ground, including speaker and hearer in the topic, and being voluble. Employment of negative politeness, i.e. hedging *perhaps* (line 373), is also found in the HKC's justification.

The NES interrupts the HKC in the middle of *and so they (the maids) are I think relatively they are* (line 386) with a firm statement *so I think she is on a very very good position* (lines 387–388). Note that the HKC is still attempting to compare the maids employed by expatriate employers to those employed by Chinese employers. The NES, who cuts in on the HKC's turn-at-talk, has made a firm, direct, clear and unambiguous statement to indicate disagreement with the HKC's remark at the start of the extract (*I think I think she's spoiled*, line 334). At this point, the HKC has no choice but to agree with the NES and to correct his view that the maid has been spoiled by the NES. The HKC has actually cornered himself into admitting his faulty evaluation.

Extract 14 is hence different from the others in that the participants are engaged in a culturally sensitive topic that is related to, and potentially face-threatening to, both of them. They confront each other, and their cultural group, with criticism. As discussed, the strategies employed by the participants are very different.

Conclusion

In this study, discourse topic management by HKC and NES in the intercultural conversations has been investigated. First of all, the investigation compared HKC and NES in their use of various topical strategies to initiate topics into the conversation. The findings do not fully support the hypothesis that compared to NES, HKC will have a greater tendency to introduce topics in an interdependent way. In other words, HKC and NES do not differ regarding whether or not consecutive topics should be propositionally related to each other.

Second, HKC and NES were compared in the content of the topic that they introduce into conversation. As hypothesized, HKC are more likely to initiate topics that involve themselves and the interlocutor (Speaker and Addressee-oriented) and the interlocutor (Addressee-oriented) rather than themselves (Speaker-oriented). Also as hypothesized, NES are less likely than HKC to introduce topics that are oriented to the interlocutor (Addressee-oriented).

The third aspect of investigation was to compare the way in which HKC and NES manage the interpersonal aspect of the intercultural conversation when they are engaged in culturally sensitive topics, particularly the formulation and expression of their ideological assumptions, values and attitudes concerning some delicate and sensitive, and potentially face-threatening, topics. In a modern society, of which Hong Kong is an example, where egalitarianism is upheld and racial equality is promoted, for a person to openly express views and beliefs which contradict social norms implies that facework is required to rectify any resultant negative impressions.

Both HKC and NES can be seen to be involved in the processes of negotiating common ground along the lines of racial identities, stereotypes and prejudice. These processes are central to the ongoing production and development of meaning (Lee 1992, p. xi). Such processes reveal both the underlying cultural assumptions held by the speakers, and the strategies the speakers employ for the formulation and presentation of such stereotypes. These strategies include turn-taking organization, repetition, overlapping talk, pauses, hesitations, back-channels, non-linguistic signals (such as intonation and laughter), lexical choice, preference organization, indirectness, facework and politeness.

Regarding interactional patterning, the topics of stereotypes, identities and prejudice are introduced and developed spontaneously, which is different from those interactional contexts in which topics are planned in advance and elicited in the process of conversing, for instance, in interviews (van Dijk 1984). A range of topic management strategies has been observed, including topical initiation and continuity, topical sequencing, topic changes and so on which show the way in which racial and ethnic stereotypes (and at times prejudiced discourse topics) are introduced, discussed, changed and finished by the speakers. Further, the results show that conversational topics can be initiated and finished by either of the participants as the conversation unfolds, instead of pre-determined and then assigned to particular participants. When a topic relating to race and ethnicity comes up, its contents do not always concern the expression of racial or ethnic prejudice against minority groups by the majority group or the in-group members. In fact, many of the topics relating to ideological assumptions made of racial and ethnic stereotypes found in the intercultural conversations are not at all loaded with any negative connotations.

The discourse relating to ideologies of race and ethnicity actualizes interpersonal and social functions that are both similar to and different from those of related studies, such as prejudiced discourse (van Dijk 1984) and collaborative argumentation (Kleiner 1998). The communicative and social functions of prejudiced talk described in van Dijk (1984) are socializing personal experiences, self-presentation, identity and social integration, persuasion, informal mass communication, a mode of conflict resolution, amusement and social precepts. The discursive strategies for collaborative argumentation examined in Kleiner (1998) mainly function to balance competing conversational, instrumental goals (to change the adversary's beliefs) and identity (face) goals (to avoid affront, to present a positive self-image), and hence to ward off negative attributions of racism. The main motives are self-identity management and reassurance to each other of ideological alliance and solidarity.

It is evident that individual participants in this study are aware of the face-want and the identities of both themselves and their interlocutors while expressing racial and ethnic ideologies. Some of the discoursal and pragmatic features observed in the data play an important role in the construction, reinforcement and dissemination of the ideological assumptions relating to race and ethnicity in intercultural conversations. Many of the ideological messages presented by the participants are invoked as the conversation unfolds, serving such functions as socializing personal experiences, self-presentation, management of delicate opinions and persuasion, and finally, amusement. Nevertheless, rarely are many facts or examples required to back up the speaker's ideologies of racial and ethnic stereotyping. In fact, conversational implicatures are often sufficient for the expression, comprehension and construction of such stereotypes, and even prejudiced beliefs.

Note

1. In Hong Kong, maids are overwhelmingly Filipinos.

Chapter 8

Discourse information structure

Introduction

Any intercultural analysis of indirectness needs to take into consideration such factors as information sequencing (Chinese inductive pattern and Western deductive pattern) (Scollon and Scollon 1991; Kirkpatrick 1991), the meaning of indirectness and its manifestation in different contexts (Scollon and Scollon 1991; Kirkpatrick 1991), the length and types of small talk or supportive moves preceding and oriented towards the main topic (Færch and Kasper 1989; Zhang 1995), and face implications of speech acts (Brown and Levinson 1987; Gu 1990). In this study, HKC and NES were compared in the way they sequence information in their discourse as a realization of indirectness, as well as the cultural value and motivational factors that may lead to indirectness in language use. The purpose of the analysis was three-fold, and these are:

1. investigating whether or not, and to what extent, indirectness in conversation is culture-specific;
2. comparing and contrasting the forms in which indirectness is realized in the HKC discourse and the NES discourse in conversation; and
3. comparing and contrasting the ways HKC and NES manage indirectness in discourse.

Based on stereotypical perceptions of Chinese and Western cultures, HKC were hypothesized to be more indirect and NES more direct, relative to each other, in the way they structure the information of their talk. Specifically, HKC will use an inductive discourse pattern more frequently than NES, while NES will use a deductive discourse pattern more frequently.

The 25 intercultural conversations were analyzed to find out the frequencies of occurrence of the inductive and deductive discourse patterns of organization. Interpretations of the functions, and possibly motivations, regarding the use of a certain pattern, based on socio-cultural and situational evidence were made. Plausible reasons that may have contributed to the speakers' indirectness and directness in discursive language use and interaction were discussed. In a few cases, the HKC participants were interviewed in order to gain further insights.

Chinese inductive pattern and Western deductive pattern

Extract 1 shows an inductive discourse pattern used by the HKC to express disagreement with the NES. The two friends and colleagues are discussing the relative merits of the various forms of housing assistance provided by their employer.

(1) 001
b: male Hong Kong Chinese B: male Australian
b: but for me my my my kids are only five and nine and I
think er [that is
B: [is there any advantage in buying there is
no financial advantage in buying a place
b: oh yes you have financial advantage because you get
the real money
B: an asset ah
b: an asset yes you got an asset
B: which you can sell
b: yes which you can sell [at a price yea I mean
B: [down in Australia our house
is two hundred thousand you pay twenty thousand
deposit borrow from the bank the rest
b: yeah yeah yeah
B: but when you sell it you you'll get money back plus
capital gain
b: yes yes yes yes yes yes [that's what er that's what
B: [so it's for savings into an
asset
b: yes that's true correct but if you if you opted to
buy your own flat you're only entitled to housing
assistance for ten years (.) for ten years it's it's
the rule
B: oh
b: you would be given the money to pay for the mortgage
etc but that would last for ten years only
B: right
b: but for us if you if we if we if we have opted to
stay in government quarters then we can stay here for
life I mean until retirement of course er I'm now in
my thirties so I mean if I retire in er when I was
sixty when I I I'm sixty then I still have twenty

818:    more years to go
819: B: yeah
820: b: more than twenty years to go
821: B: and can you stay in that quarters
822: b: oh yes yes
823: B: once you retire you stay in
824: b: no no no no I have to move out but I I'm talking
825:    about twenty plus years (.) er that I will enjoy this
826:    benefit
827: B: yes

The NES prefers the home ownership scheme whereby staff can use an allowance to buy a residential property — *but when you sell it you you'll get money back plus capital gain* (lines 800–801) and *so it's for savings into an asset* (lines 803–804). The HKC concedes that this is *true correct* (line 805) but disagrees that this is the best choice by using an inductive discourse pattern. The HKC begins by giving background information about the home ownership scheme and the government quarters scheme (lines 805–818). The main point the HKC is making is that for employees such as him, *I'm now in my thirties* (lines 815–816), the fact that government quarters are available until retirement, rather than for just ten years in the case of the home ownership scheme, means that *I still have twenty more years to go* (lines 817–818). In other words, the benefits from living in government quarters last for much longer. The NES then seeks confirmation that it is really for twenty or more years (line 821) and whether this extends beyond retirement (line 823). In lines 824–826, the HKC summarizes his main point when he says *but I I'm talking about twenty plus years (.) er that I will enjoy this benefit.*

An inductive pattern of organization has the first or main topic introduced only after background information, reasons or examples have been given. The choice of an inductive strategy here is probably because the HKC disagrees with the NES that the home ownership scheme is the better scheme for him, and this may threaten the face of the NES. The HKC therefore begins by conceding that home ownership has its merits and then gives reasons and background information before concluding that the benefits of living in government quarters are far more long lasting.

Extract 2 exemplifies a deductive pattern found in the NES's discourse. The NES is telling the HKC about assessing 180 first-year Hong Kong medical students a few days before. The NES is giving information in response to a question posed by the HKC addressee in a direct, deductive way. As the NES's main topic is potentially face-threatening, she has given reasons to manage the culturally sensitive topic (see also Chapter 7).

(2) 014
a: female Hong Kong Chinese A: female Scottish
210. a: are you satisfied with their performance
211. A: er some of them were (.) utterly useless but in on
212. the whole they were okay (.) the only thing I would
213. criticize is that er (.) when when I introduce the
214. (.) subject to (.) blood pressure they were to
215. measure (.) [I said this is a patient who has come to
216. a: [mm
217. your clinic can you please take his blood pressure as
218. if he is (.) a a normal patient (.) real life patient
219. (.) and they were very bad about even saying hello er
220. introducing [themselves
221. a: [((laugh))
222. and I'm explaining what they're going to do
223. [they just they know their they know their classmates
224. a: [just because
225. very well (.) er no they weren't classmates
226. [they were final year students (.) [and they were
227. a: [oh that's why they can't [okay
228. briefed to behave as if they were doctors and the erm
229. student was a erm
230. a: pa [tient
231. A: [patient yeah and they were very bad about
232. communicating and quite a lot of them I warned them
233. for the next stations because they had (.) loads of
234. thing to do during the day I warned them that they
235. should er (.) treat patients as human beings (.) so
236. that was really my only criticism and they were
237. otherwise (.) in general okay (.) so it was a (.)
238. fairly good assessment and mm there were also lots of
239. er (.) dead stations they were called fifteen live
240. stations and fifteen dead stations [and the dead
241. a: [mhmm
242. stations when they had to look at some (.) erm
243. laborator [y information (.) come up with the er
244. a: [yes
245. answers (.) and some of them were very poor at that
246. actually (.) so I wonder if that's a (.) shortcoming

247. with problem-based learning (.) I don't know I think
248. time will tell but they've introduced this course
249. [in
250. a: [it sounds good
251. A: yeah it is good they they've introduced it all over
252. the world including Harvard (.) and a couple of
253. places in Australia and it seems to be working
254. extremely well so hopefully that'll work

When the HKC asks the NES whether she is satisfied about the performance of those medical students in the assessment (line 210), the NES gives an overarching comment in a clear, direct and quite a blunt way, saying *er some of them were (.) utterly useless but in on the whole they were okay* (lines 211–212). The wording she employs to present the main topic, i.e. her strong criticism of some of the students being 'utterly useless', potentially threatens her own positive face (see also Chapter 7). At the same time, as the students being criticized come from the same cultural group as the HKC, the criticism could be perceived as threatening the positive face of the HKC as well. The NES's main topic is followed by very elaborate reasons and explanations (lines 212–250), particularly the students were *very bad about communicating* (lines 232–233) and they gave very poor answers in the assessment (lines 243–246). The NES continues, wondering whether the students' poor answers could be attributed to problem-based learning (lines 247–248).

The NES can be seen to be direct when giving her response in the form of a comment on some students (*utterly useless*). The deductive strategy, characterized by giving the main or first topic at the beginning followed by supportive information, can be seen as her attempt to lessen the FTA and to manage a culturally sensitive topic.

Analysis of discourse patterns in the intercultural conversations

In order to better understand the relationship between indirectness in discourse and cultural values and motivational factors, only culturally sensitive functions that are served by the use of inductive and deductive discourse patterns were examined. A total of seven functions have been identified, and these are:

1. Agreeing
2. Disagreeing
3. Making a request or a suggestion
4. Partial or complete rejection of a request or a suggestion
5. Avoiding self-praise

6. Responding to self-denigration
7. Managing a personally or culturally sensitive topic

Altogether, 153 instances of inductive and deductive discourse patterns have been found to serve the seven functions, 88 of which were initiated by HKC and 65 initiated by NES (Table 8.1).

Table 8.1. Comparison of discourse patterns: HKC and NES

	Hong Kong Chinese		Native Speakers		Total tokens
	Tokens	%	Tokens	%	
Inductive discourse pattern	33	37.5	8	12.3	41
Deductive discourse pattern	55	62.5	57	87.7	112
Total	88	100	65	100.0	153

As Table 8.1 shows, when HKC and NES were compared in their preferred way of ordering information in discourse, it shows that both use a deductive pattern more frequently than an inductive one. In fact, both the HKC (62.5%) and the NES (87.7%) have chosen to use the deductive discourse pattern most frequently. However, when the relative proportion of inductive and deductive patterns was compared, HKC are more likely than NES to organize their discourse with an inductive style — 37.5% are inductive and 62.5% deductive. NES are less likely than HKC to use an inductive pattern — 12.3% are inductive and 87.7% are deductive. It is therefore true to say that compared to NES, the tendency for HKC to use an inductive pattern of sequencing discourse information is greater. The hypothesis that HKC were more indirect and NES more direct, relative to each other, in the way they structure the information of their talk is hence confirmed.

Each occurrence of the 153 inductive and deductive discourse patterns was qualitatively studied to better understand the way indirectness in HKC and NES's discourse is manifested in different contexts for particular interactional functions, and to find out possible reasons or motivations that may have contributed to the participants' indirectness in their talk. Mey (2001: 276) stresses the importance of the "proper context", namely the social and cultural background of the speaker, in assigning any significant pragmatic value to a particular speech act; in other words, "the proper context (or 'affordances') is what establishes the speech act as part of a pragmatic act". Mey states that as cultures are different, the pragmatic acts are manifested differently. Many studies examining speech acts in different languages and cultural groups have been carried out and can broaden people's understanding of the pragmatic norms of different cultures and provide evidence for cross-cultural comparisons (for example, Blum-Kulka et al. 1989; Chen, Ye and Zhang 1995).

Table 8.2. Comparison of functions served by HKC and NES's inductive and deductive patterns

Functions	Hong Kong Chinese						Native Speakers						TOTAL
	Inductive Pattern		Deductive Pattern		Sub-total		Inductive Pattern		Deductive Pattern		Sub-total		
	Token	%	Token	%	Token	%	Token	%	Token	%	Token	%	
1. Agreeing	0	0	17	100	17	100	0	0	20	100	20	100	**37**
2. Disagreeing	6	43	8	57	14	100	1	17	5	83	6	100	**21**
3. Making a request/ suggestion	2	33	4	67	6	100	0	0	1	100	1	100	**7**
4. Partial/ Complete rejection of a request/ suggestion	1	8	11	92	12	100	1	10	9	90	10	100	**22**
5. Avoiding self-praise	1	33	2	67	3	100	0		0		0		**6**
6. Responding to self-denigration	0	0	1	100	1	100	1	50	1	50	2	100	**3**
7. Managing a sensitive topic (personal/ cultural)	23	66	12	34	25	100	5	19	21	81	26	100	**61**
Total	33	38	55	62	88	100	8	12	57	88	65	100	153

Table 8.2 presents the frequencies in which HKC and NES sequence their discourse information inductively and deductively to perform the seven culturally-laden functions. Table 8.2 shows that when individual functions were analyzed, HKC are more likely to use a deductive than an inductive pattern for all but one of the seven functions. For function 7, managing a culturally or personally sensitive topic, only 34% of all tokens of discourse patterns are of the deductive type, while 66% are of the inductive type. In the case of NES, for all of the functions except function 6 (responding to self-denigration), there is a tendency to use a deductive rather than

an inductive pattern of organizing information. In the case of function 6, there is actually one instance of each of the inductive and deductive patterns.

In the following, excerpts illustrating the functions that have been identified in the inductive and deductive patterns in the discourse of HKC and NES (Table 8.2) will be analyzed. The analysis also focuses on comparing and contrasting HKC and NES in their respective ways of negotiating meaning in the case of either of the conversational participants being indirect in discourse. The findings which show similarities between HKC and NES will first be discussed, followed by the findings which indicate differences.

Similarities between HKC and NES in discourse patterns

Agreeing

When performing the speech act of agreeing with the interlocutor (function 1), HKC and NES behave similarly in deductively organizing all of their lengthy turns for giving agreements. In fact, none of their agreements are ordered inductively. This means both HKC and NES state their agreements directly and early in the discourse before they give reasons or examples to justify the agreements. An agreement is hence characterized by the structure of a "preferred turn" (Pomerantz 1978).

Extract 3 below illustrates an NES participant giving an agreement in a deductive way. The HKC and the NES were teachers in the same secondary school. The NES was an English teacher and the HKC was a Maths teacher. They have been talking about a sixth form class which both are teaching.

(3) 012
A: female British b: male Hong Kong Chinese
17. b: I teach half the classes but I found they er some of
18. them are very passive (.) but they are very attentive
19. in class
20. A: er I don't think they're passive erm maybe some of
21. the girls but maybe that's the subject [because I
22. b: [yes mm hm yea
23. mean for you it's very hard to have them active and
24. b: ((laugh))
25. running round the classroom but I mean for me that's
26. part of the teaching process yeah I encourage them to
27. be active and to stand up move around whereas for you
28. that wouldn't work [would it it would be chaos [you
29. b: [yes sure [mhmm
30. know so I think that's a good aspect for me about

31. being here is that I can let them relax so they
32. probably enjoy it more [than they are sitting doing
33. b: [mhmm
34. maths
35. b: but during this this past week many of my students in
36. the secondary six class they're going to do some
37. activities [so some
38. A: [yeah yeah at the moment they're really
39. busy because they've been involved with this er er
40. environmental campaign they've all been really
41. involved [you've got all the house activities so like
42. b: [yes
43. er after school I've got these mm oral practices
44. for the group interaction because there should be
45. four so there's always two because two are involved
46. with the basketball like tonight we have to cancel
47. because they've got just too much to do [there's just
48. b: [yes
49. too many English verse-speaking competition house
50. practice for the basketball so (.) you know they're
51. really tired as well as being very occupied
52. b: does this affect the mm classroom teaching

In lines 25–34, the NES English teacher is saying that she is able to allow students to relax and enjoy practising their English which she suggests is not possible in Maths lessons. The HKC then points out that a number of his Maths students have been involved in some (English) activities in class over the last week, and thus implies that there cannot be much time for relaxation. In line 38, the NES agrees and then lists all the reasons why the students are *really busy* (lines 38–39) and *very occupied* (line 51), namely *environmental campaign* (line 40), *house activities* (line 41), English *oral practices* and *verse-speaking competition* (lines 43 and 49) and *house practice for the basketball* (lines 49–50).

In the 25 intercultural conversations, for both HKC and NES, the deductive pattern is the standard style of sequencing discourse information for agreeing, and that is, if an extended turn is employed at all to agree, to first agree and then give reasons for agreeing. There are at least two explanations for this phenomenon. First, a deductive pattern serves to underline the strength of agreement and, second, it gives face to the one who is being agreed with. To withhold the agreement until after reasons have been given, for which there are no examples in the data, might suggest that the agreement is given reluctantly or only because there are reasons over and above what has already been provided. The cultures of HKC and NES in this study similarly support a direct deductive pattern of structuring an extended turn to express agreement with the interlocutor.

Disagreeing

It needs first to be pointed out that the kinds of disagreements examined in this chapter are not the same as those investigated in Chapter 4. In Chapter 4, most of the disagreements are contained in not too extended utterances, with or without the use of redressive language. The redressive language can be realized in the form of hedging or reasons. In this chapter looking at rhetorical patterns, the disagreements are embedded in a much larger discourse context, prominently framed by much more extensive background, reasoning and justifications.

Regarding disagreements, it is again interesting to see that both HKC and NES are more likely to organize their disagreements with the addressee deductively rather than inductively. There are 8 instances of deductively organized disagreements for HKC and 5 for NES, while there are 6 instances of inductively organized disagreements for HKC and only 1 for NES. However, when HKC and NES were compared, HKC are inclined to use an inductive pattern more frequently — 40% of HKC's disagreements are sequenced inductively, while only 17% of NES's disagreements are organized and presented inductively.

Extract 4 below exemplifies a HKC disagreeing with an NES in an inductive way. The HKC was in her NES brother-in-law's home where the conversation took place. In this extract, the two participants have been discussing the NES's plan to launch a very new business concept: an Internet-based barter company in Hong Kong.

(4) 004
a: female Hong Kong Chinese B: male British
280. a: have you talked (.) about this with your friends
281. B: yea and everyone I've spoken to people who're in
282. businesses who are in advertising agencies
283. a: yea
284. B: I haven't told every one 'cos I don't want every one
285. to know
286. a: yes
287. B: er but oh I there's no company like that and no
288. nobody can think of it anyway that does this
289. a: but what's their opinion would would they think that
290. it can earn money
291. B: yea because you can earn money by being the central
292. person the broker you charge so much for being the

293. broker you charge the commission for selling the
294. goods for exchanging
295. a: because er Chinese er most probably are quite
296. stubborn and cannot accept new things or new ideas it
297. is quite difficult for Chinese to do this especially
298. in business
299. B: but if you go to a Chinese person and say hey look
300. you've got a computer which you've not sold [and it's
301. a: [yea
302. you are not doing anything with it (.) I can give you
303. something for it (.) won't cost

The NES is very enthusiastic and positive about the prospects of such a company but the HKC does not agree that this is a workable proposition in Hong Kong. The HKC twice expresses her concerns off-record when she asks the NES *have you talked (.) about this with your friends* (line 280) and then *but what's their opinion would would they think that it can earn money* (lines 289–290). The NES remains undaunted by these implied doubts about his proposed business adventure, and so in lines 295–298 the HKC uses an inductive discourse pattern to more openly voice her disagreement with the NES's optimism. The HKC begins by giving reasons relating to the general characteristics of the Chinese — *because er Chinese er most probably are quite stubborn* (lines 295–296) and that it is *quite difficult* (line 297) for Chinese to either accept *new things* or *new ideas* (line 296). She ends her utterance with her main point *especially in business.* In other words the HKC is listing these characteristics, all of which serve to undermine the NES's business idea, to make the emphatic point that, while these hold generally, they are particularly true for the Chinese when they do business. The HKC is engaged in an FTA in which she does not agree with the NES's view of this new business concept. The HKC first disagrees off-record and then disagrees inductively in order to mitigate the face threat to both herself and the NES.

Partial or complete rejection of a request or a suggestion

The use of function 4, partial or complete rejection of a request or a suggestion, is another similarity. HKC and NES predominantly use a deductive pattern when performing this function. 92% of HKC's rejections and 90% of NES's rejections are sequenced directly and deductively. The findings can be seen as contradictory to expectations. One would imagine that as a rejection is potentially face-threatening, the person who rejects the addressee might be indirect in stating the main topic. As HKC are expected to be paying even greater attention to maintaining the addressee's face want, they would be expected to be even more indirect, compared to NES.

Extracts 5 and 6, which show a HKC and an NES structuring and presenting a rejection in an inductive way, are the only examples found in the data set. In Extract 5, the HKC inductively sequences her partial rejection to a suggestion implied in the NES's question. The speakers are colleagues and were having the conversation in a staff common room. The HKC has been explaining to the NES that when she goes on vacation with her children, it is not for her enjoyment but rather for her children to have some experience in another environment. The NES then asks about overseas education for her children.

(5) 015
B: male British a:female Hong Kong Chinese
403. B: have you ever thought of education overseas for your
404. children
405. a: yes erm both erm my husband and myself (.) er (.)
406. think that we must send our kids (.) to overseas [for
407. B: [mm
408. their tertiary education or erm (.) after they got er
409. graduate [the postgraduate er get [postgraduate
410. B: [mm [yea
411. education (.) er over[seas yea (.) yea er it is
412. B: [yea
413. a must and it will do them a lot of good because er
414. B: it does yea [yes (.) just as I think actually it does
415. a: [yea
416. people a lot of good if they are say er in in Europe
417. to come to somewhere like Hong Kong to do their
418. education [I think a change of environment with an
419. a: [yea
420. educational programme (.) does give that extra (.) um
421. depth [and that the persons mm [er er all round (.)
422. a: [yea [uh huh
423. person [as it were
424. a: [yea the learning curve will goes up (.)
425. [((laugh)) (.) yea you know in another environment
426. B: [mm (.) that's right that's right
427. (.) but er I will not er (.) er (.) send them there
428. (.) when they are too young
429. B: no
430. a: you know in (.) I I can see some friends and some
431. colleagues here (.) they send their kids to UK and

432. (.) they're just at their (.) er primary five [or
433. B: [yea
434. seconda[ry er in erm (.) first or second [(.) year
435. B: [yea yea [yea
436. (.)it's too young
437. B: too young [yea yea (.) it's cert- certainly with
438. a: [yea
439. children that age er er one of the (.) other things
440. which has been a concern to me I suppose so (.) if
441. I'm completely honest (.) with Hong Kong society is
442. that children do seem to be put under (pause) erm an
443. enormous amount of pressure [with education

The NES asks the HKC *have you ever thought of education overseas for your children* (lines 403–404), which can be interpreted as the NES making a suggestion. The HKC states that she and her husband *think that we must send our kids (.) to overseas for their tertiary education* (lines 406–408), and this appears to be accepting the suggestion. After responding to the NES's suggestion in a positive way, the HKC elaborates on the main point of her response by giving reasons for sending her children overseas. She states that this *is a must* (line 413), that it *will do them a lot of good* (line 413) and that *the learning curve will goes up* (line 423). The NES lends support to the HKC's reasoning (lines 414–423). In lines 427–428, the HKC presents a rejection, saying *but er I will not er (.) er (.) send them there (.) when they are too young*. Her delayed sub-topic shows that she is only partially accepting the NES's suggestion. She carries on and explains why it will only be for tertiary education that she will send her children overseas. She explains that any earlier they would be *too young*, and she gives examples of friends and colleagues who have sent their children overseas for primary and secondary education and that, again, *it's too young*. In giving reasons and drawing upon the experience of friends and colleagues, the HKC tries to provide support for her partial rejection of the NES's suggestion.

An inductive discourse pattern is used by the HKC to indirectly reject the NES's suggestion. The topic itself is not a sensitive one, but rejecting a suggestion is. Overseas education is a fairly commonplace option for the middle and upper classes in Hong Kong and, in the case of these participants, it is actually financially assisted by their employers for school-age dependents. It is, obviously, also an issue of "good parenting" in that one might think that either sending, or not sending, school-age children overseas is a good choice for parents to make on behalf of their children. The HKC's choice of an inductive strategy is probably motivated out of a need for saving the NES's face as she does not wholly accept her colleague's suggestion.

In Extract 6, the two friends' topic content has been concerned with the NES's domestic helper. The NES is telling the HKC that now he needs a domestic helper to work in his family for a very short time.

(6) 002
a: female Hong Kong Chinese B: male British
87. a: can I_'s man mum come and help a bit (.) [is she
88. B: [er
89. living nearby
90. B: she lives nearby but er she's in her seventies now
91. a: ohh
92. B: not very steady on her feet [and her eyes are not so
93. a: [uh huh
94. good [(.) so although she comes every day and helps
95. a: [uh huh
96. a little bit occupies the baby for some time mm there
97. are things that the maid has to look after her with
98. as much as she helps to look after
99. a: the the children
100. B: the children [so it is not very practical

In line 87, the HKC asks whether I_'s mum *could come and help a bit* and whether she lives nearby. The NES employs an inductive rhetorical strategy in his response (lines 90–100). First of all, the NES confirms that I_'s mum lives nearby, but he lists reasons why I_'s mum is not the solution to his domestic needs — *she's in her seventies, not very steady on her feet, eyes are not so good* and I_'s mum needs as much help herself as she can give. It is not until line 100 that the NES presents his main point when he says *it is not very practical.* Although it can be argued that the NES's *but er she's in her seventies now* implies a rejection of the HKC's suggestion, the NES's rejection is given only after he has listed some reasons as justification. The NES prefaces his main point — rejection — with *so* which substitutes for all of the reasons that the HKC's suggestion has to be rejected. Here it can be argued that the choice of strategy is part of an overall strategy to save the face of the HKC. The NES agrees with HKC where possible — it's possible in terms of I_'s mum getting to the NES's home and *she helps a little bit,* but ultimately the NES rejects the suggestion which is an FTA. This FTA is mitigated by the reasons and the overall rhetorical strategy.

Responding to self-denigration

The last similarity between HKC and NES is found in function 7 — responding to self-denigration. Pomerantz (1978: 96) observes that in Western culture, "praising self with strong-positive descriptors has a violative status", and that when the recipient of praise responds with moderate-positive term (↓), it may then be replaced in the coparticipant's "praise reaffirmation with a strong-positive term (↑)". Among the Chinese, elevating the addressee, or "other elevation", is a valued Chinese quality (Gu 1990). HKC and NES are similar in that there are very few examples of this function in the data set. There is only one instance for HKC, which is organized deductively. There are two instances for NES — one sequenced inductively and the other deductively.

Extract 7 illustrates an NES using a deductive discourse pattern when responding to the HKC's self-denigration. The participants were colleagues working in the Independent Commission Against Corruption (ICAC) and were having a conversation in the HKC's office. The HKC has been telling the NES that after graduation from the university, which was fifteen years ago, her ambition was to become a journalist, saying that she regrets starting working in ICAC too soon.

(7)	016	
B:	male British	a:female Hong Kong Chinese
612.	a:	my er regret is that er (.) I er start with ICAC too
613.		soon
614.	B:	yea yea
615.	a:	if I got an opportunity to try er more things maybe
616.		er the result's the same with the ICAC in the
617.		[environment (.) but mm [I think it's good to get
618.	B:	[yea yea yea [but but they say
619.		more experience
620.	B:	experience broadens the mind and any form of
621.		experience broadens the mind mm
622.	a:	and I only think that I'm very narrow vision mm
623.		narrow vision ((laugh))
624.	B:	well I have to say I don't agree with your view of
625.		yourself there because you know well the way you know
626.		the way I see you conduct courses they are mm with
627.		information you certainly seem to have an
628.		unbelievably wide aspect of of of knowledge and
629.		information available to you to to to to plan
630.		different courses and it's not everybody that's that
631.		that knows enough about the different subjects to be
632.		able to know (.) that a particular course would be
633.		well-structured using all those different concepts
634.		erm and I am very grateful to you for the help you
635.		gave me with the command course er you know I must

636. admit coming from a basically a career as just being
637. a hard-nosed detective [to sort of like throw
638. a: [((laugh)) oh
639. throwing things like that together is is or was
640. actually quite a challenge er [and I am very grateful
641. a: [I'm
642. a: I'm happy to see that you you seem to enjoy it so
643. much mm the training work work and the designing of
644. the courses

The HKC criticizes herself saying she has *narrow vision* (line 622). The NES expresses his view that he does not agree with this self-assessment, or self-denigration, which has the effect of elevating the HKC (lines 624–625), and this is the main point of the NES's response. The NES then continues to give reasons for elevating the HKC (lines 625–633): she has an *unbelievably wide aspect of of of knowledge and information, it's not everybody that's that that knows enough about the different subjects* to be able to design a course that is *well-structured*. He concludes by expressing his gratitude twice, *I am very grateful* (lines 634 and 640), to the HKC for her input into a training course that they have jointly been responsible for.

The NES employs a deductive rhetorical strategy to respond to the HKC's self-denigration. It might be argued that in order not to have the praise rejected, the NES feels obliged to list reasons for his claim. It is interesting to note that his strategy seems to work as the HKC accepts his praise (lines 642–644) although she deflects it by saying that she's happy that he enjoyed the *training work work and the designing of the courses* rather than fully accepting the praise given her.

Differences between HKC and NES in discourse patterns

Disagreeing

Regarding disagreeing (function 2), HKC and NES differ in the relative frequencies in which they disagree with the interlocutor inductively as opposed to deductively. HKC can be seen to be more likely to disagree with NES deductively (57%) than inductively (43%). Compared to NES, however, proportionally, the difference between disagreeing deductively and disagreeing inductively is not so big for HKC. For NES, however, the tendency to disagree deductively (83%) is a lot greater than the tendency to disagree inductively (17%).

Making a request or a suggestion

For HKC, 4 of the 6 instances of making a request or a suggestion embedded in an extended turn are organized in an inductive pattern. For NES, there is only one instance of the use of a direct, deductive discourse pattern for making a request or a suggestion in the data set. An example of a HKC using an inductive pattern to make a request of the NES is presented in Extract 8. The female NES had been an English tutor for the female HKC's daughters for almost a year when the conversation was recorded. At the end of lessons, the women would sometimes have a chat. In the extract, the HKC makes an indirect request of the NES, which is organized and presented in an inductive way.

(8) 009
a: female Hong Kong Chinese A: female Irish
4. a: yes er (.) in fact er this colleague of mine er she
5. has something er which er she wantsme to ask you
6. A: oh yes
7. a: er when when we er talked about the research er I told
8. her about er having a private tutor for my daughters
9. [and she er finds it very interesting and she also has
10. A: [yes
11. a: two daughters [and she also er is thinking about er
12. A: [yea
13. getting them some er pri- private tuition in English
14. and so she asked whether I would pass the message to
15. you and see whether you would like to take her
16. children too ((laugh))
17. A: oh yes er that sounds interesting yes
18. a: uh huh what do you think
19. A: I think that will be very good yea
20. a: uh huh uh huh
21. A: does she want er to have my opinion on tuition or does
22. she want to erm what did was she asking me any
23. questions about it did she
24. a: she she she re- she re- she in fact really wants to
25. know whether you have er [time (.)to give her er
26. A: [time yes
27. [daughters some lessons
28. A: [yea
29. A: okay er are they do they speak English have they got a
30. little bit of English
31. a: they do because eh her elder daughter eh they they
32. they er have been er living in Australia for some
33. years
34. A: aah yes

35. a: and so er her elder daughter er went to the
36. international school in er not Australia I think it's
37. Japan I mean yea yea
38. A: in Japan [but they spoke English oh

The cultural attribute being examined is concern for the addressee's face. From the perspective of the wider context of interaction, the HKC might be expected to be indirect, relative to the NES, and use redressive language, motivated by the concern for face. In the situated discourse, the HKC makes a request of the Irish friend (NES) indirectly by organizing the discourse inductively. She uses an indirect way of requesting the female NES to give private tuition to her colleague's daughters.

The HKC uses a very indirect way of requesting the NES to give private tuition to her colleague's daughters. Before the actual request is made, she uses an "alerter" and a number of "preposed supportive moves" (Blum-Kulka et al. 1989) to mitigate her request. The alerter is *yes er (.) in fact* (line 4) which is an attention getter to alert the hearer's attention to the ensuing speech act. In lines 4–5, the HKC uses a "preparatory" (Blum-Kulka et al. 1989) to prepare the hearer for the ensuing request, by saying that her colleague will make a request of the NES through her (*this colleague of mine er she has something er which er she wants me to ask you*, lines 4–5). In other words, the HKC is asking for the hearer's permission to make the request on behalf of her colleague. The "preparatory" is broken up by a few hesitations *er* to fill the pauses, indicating some difficulty or uncertainty on the part of the HKC to even utter the "preparatory".

When the permission for the ensuing request has been granted by the NES (*oh yes*), the HKC begins a narrative sequence (lines 7–16), or the "grounder" move (Blum-Kulka et al. 1989), in which she first gives the context in which the topic of the NES being the private tutor for her daughters was discussed with her colleague (*er when when we er talked about the research er I told her about er having a private tutor for my daughters*). Then she describes her colleague's reaction (*she er finds it very interesting*), and provides reasons and explanations for the ensuing request of her colleague (*she also has two daughters (.) and she also er is thinking about er getting them some er pri- private tuition in English*).

It is interesting to note that no request has been explicitly made yet. Even in lines 14–15, the HKC is still speaking of passing a message rather than making a request, which acts as another "preparatory" *and so she asked whether I would pass the message to you.* The HKC's reported speech *see whether you would like to take her children too ((laugh))* is close to making a request, but *take her children too* is so unclear and non-specific that the utterance hardly serves as a direct and clear request. Interestingly, the embarrassed laughter of the HKC at the end of the indirect request could be interpreted as an additional sign that making the request is not at all easy. A direct request would be something like, for example, 'she wants some help with her children's English from you', 'do you think you could help with her children's English', or even 'she would like you to teach her daughters English'.

As a result of the indirectness in the request, the HKC's *uh huh what do you think* (line 18) does not manage to get an appropriate, or even a desirable response from the NES. The expression 'take her children too' has proved to be confusing to the NES, as is evident in the NES's query about the actual nature of the colleague's question (*does she want er to have my opinion on tuition or does she want to erm what did was she asking me any questions about it did she*, lines 21–23). In this case, the NES is asking an 'Is it this or that?' alternative question, which is an attempt to pin the HKC down to be direct about her colleague's question or the request. Not until the very end (lines 24–27) of the discourse does the HKC make the request in a relatively direct manner *she she she re- she re- she in fact really wants to know whether you have er time to give her er (.) daughters some lessons.* Hearing this, the NES says *okay*, which indicates that now the meaning is clear to her. The NES then shifts to ask questions about those girls.

Note that the HKC's request is marked with repetitions, reformulations and hesitations. All of these features indicate that she is having difficulty in producing this utterance. She prefaces the ensuing request with *in fact* to indicate that she is giving more information about what she has just said in previous utterances, followed by *really*, which can be viewed as a "re-opener" (Stenström 1994: 66) that functions to re-open her topic, i.e. the request. The request itself contains a reference to a preparatory condition for the feasibility of the request, and in this case, one of availability (*whether you have er time*). It can be seen that even when making the request eventually, the HKC is still questioning, rather than stating, the presence of the "preparatory" condition, that is, whether the NES will have the time to give her colleague's daughters some lessons. The use of vague language *some* (Channell 1994) acts as a kind of "imposition minimiser" (Blum-Kulka et al. 1989), serving to mitigate the force of the request.

With respect to Extract 8, it is argued that the determining factors for the choice and use of indirect language, like culture (Hall 1976) and power and social distance in terms of age, gender, occupation, status, and degree of intimacy (Thomas 1995) may not be relevant in this particular context of conversation. It is because what the request entails — giving private tuition for fees — is exactly what the NES has been doing for the HKC's own children. What accounts for the choice and use of an inductive discourse pattern by the HKC is more likely the "interactional and dynamic context in which participants are using language to achieve their various goals" (Kong 1998b).

Analysis of the situated discourse shows that the HKC chose to be indirect in her request, namely by giving background information about her colleague before making the request, and also by using a lot of redressive language in the form of negative politeness. A post-interview with the HKC revealed that the NES was in her final stage of pregnancy when the conversation was recorded. When making the request, the HKC was not sure whether or not the NES would agree with the request even though this is the work that she does for the HKC. Also, the HKC felt that asking the NES to take up additional work at that stage was too great an imposition. Knowing that the request may be a weighty imposition and in anticipation of a likely refusal, the HKC had therefore chosen to be indirect in her request.

The immediate context of situation can therefore afford explanations of the turn by turn behaviour of the HKC. In this specific context, her worries about threatening the negative face of the NES has led her to use an inductive strategy and negative politeness strategies to compensate for her face-threatening behaviour and to achieve her communication goals. In other words, the HKC's behaviour in the situated discourse is motivated by competing goals (Thomas 1995), namely there is a clash between the HKC's propositional goal and her interpersonal goal. In terms of the wider context of interaction, the above analysis of situated talk provides evidence for the cultural attribute of greater concern for face through the HKC's use of an inductive rhetorical strategy and use of redressive language, both of which serve to mitigate her face-threatening act.

Avoiding self-praise

Another difference is observed in the function of minimizing or avoiding self-praise (function 5), which is assumed to be a characteristic of both Chinese and Western cultures (Pomerantz 1978; Gu 1990). In the 25 intercultural conversations, three instances of avoiding self-praise can be found, one inductive and two deductive. No NES examples can be found.

Extract 9 exemplifies a HKC's indirectness realized in the form of an inductive discourse pattern in order to avoid self-praise. The speakers were police inspectors of equal rank in the Hong Kong Police Force. The conversation took place in an office in the police station. The speakers have had a long talk about charity walks. The topic is terminated and a pause follows.

(9) 018
B: male British a:female Hong Kong Chinese
149. (pause)
150. B: how's the family
151. a: oh it's nice (.) you know I er last Friday er it was
152. a big day for me and for S_ (.) my son
153. B: yea
154. a: because he is now in his primary six he's going to go

to
B: high school in
a: high school
B: August [September
a: [in the coming yea in the coming er school
term and in Hong Kong you know the arrangement is
ridiculous (.) you have to grade the students into
(.) band one two three four and five (.) and then (.)
it depends on his academic er results (.) from his
primary five (.) to primary six (.) there're three
exams (.) they have to take
B: yea
a: and then they count er the number of marks he got and
(.) and do an average and then they will classify him
as band one two three er four and five depending (.)
his er er academic result (.) and then I I was very
nervous (.) because I don't know how how he work in
school he's kind of er (.) you know mediocre er what
I will say he is two or three between band two and
three and that worries me because er (.) band two and
three is not er very good school (.) according to you
know general Hong Kong standard (.) and (.) and last
er last Friday (.) the school give me a slip (.) of
the estimated grading (.) of S_ (.) and it was my
surprise (.) he he is the fifty (.) his ranking is
fifty (.) er among a group of hundred and thirty-two
students (.) and the the headmaster told me if the
students er is grade about for example before sixty-
six (.) he he will be band one (.) so fifty is before
sixty-six
B: so he's
a: so he's band one
B: he's better than you gave him credit for
a: right yea he's better much better than what I expect
(.) so I well it's a surprise and I hope er (.) by
the by August (.) er (.) he can get into his er
desired (.) [high school

Extract 9 starts with the NES initiating a topic change. He asks after the family of the HKC, who responds by announcing something important and delightful which has happened recently, which involves her son and herself *oh it's nice (.) you know I er last Friday er it was a big day for me and for S_ (.) my son* (lines 151–152). The HKC, however, does not get to the main proposition after the introductory utterance, namely why it is so and what has made it a big day. Instead, she launches into giving a lot of background information and detailed descriptions about her son's education, the ridiculous arrangement whereby primary students are allocated to secondary schools, and her worries over her son's academic banding, as he's kind of mediocre (line 172), all of which acts as supportive and illustrative information.

In lines 177–178, the HKC resumes talking about last Friday (*last er last Friday (.) the school give me a slip (.) of the estimated grading (.) of S_*). She then describes her reaction upon reading the slip (*and it was my surprise*), followed by describing the information on the slip (*he he is the fifty (.) his ranking is fifty*), and how the information should be interpreted in context (*er among a group of hundred and thirty-two students*, lines 180–181). She then brings the headmaster into the scene, quoting what the headmaster has said about what constitutes band one (*and the the headmaster told me if the students er is grade about for example before sixty-six (.) he he will be band one*[1]). In this context, 'he' has the status of 'they', referring to those students whose rankings are above sixty-six.

After announcing her son's ranking (50) out of a group of 132 students, and what the headmaster has said about the chances of students whose ranking is above sixty-six, she carries on verbally working out the logical steps, saying so *fifty is before sixty-six.* At this point, the NES says *so he's* (line 185). Only then does the HKC explicitly state why last Friday was a big day for her son (*so he's band one*, line 186). She finally gives the reason that made it a nice day for her son and herself the Friday before, after a great deal of setting the scene and building up the case.

Interestingly, the HKC's final 'admission' that her son did well has to be prompted by the NES. It may be that the NES perceives that the HKC discourse has reached a point where a direct statement is called for, and so he offers help by coaxing the HKC to make her point. Alternatively, it is possible that the HKC, coming from a high-context culture, may feel that she has already made her point clearly enough when she says 'so fifty is before sixty-six'. This is because before this, she has announced that the ranking of her son is 'fifty', and that the headmaster told her that any position before 66 will be in band one. However, probably the NES, who comes from a low-context culture, feels that the words 'he's in band one' are needed as the finale.

Extract 9 can very well exemplify an indirect discourse structure due to the modesty of a proud Hong Kong Chinese mother. Modesty, being a feature of Chinese politeness, has been well documented (Gu 1990). Probably motivated by modesty, the HKC woman has given much background information and many details, before she eventually tells her NES colleague that her 'mediocre' son is a band-one student.

Managing sensitive topics

The last function, function 7, is managing a sensitive topic that can either be personal to the speaker, personal to the addressee, or a culturally sensitive topic (see also Chapter 7). There are 35 instances of this function presented in an extended turn performed by HKC, and only 26 by NES. As shown in Table 8.2, HKC use an inductive pattern (66%) more frequently than a deductive one (34%). It is, however, the opposite for NES, who use a deductive pattern more often (81%) than an inductive pattern (19%). As sensitive topics can potentially threaten the face of both the speaker and the addressee, the fact that compared to NES, HKC use an inductive, indirect pattern more frequently demonstrates that they pay greater regard for the addressee's face. This phenomenon lends support to the cultural preferred values of the Chinese. Five examples (Extracts 10 to 14) will be discussed and analyzed.

Extract 10 is an example of a HKC's inductive discourse pattern, adoption of which serves to manage a personally sensitive topic. The speakers are relatives. The NES speaker married the younger sister of the HKC. The NES owned a small-scale on-line barter company based in Hong Kong, which had recently been bought up by an Internet company in America, which is listed on the NASDAQ. Before the extract opens, the speakers have been discussing the terms and arrangements offered by this company in America. Topics have included, in sequence, change of directorship, salary to be paid to the NES by the company, the listed company's request to change the name of the NES's company, change of the registered office of the NES's company, and choice of company accountant. Then the topic shifts to the excellent share performance of the listed company — a seven-fold increase from one dollar to seven dollars since it was listed on the NASDAQ three months before. Extract 10 starts with the HKC asking whether the listed company would give the NES some shares.

(10)	019		
b:	male Honk Kong Chinese	B:	male British
157.	b: er will they give you some shares		
158.	B: yea after a year the share option	[to buy at one	
159.	b:	[share	
160.	dollar		
161.	b: buy at one dollar		
162.	B: yea so it's good		
163.	b: wow ((laugh))		

164. B: yea but I have to wait after
165. b: you'll be a millionaire ((laugh))
166. B: eh but it's on [er net profit
167. b: [maybe but but there are time interval
168. maybe yea maybe
169. B: it's after one year but only on if we make profit
170 then we buy at one er one dollar
171. b: okay
172. B: so that's the option
173. b: okay
174. B: so if we don't make a profit then we can't buy the er
share
175. b: uh huh
176. B: it's all right
177. b: okay how about your business because I saw from the
178. from the websi- from your website [er because er er
179. B: [uh huh
180. in my office sometimes I'll have spare time
181. B: oh good
182. b: ((laugh)) er is it is it (.) [more more more
183. B: [we're doing okay
184. membership now
185. B: more membership [now
186. b: [more members
187. B: yea [and now also because of this new company because
188. b: [oh
189. they are (.) an Internet
190. B: company [they can promote it a lot more (.) so we get
191. b: [oh
192. more people (.) interested
193. b: uh huh
194. B: and also we're doing a thing with Hong Kong Telecom
195. [to do er shopping online
196. b: [uh huh

Between lines 157 and 177, the NES explains the condition under which the listed company will give him shares at one dollar each, and so whether he would become *a millionaire* (line 165) very much hinges on the business performance of the NES's company. Then the HKC asks the NES about his business (lines 178–185) and his question is sequenced inductively (*okay how about your business because I saw from the from the websi- from your website [er because er er in my office sometimes I'll have spare time (A: oh good) ((laugh)) er is it is it (.) [more more more membership now*). The HKC's *how about your business* only functions to mark a topic shift, but it neither asks a specific question nor makes a specific comment related to the NES's business. *How about*, or *what about* is a 'shift marker' that serves to move from one topic to a related topic or from one aspect of the current topic to another, as illustrated in Chapter 7. The use of *how about* by the HKC therefore indicates his intention to shift from the current topic framework (that is, whether the NES would be given shares is dependent on the company's business performance) to a related aspect of the topic framework (that is, the current business of the NES).

What is interesting to note in Extract 10 is the politeness strategy that the HKC employs when making the utterance. He asks about the NES's business, and explains what has made him ask, and that is, from visiting the NES's website. He, however, stops before getting into what he saw on the website. Rather, he changes to explain why he has visited the website to avoid giving the impression that he has been checking on the business of the NES's company on purpose (*because I saw from the from the websi- from your website [er because er er in my office sometimes I'll have spare time*). This is similar to giving overwhelming or compelling reasons, whereby "implying that normally he wouldn't dream of infringing H's negative face" (Brown and Levinson, 1987: 189). Also, the HKC's utterance is made hesitantly with repetition and fillers. Only then does he ask his question *er is it is it (.) [more more more membership now*, which is equally marked by repetition, suggesting that the question is asked with certain difficulty on the part of the speaker. The explanation, justification and markers of non-fluency are all negative linguistic strategies, showing that redressive action in the form of negative politeness is adopted by the HKC to diffuse threatening the negative face of the NES.

It is interesting to note the way meaning is negotiated by the speakers. The NES has actually correctly predicted the indirect meaning in the HKC's *how about your business … ((laugh)) er is it is it*. In fact, the NES responds with *we're doing okay* (line 183), said at the same time as the HKC's *more more more membership now*. The actual topic, that is, the question about whether there is *more membership now*, is an instance of asking indirectly whether the business is good. The indirect meaning that the HKC has intended to convey is likely to be 'Is business good?' or 'Are you making profits from business?' In other words, the utterance *er is it is it (.) [more more more membership now* implies asking whether the barter business has become better, or has started to make a profit.

The analysis has been confirmed by the HKC speaker at an informal interview with the researcher, where he also explained the background to the indirectness in his discourse, and hence his use of negative politeness strategy. Between the two speakers, and actually among members of the family, the barter business of the

NES's company has all along been a topic of much discussion and a big concern. It is not a secret that the company has not been doing well, and so when the American listed company suggests buying up the company, the family members are very pleased about that and all look forward to the prospect of an expansion and improved business. The HKC considers asking about the business of his brother-in-law's company a potentially face-threatening act exactly because of the poor business of the company. The HKC does not feel comfortable asking directly, and he particularly fears that he might give an impression to the NES brother-in-law that he is overly concerned about, or even that he is checking on, the financial situation of the NES's company. Regard for face and competing goals (Thomas 1995) hence account for the indirectness in the HKC's discourse. The clash between the HKC's goal to express his ideas and opinions and his goal of face management has resulted in him being indirect.

Extract 11 is another example of a HKC's inductive discourse pattern to manage a sensitive topic; and in this case, the topic is a personal one. The speakers in the conversation were colleagues working in the ICAC of Hong Kong. They were equals in the organizational hierarchy. The job of the HKC was educating the community, particularly the private sector, about not committing bribery and corruption. At the beginning of the excerpt, the HKC is sharing her views, and doubts, about the impact of her work on her audience.

(11) 011
a: female Hong Kong Chinese B: male British
536. a: how much effect (.) [I have created after er talking
537. B: [mm
538. to er er a manager or talking to a group of er
539. [executives having them er the provisions of the law
540. B: [mhmm mm
541. and er trying to influence them not to commit their
542. (.) bribery and [corruption (.) really quite funny
543. B: [yea
544. B: but there's no regrets on joining the ICAC (.) as a
545. career
546. a: a little bit [((laugh))
547. B: [((laugh))
548. a: eh (.) first of all I must admit I'm quite proud to
549. to be a member of the ICAC
550. B: mm
551. a: and (.) the image of ICAC is is er very good

B: yea
a: outside in Hong Kong or in[ternationally when I say I
B: [yea yea
am working for ICAC people always have some good er
opinions
B: mm
a: I truly believe that ICAC got really a lot of
contribution in Hong Kong society (.) over the last
twenty years [something (.) mm (.) but erm (.) if I
B: [mm
er (.) if I (.) had not joined the ICAC maybe I will
got a more erm dynamic er (.) career or or (.) more
more colourful yea [career yea
B: [yea yea would have you thought
of becoming a business lady
a: ((laugh))
B: er having your own business or becoming a solicitor
or (.) or becoming a (.) er you know a fashion
designer or something of that nature ((laugh))
a: when I er graduated er from the university I think erm
(.) think of er to (.) er work in the er in the in the
(.) in the television
B: oh right yea
a: industry
B: yea
a: in the university erm I (.) spent most of my time in
the writing workshop
B: oh right [yea
a: [I like er reading and I like writing
B: yea yea so would you have liked to have been say a
television journalist (.) or or (.) or would you like
to have been an actress or [appeared in television
a: [not not actress of course
not (laugh)) actress ((laugh)) [yea (.) no to become
B: [yea yea
to write scripts [scriptwriters
B: [oh like like a scriptwriter [or or
a: [yea
yea or a journalist or an editor or something of that

591. nature
592. a: yea [yea
593. B: [yea yea
594. a: and many of my friends er in the mm writing society
595. they become journalists
596. B: yea yea
597. a: I admire them really
598. B: yea yea (.) actually journalism is a good profession
599. erm (.) the problem is though it's only really you're
600. only really as good as the last good piece of work
601. that you did and the and if the journalist goes off
602. the boil they tend to then get forgotten about mm
603. especially as an awful lot of journalists now
604. freelance
605. a: mm
606. B: erm you know I have a friend in Hong Kong who er
607. writes an article for the Sunday Post every Sunday
608. every week and mm he is a a a car specialist not not
609. not a mechanic he's a he's a person who test drives
610. motor vehicles and and reports on their performance
611. their you know the luxury of them the the the facades
612. and all this sort of stuff that goes with it mm and
613. then he has to do an article every week for that now
614. then okay fair enough you can well it's not his only
615. job obviously he does other things [but even if that
616. a: [((laugh))
617. was his only job that would be I think quite
618. stressful to actually [not only identify a car but
619. a: [yea
620. get the car drive the car test the car work out the
621. good points [the bad points then write it up and make
622. a: [yea
623. sure it's there for us to read on Sunday morning
624. every Sunday morning when you [buy the Post
625. a: [yea it's very
626. stressful
627. B: yea
628. a: er er journalism you have to have [erm a product
629. B: [mm

630. [to write
631. B: [that's right that's right and you've got to maintain
632. a standard haven't you because as soon people
633. recognize you for the standards that you set [and
634. a: [and
635. also they did not er earn good money
636. B: no [no
637. a: [the salary is very low
638. B: that's right that's right it's only really the top
639. ones that
640. a: yea but I think erm for young people at the start of
641. their career (.) er they should try out more things
642. before they settle on one thing
643. B: I think that's very true actually yea
644. a: my er regret is that er (.) I er start with ICAC too
645. soon
646. B: yea yea
647. a: if I got an opportunity to try er more things maybe
648. er the result's the same with the ICAC in the
649. [environment (.) but mm [I think it's good to get
650. B: [yea yea yea [but but they say experience
651. more experience
652. B: broadens the mind and any form of experience
653. broadens the mind um
654. a: and I only think that I'm very narrow vision mm
655. narrow vision ((laugh))

The topic discussed in Extract 11 is potentially face-threatening for the HKC. After hearing her frustration over her job, the NES asks about her career *but there's no regrets on joining the ICAC (.) as a career* (line 544). In response, the HKC gives an answer *a little bit [((laugh)))* to directly address the question. This response is an understatement, given what she says *my er regret is that er (.) I er start with ICAC too soon* (lines 644–645).

After saying *a little bit*, the HKC starts to give an account for her response. She, first of all, shifts the topic to how she feels about working in the ICAC and justifies it by listing the positive qualities about ICAC, namely the international image and contribution of the organization (lines 548–560). Then she moves on to give a reason for regretting *a little bit* joining the ICAC as a career when she says *mm (.) but erm (.) if I er (.) if I (.) had not joined the ICAC maybe I will got a more erm dynamic er (.) career or or (.) more more colourful yea [career yea* (lines 560–564).

It is interesting to note the way in which the HKC has presented and managed the discourse so far. Immediately after her answer, which shows her slight dissatisfaction with her career, she provides a positive evaluation of the organization in which both she and her interlocutor are working. By doing so, she is giving a clear message that she is not complaining about the organization (ICAC), and her frustration does not have anything to do with the organization. Her praising of the organization is a deliberate action to give concern to the face of her interlocutor as well as herself, both of whom are current staff of the organization.

The NES then asks a follow-up question about the kinds of 'dynamic' and 'colourful' careers that the HKC had thought of taking up before joining the ICAC. He lists such careers as *a business lady, a solicitor, a fashion designer or something of that nature*, all of which have positive features and qualities including ambition, character, capability, competence, professionalism and artistic fine taste. These careers illustrate what the NES perceives as more *dynamic* and *colourful* work for the HKC than working in the ICAC.

The NES's question is not directly addressed by the HKC. The HKC goes on to say that she thought of working in the television industry. The NES persists in his glamorous, attractive careers by asking whether the HKC would have wanted to be a television actress. The HKC then reveals that it was a scriptwriter that she was interested in being. Interestingly, hearing this, the NES still guesses jobs related to but possibly better than a scriptwriter (*oh like like a scriptwriter [or or yea or a journalist or an editor or something of that nature*, lines 588–591). The topic is then shifted to journalism, with both participants contributing their knowledge and beliefs regarding journalism to jointly develop the topic.

It is not clear why the HKC does not respond to the NES's question by referring to the list of probable careers that she had thought of pursuing upon graduation. Nevertheless, the fact that the HKC does not acknowledge any of the guesses but offers information about the field in which she was interested indicates that she is generating a conversational implicature that none of those careers proposed by the NES was correct. This may be due to her wish to preserve the NES's face, by avoiding directly saying to him that all his guesses are wrong. It can, however, possibly be due to the HKC's wish to preserve her own face. In Hong Kong, for many years, a scriptwriter or a television journalist has never been accorded the same kind of social status as a solicitor, a businesswoman, or even a fashion designer. Rather, the nature of the job is *very stressful* (lines 625–626), and journalists generally receive lower pay (*they did not er earn good money*, line 635; the *salary is very low*, line 637) and do not enjoy promotional opportunities and success of any kind that are comparable to those of business people, solicitors and fashion designers. Therefore, for the HKC to disclose that her career ambition was to become a scriptwriter may put herself in a less than favourable light. She would be exposing a certain side of herself, which does not match the expectations of the NES. Driven by the intention to preserve her own face, the HKC hence avoids directly responding to the NES's question. Besides, listing the drawbacks of being a journalist, by the HKC as well as by the NES, is an indirect way of conveying the meaning that the HKC has made the right choice in that she had not taken up journalism as her career.

In lines 644–647, the HKC wraps up the topic by echoing, and in a more direct way, what she said at the beginning of the discourse (*a little bit*). She says *my er regret is that er (.) I er start with ICAC too soon if I got an opportunity to try er more things.* She adds to this by evaluating her choice — *maybe er the result's the same with the ICAC in the [environment (.) but mm [I think it's good to get more experience.*

To sum up, Extract 11 shows an instance of an inductive pattern in the HKC's discourse. The topic initiated by the NES has proved to be sufficiently sensitive to have caused the HKC to supply lots of information to justify her main idea before moving to her main topic. The HKC's answer is related to herself, particularly admitting that, to a certain extent, she has made a wrong career choice, which can be perceived as a sign of weakness.

Extract 12 is an example of a HKC managing a personally sensitive topic inductively. The speakers were colleagues in a university in Hong Kong. The female HKC was an accountant and the female NES a financial officer. Before the extract begins, the topic has been work-related, with the HKC telling the NES that her fingers have become stiff as she works on the computer keyboard a lot and she does not usually get help from clerical staff. In line 466, the NES initiates a topic resumption, which is related to the school attended by the son of the HKC. The old topic is not shown in the extract.

(12) 022
a: female Honk Kong Chinese   A: female British
453. a: yea yea I do everything you know so I am not assisted
454. by any clerical staff [you know
455. A: [you you can use you can use
456. N_
457. a: but I I I used to do it myself [if I can handle
458. A: [right OK so you're
459. you're more comfortable [(.) doing your own doing
460. a: [yes I guess so yes
461. your own stuff something like oh it's [really
462. a: [great
463. interesting
464. a: yea

465.	a:	well [that's what they hope
466.	A:	[but they're having an extension right yea
467.	a:	I'm afraid they would mm ask the parent to you know
468.		to to donate
469.	A:	donate money or do other [fund raising yea
470.	a:	[money
471.	a:	yea but it seems a very big project [it needs a lot
472.	A:	[it does doesn't
473.		of money
474.	A:	it
475.	A:	yea
476.	a:	so I've been wondering even my son graduated after
477.		five or six years you know the project hasn't er will
478.		not be completed [by that time (.) but they
479.	A:	[no probably not
480.		collected the money already
481.	A:	an indoor swimming pool a include the sports hall a
482.		roof-top tennis court

The NES asks about the school's plans for expansion in line 466 *but they're having an extension right yea.* In lines 467–480, the HKC uses an inductive pattern of organization to express her main point regarding the school's expansion plans and the financing of them. In lines 467–468, the HKC expresses her fears that the school *would mm ask the parent to you know to to donate,* a likelihood confirmed by the NES in line 469. In line 471, the HKC gives more background information that *it seems a very big project it needs a lot of money* and again the NES agrees. The HKC then gives more information that even though her *son graduated after five or six years* the project *will not be completed by that time,* and again the NES agrees, *no probably not* (line 479). The fears and information presented earlier by the HKC are now seen to be by way of supporting her main point; and that is, *but they collected the money already.* The HKC's main point is her concern that as a parent she will be asked to donate a significant amount of money to a building project in her son's school that will not be completed before her son graduates, and so he will not benefit from the improved facilities in the school. The use of an inductive discourse pattern is an attempt to save the face of the speaker who feels the need to provide background information to explain why she feels that it is unreasonable to be asked to donate money to her son's school if he is not going to personally benefit from the donation.

Extract 13 illustrates an NES speaker organizing a personally sensitive topic inductively. The participants were colleagues and before the extract begins, they have been talking about property speculation in Hong Kong and comparing the property prices in Hong Kong, U.K. and U.S.A.

(13)	015	
B:	male British	a: female Hong Kong Chinese
188.	a:	[yea and what about now (.) years ago you (.)
189.		have think about it (.) to buy property in Hong Kong
190.		[and now the prop- [the prices is going down
191.	B:	[well [well there (.) that's right
192.		that's right mm erm and at the moment you see I've
193.		got a property in the U.K. and I've and I've also
194.		bought some land in Canada (.) mm (.) and (.) I'm not
195.		too sure that I could actually afford it at the
196.		moment because I I've spent all the money [I've got
197.	a:	[((laugh))
198.		available for [deposits on on on [other property
199.	a:	[((laugh)) [but do you intend
200.	B:	overseas
201.	a:	to stay in Hong Kong er [for a long time

The participants have been exchanging information and opinion about property prices in Hong Kong when, in lines 189–190, the HKC asks the NES if he's thinking *to buy property in Hong Kong and now the prop- the price is going down.* The NES responds by sequencing the information inductively. He begins by acknowledging that prices are falling, but then lists background information — *you see I've got a property in the UK* and *I've also bought some land in Canada.* He then states — *I'm not too sure that I could actually afford it at the moment* (lines 194–196), and then he finally gets to his main point (i.e. that he will not be buying a property in Hong Kong) *because I I've spent all the money [I've got available for [deposits on on on [other property overseas* (lines 196–200). The state of an individual's personal finances constitutes a sensitive topic in both Hong Kong and British cultures and here the British NES can be seen using a more indirect style to package the information that he has no money to be able to take advantage of the lower property prices in Hong Kong. The adoption of an inductive rhetorical strategy serves to save the face of the NES by first listing his assets (property in UK and land in Canada) and, by so doing, he establishes that he is a man of some means rather than simply and directly responding that he cannot afford to buy property in Hong Kong because he has no money.

Extract 14 shows an NES speaker using a deductive pattern to organize the discourse in order to present a culturally sensitive topic. The participants were university colleagues. Their conversation was recorded in a Chinese restaurant on campus. The female HKC has been telling the male NES about her previous job as a personnel and administrative manager in a factory in Doungguan, a city in southern China.

(14) 025

B: male British a: female Hong Kong Chinese

80.	B:	[right [what kind of factory was it
81.	a:	um electronics manufacturing
82.	B:	all right yes
83.	a:	they're exporting lighting and the security alarm
84.		products [to Europe
85.	B:	[right seems strange doesn't it that so much
86.		of sensitive [elect- electrical equipment [is
87.	a:	[yea [yeah
88.		manufactured in (.) southern Ch[ina which we always
89.	a:	[((laugh)) low quality
90.		think of as being kind of er low low quality [and er
91.	a:	control ((laugh)) [yeah
92.		(.) low wages and so on it's very funny you know (.)
93.		I mean a lot of lot of the electrical stuff you pick
94.		up in UK er (.) Kenwood things you know are all made
95.		in China
96.	a:	all made in China and then those who do the
97.		manufacturing work you know they are the people who
98.		come from the village
99.	B:	yes
100.	a:	they don't even know how to hold a soldering iron
101.	B:	no no [they probably have never never encountered to
102.	a:	[no
103.		[er
104.	a:	[they've never touched never seen such an equipment
105.		before
106.	B:	sophisticated [equipment (.) but there we are which
107.	a:	[((laugh))
108.		makes mm (.) I don't know how you control quality
109.		under those circumstances [er it must be so difficult
110.	a:	[no
111.		you can't you can't simply add it on at the end and
112.		reject the things that are not good enough I mean
113.	a:	mm and there are cases that goods are rejected

114. B: yeah
115. a: yeah (.) and then well [huge loads of (inaudible)
116. B: [mm
117. coming back
118. B: yes well [but the trouble is it's too late then isn't
119. a: [yea
120. it once the goods [have already gone out
121. a: [the boss's screaming like hell
122. B: yeah
123. a: ((laugh))

In this conversation, the participants are discussing the HKC's former job which involved travelling to factories across the border in southern China. The NES expresses the view that it *seems strange* that *so much of sensitive elect- electrical equipment is manufactured in (.) southern China* (lines 85–88). The NES's assertion is actively supported by the HKC who suggests *low quality control* (lines 89 and 91), which is endorsed by the NES in his utterance *which we always think of as being kind of er low quality [and er (.) low wages and so on*, lines 88–92. The NES adds to the 'strange' phenomenon, i.e. 'so much' comes from this region, by saying *it's very funny you know (.) I mean a lot of lot of the electrical stuff you pick up in UK er (.) Kenwood things you know are all made in China* (lines 92–95). The derogatory nature of the NES's main assertion might have led him to adopt a deductive pattern of organizing information (i.e. main idea followed by supporting details and reasons) to avoid potential face loss, although the HKC appears to be in full agreement with him.

Conclusion

A quantitative analysis of the data has supported the hypothesis that HKC are more indirect than NES in the form of using an inductive discourse pattern. This indicates a greater tendency on the part of HKC to frame their topics in a larger discourse framework through "external build-ups" (Zhang 1995: 82), which are predominently background to the topic, examples, reasons, and other supportive details. These findings lend support to views that purport high-context, collectivistic cultures to be indirect (Gudykunst 1998; Kim 1994) due to perception of and importance assigned to values such as rapport and harmony versus independence, and clarity and preferred topics in conversation (Wierzbicka 1991). It needs to be pointed out, nevertheless, that in terms of face management, both of the patterns of organization, though to varying degrees, serve to mitigate potential face loss as they both involve giving background information, reasons, or examples to support the speaker's main or first topic.

Qualitative examination of the intercultural conversations has focused on seven culturally sensitive speech functions, namely agreeing, disagreeing, making a request or a suggestion, partial or complete rejection of a request or a suggestion, avoiding self-praise, responding to self-denigration and managing a personally or culturally sensitive topics. It has been found that HKC have a higher tendency to be indirect in terms of organizing discourse information in an inductive way, and NES have a higher tendency to organize discourse information deductively. This conclusion supports stereotypical generalizations regarding the preferred patterns of organizing discourse information by Chinese and Western cultures. However, the qualitative analysis of conversational excerpts by no means intends to develop theories about the subjective mind of the speaker and the hearer. Some of the plausible explanations were deduced from the surrounding text of the instance of indirectness, and hence there is a sufficient level of evidence in some cases. Where possible, the speakers were interviewed to identify and, at times, also to confirm the reasons for being indirect in a particular way in a particular context.

Indirectness, actualized in the form of an inductive pattern, has been found to be a more likely phenomenon in HKC's, rather than NES's, discourse. One may argue that this is due to culturally determined preferred thought patterns which influence the way ideational messages are organized; and consequently, the Chinese are more likely than Westerners to have a delayed introduction of the topic in their discourse. Qualitative analysis of some of the examples has suggested an interrelationship between discourse patterning and the physical, social, cultural and linguistic contextual variables. The findings have also indicated that indirectness is rational behaviour, through which HKC and NES obtain interpersonal or communicative benefits or avoid some negative consequences, such as threatening their own or the addressees' face.

Both HKC and NES perform a range of culturally sensitive functions by means of sequencing their information and introducing their main topic either inductively or deductively in their conversation. A few major similarities between HKC and NES have been observed, including a greater tendency to use a deductive pattern in agreeing with the addressee, making a request or suggestion, and partially or completely rejecting a request or suggestion. HKC and NES are also similar in that they use only a deductive pattern to give agreements to the addressee. There are differences, too. The major difference is that when the topic is sensitive, either culturally or personally, HKC use mainly an inductive pattern to organize and present the information, whereas NES predominantly use a deductive pattern. Other differences include HKC being more likely than NES to disagree with the interlocutor and to manage a sensitive topic by ordering their discourse information either inductively or deductively. The last difference is that in the data set, there are only examples of HKC sequencing their discourse information inductively and deductively (N=3) to avoid self-praise.

Generally, the findings illustrate differences between the two cultural groups in their perception of the purpose of communication, the notion of self in relation to others, and the conception of face and politeness. As revealed in the contrasting behaviours, compared to NES, HKC can be seen to be more concerned about striking a balance between achieving propositional goals and interpersonal goals. This indicates that HKC are more concerned about face management and politeness than NES, as revealed in avoiding making an imposition on the interlocutor, in refraining from intruding upon the addressee's territory, and in being modest and humble. These motivational factors indicate the cultural value orientations characteristic of the Chinese, namely the concept of "self" as an interdependent self, preference for harmonious and positive interpersonal relationship communication, and modesty and humility as expected norms of behaviour.

All of the seven functions examined are culture-specific. Imposition, for instance, is "culture-dependent" (Mey 2001: 263), as cultures perceive speech acts differently. The degree of imposition of the speech act of "making a request" may be evaluated differently by the HKC and the NES women in Extract 8. In a similar vein, the HKC's preference for an inductive discourse pattern, from a pragmatic politeness viewpoint, could be motivated by giving reasons and detail to support propositions, which are manifestations of the HKC's sense of the size of the imposition and the need for politeness. Other factors are more related to the immediate context of conversation, rather than the cultural backgrounds of the participants. These factors include the desire to make the language more interesting and more forceful.

As there is an "indispensable link between the spoken words and the world of their users" (Mey 2001: 265), the forms of indirectness in the patterns of organization examined in this chapter both reflect and reveal the world of their HKC and NES users.

Note

1. In 1997, primary students were categorized into five bands, with Band One being the best performing students. 'Band One' schools refer to secondary schools that admit Band One students.

Chapter 9

Conclusion

Introduction

This study investigates the English conversation between Hong Kong Chinese (HKC) and native English speakers (NES). It has been noted that there is a paucity of research in naturally occurring English conversations with the Chinese in Hong Kong as participants. The present study has compared the two groups of culturally divergent participants in the ways they manage the organizational and interpersonal aspects of English conversation. The examination is conducted by focusing on five culturally-laden conversational features, namely preference organization (disagreements), compliments and compliment responses, simultaneous talk, discourse topic management and discourse information structure. For each of the features, a set of hypotheses was proposed regarding the communication process, behaviour, style, and pattern characteristic of HKC and NES engaged in conversation.

It is argued that there has been a lack of consistency in the definition of the term "conversation" in the literature and hence in the data depicted as conversation in some other studies. In this study, attention has been paid to both the origin and the appropriacy of the data. The conversations were not recorded surreptitiously; in other words, they were recorded with the prior knowledge of the participants. It is, however, expected that the conversations were as naturally occurring and authentic as possible, given the data collection method and procedure, the relationships between the participants; and most importantly, the context of situation in which the conversations took place.

All of the conversations examined in this study are "interactions carried out for social purposes, rather than for the exchange of goods and services" (Nunan 1993: 118). When collecting conversational data, the study has been very careful in monitoring the social parameters, namely social distance and power relationships, of the participants; the goals of interaction; as well as the context of conversation. The participants are colleagues, friends, and, in two cases, relatives. Some of their interactions took place in homes, but most of them in restaurants and cafés. In Hong Kong restaurants and cafés are the preferred locations for socializing.

For the purposes of theory testing, this study has made hypotheses about the various features manifested in the conversation between HKC and NES in a stereotypical sense, based on the work of others in related fields. The overriding hypothesis was that HKC and NES are different in the ways they manage the organisational, social and interpersonal aspects of English conversation, on the grounds that HKC and NES are different in their respective cultural make-up and value orientations which affect their conceptions of self and their conceptions of the notion of "face" and polite behaviours in interactions for social purposes.

Culturally-laden features of conversation

Investigation of the five conversational features has shown that, on the whole, the HKC participants examined in the present research exhibit conversational and pragmatic behaviours that conform to most of the stereotypical assumptions about the Chinese. In conflict management contexts, when disagreeing with the addressee, HKC do employ a greater number of instances of, and more elaborate, redressive language in their disagreements for face management purposes (Chapter 4). In other words, HKC are more likely to use disagreements, which are heavily redressed so as to mitigate the imposition of the disagreement on the NES interlocutor, to disclaim an all-knowing and authoritative status, and to coerce and involve the interlocutor in the reasoning and in claiming common ground. This shows that for HKC, disagreeing with the addressee involves a lot more facework and interpersonal management work than for NES, especially in order not to sound imposing. The extent to which HKC and NES pay regard for the interlocutor's face is clearly different. HKC's disagreements are more likely than NES's to be realized in the form of a dispreferred response. On the contrary, NES are more likely than HKC to both give a disagreement upfront followed by redressive language and give a direct and blunt disagreement. The findings have largely confirmed the "independent and interdependent conceptions of the self" that characterize Chinese and Western cultures respectively (Markus and Kitayama 1991, 1994).

The findings relating to HKC and NES's preferred compliment topics and compliment response types, reported in Chapter 5, largely converge with those of previous studies. The participants in this study have complimented on the most commonly evaluated aspects specific to the culture of their interlocutor. Concerning compliment responses, HKC's responses range from absence of a verbal response to a back-channel signal to an (implicit) agreement to an outright rejection, while all of NES's compliment responses take the form of accepting the compliment. The phenomena can be explained by the Western notion of minimizing or avoiding self-praise (Pomerantz 1978) as well as the Chinese notion of politeness, which takes the forms of "self-denigration" and "other elevation" (Gu 1990) and "reciprocity" (Hong 1985). Among the Chinese, being modest and respectful as a manifestation of humility is considered ideal in daily communication (Gu 1990).

In simultaneous talk (Chapter 6), HKC are more oriented to the "one-at-a-time" model of turn-taking than NES, and pay greater attention to rules governing turn-taking in conversation. It is hence arguable that the turn-taking rules better describe HKC than NES behaviour. These phenomena can be attributed to the way they perceive the purpose of communication and their conception of self in relation to others in communication.

In discourse topic development (Chapter 7), HKC are more inclined than NES to initiate both Speaker and Addressee-oriented topics and Addressee-oriented topics.

Finally, as discussed in Chapter 8, HKC have been shown to be more indirect than NES, in terms of the use of an inductive pattern of sequencing the information of their discourse. HKC use an inductive rhetorical strategy much more frequently than NES and for a wider range of functions. The findings have, to a great extent, confirmed preconceptions of Chinese cultures being relatively indirect, compared to Western cultures, due to their concern for politeness and preservation of face.

The findings relating to the conversational features have therefore supported the purported intercultural differences between HKC and NES, in terms of the underlying cultural value orientations, conceptions, beliefs, and attitudes, which are believed to have influenced the ways the participants manage the organizational and interpersonal aspects of conversation.

However, some findings do not support the stereotypical assumptions made of the cultural groups of HKC and NES. For instance, contrary to expectations, HKC disagree more frequently than NES (Chapters 4 and 8). In the investigation of discourse topic management (Chapter 7), again contrary to expectations, when HKC introduce topics into the conversation, they do not seem any more concerned than NES regarding whether or not consecutive topics should be propositionally related to each other. In the investigation of the preferred pattern of sequencing discourse information (Chapter 8), HKC have actually used the supposedly archetypal Western deductive pattern slightly more frequently than NES do, although when only culturally sensitive functions were compared, HKC are inclined to use an inductive pattern more frequently and a deductive pattern less frequently than NES.

Despite differences observed in the conversational features of disagreements, discourse topic management and discourse information structure, the findings reported in this study have largely supported the stereotypical, generalized preconceptions made about the communicative behaviours of members of the Chinese and Western cultures. For the Chinese, "the interactional dynamics of facework" is "positively reciprocal with both parties engaged in mutually shared orientation to negotiate, elevate, and attend to each other's face as well as one's own face" (Zhang 1995: 85). Hence, central in Chinese facework is "face-balance", which means giving others' face simultaneously enhances one's own face and depriving other's face simultaneously damages one's face (Zhang 1995: 85). Westerners and Chinese differ in the way they conceive face. In the West, egalitarian relationship is a valued cultural ideology. Westerners emphasize the independence aspect of face. They respect the rights of the addressee to freedom of choice, autonomy, territory, and so on. The Western "self" in communication is highly individualistic, self-motivated, open to ongoing negotiation, and emphasizes independence (Scollon and Scollon 1995).

As delineated in Chapter 1, the study acknowledges the potential usefulness of the taxonomies of cultural patterns (for example, Hall 1976, 1977; Hofstede 1980, 1983, 2001) and generalized assumptions for both characterizing the intercultural conversational behaviour of HKC and NES and explaining the ways in which cultural attributes are negotiated, mediated and transformed in the situated discourse. As the starting point, this study works on the assumption that there are cultural differences between the East and the West in norms, values and beliefs which impact on the behaviours of the people. However, it argues against unquestionably adopting a "deficit" (Holliday 1999) stance of intercultural communication, and indulging in the "analytic stereotyping" (Sarangi 1994: 409) of intercultural encounters as mainly characterized by the intercultural differences present. The study supports the view that individual participants bring to the discourse their unique cultural attributes and language but during the process of the discourse, they are involved in a process of creating, recreating, filtering and transforming culture and language (Sherzer 1987).

The study supports the notion that any intercultural analysis should be looking at what people actually do in real-life communication. Intercultural encounters involve a complex, interactive and collaborative process of communication, and the communicators mediating and negotiating their values, beliefs, norms and attitudes. A principled approach to explaining data will also be based on what the participants in specific contexts of situation are doing. In this study, the interactions between HKC and NES need to be viewed in the specific context of situation for an understanding of how HKC and NES manage the organisational and interpersonal aspects of English conversation. The context of situation comprises a range of factors, including the physical setting of the interaction, the cultural make-up of the individual participants, the social relationships between the participants, the goals of interactions as perceived by them, the nature and proposition of the topic at hand, the nature and amount of shared knowledge and experiences between the participants, and the English language that is being used in the conversations. For instance, as revealed in the analysis of compliments and compliment responses, context-specific factors such as whether a speaker is serious or playful can influence the linguistic realizations of a compliment or a compliment response.

In fact, the examination of extended excerpts of conversation, which were situated in their specific contexts of interaction, has revealed a more complex scenario than what could be offered by some of the micro-level analyses of utterances. On the whole, permeating the 25 intercultural conversations is an atmosphere of harmony, support, rapport, co-operation, and shared responsibility. Contextual analysis of extended talk-in-interaction has revealed that across all of the five conversational features, HKC and NES act as collaborative conversational participants. In general, the participants can be seen to respect each other's speaker rights, contribute to the discourse in a coordinated way, share in the construction and negotiation of topic, make sense of the coherence of what they hear and negotiate mutual understanding, monitor the progress and direction of the discourse, build and maintain interpersonal relations, and realize a successful outcome.

To a greater or lesser extent, both HKC and NES are concerned with, and respect, each other's cultural identity and pay regard for each other's face-want. A sense of shared responsibility between the HKC and NES participants has been observed, in the aspects of aligning themselves with the interlocutor to manage interpersonal relationships and negotiate common ground in the employment of redressive language and the organizational pattern of disagreements as a dispreferred response, introducing topics, introducing and negotiating ideological topical content, turn-taking based on initiation of simultaneous talk, employment of necessary turn-holding and turn-yielding strategies in the case of simultaneous talk, equal access to the different acts of speaking and equal access to the different ways to respond to these acts of speaking, as well as maintenance of face and hence social relations. Regarding HKC, they have demonstrated an ability to use their knowledge of the English language in a way that has successfully attained mutually satisfying outcomes in the interactions.

From the findings, two major observations have been made. First, there are both similarities and dissimilarities in the pragmatic and conversational phenomena, as observed in the five conversational features investigated, between Hong Kong Chinese and native speakers of English, which can predominantly be explained by cultural differences. Second, it is of prime importance that the linguistic and communicative behaviours of the conversational participants and the interactional patterns in the conversations need to be interpreted in the specific contexts of situation in which they occur. In this research, although cultural differences have been found to be influential, it has also been found that cultural attributes do not predetermine entirely the ways in which conversation is managed. In fact, management of conversation is also dependent on the moment by moment negotiaton between individual participants in conversation.

As discussed, dissimilarities can be attributable to the "cultural world" (Mey 2001: 265) that the participants come from. Similarities can be caused by a number of reasons. First of all, the nature of the discourse, namely conversation, presumes equality in speaker rights, symmetry, and shared responsibility between participants in the conduct and organization of conversation. Second, the fact that the conversational participants in the study are friends and colleagues means that a certain degree of accommodation in the direction of convergence (Beebe and Giles 1984; Bourhis 1985; Ribeau and Hecht 1986) in their conversational behaviours and strategies can be expected. Convergence is typically found in most cooperative interpersonal situations as a means to lessen interpersonal distance. The participants in this study were, therefore, likely to adapt to each other's linguistic and communicative behaviour and social patterns. Third, the fact that the bilingual HKC participants speak the native language of their interlocutor makes it possible that "cultural accommodation" (Ralston et al. 1995: 714–715) occurs. "Cultural accommodation" proposes that individuals will react in a manner that favours or accommodates the culture associated with the language of presentation. When bilingual individuals respond in their native language, they will accommodate the culture associated with the native language. When they respond in a target language, these same bilinguals will accommodate the culture associated with the target language (Ralston et al. 1995).

Contribution of the study

The present study has examined 25 intercultural conversations amounting to thirteen hours of situated discourse. The conversational participants were Hong Kong Chinese educated professionals, who spoke English as their second or foreign language, and native English speakers who were living and working in Hong Kong when the recordings were made. It can, therefore, be argued that the generalizability of the findings will be restricted due to the quantity of conversations, the number of participants, the distinct characteristics of the Hong Kong Chinese participants, as well as the English-speaking community groups investigated.

Having said that, the present research has made useful and significant contributions to the study of intercultural communication, particularly intercultural conversation. What's more, this study is one of the first studies investigating a range of organizational and interpersonal features, both quantitatively and qualitatively, characteristic of Hong Kong Chinese speakers as participants in English conversation.

At the theoretical level, this study has attempted to address the questions relating to immediate (local) and wider (global) contexts of interaction. In recent years, there have been debates between researchers of two different approaches to discourse analysis, namely descriptive discourse analysis (DDA) and critical discourse analysis (CDA). Fairclough (1995), for instance, criticizes DDA that the goals of DDA are mainly to describe the orderliness exhibited in the discourse and not to look for causes, and so are not explanatory, and Widdowson (1995a, 1995b) and Stubbs (1997) criticize CDA that it is driven by a political agenda, allowing interpretation in support of belief to take precedence over analysis in support of theory. The present study has illustrated the benefits derived from integrating rather than segregating approaches to language study, and supported the position that these approaches are "complementary" but not "competitive" (Wetherell 1998; Tsui 2001: 3). These approaches would be seen to contain the elements of a possible combined, complementary approach that could harness the best of both approaches. These elements are namely description of conversational features, structures and organization and their cultural implications.

The context of intercultural studies is a suitable locus where the micro level (linguistic practices) and the macro level (cultural structures) intersect. This study has conducted analysis of the features, structures and organization exhibited in the intercultural conversations in order to gain insights into how meaning is created in the immediate linguistic context. Making use of this kind of analysis, the study has also analyzed the conversations by relating discourse description to the larger socio-cultural context in which the discourse took place. In other words, the study has integrated the immediate context (in the sense of locally organized and negotiated interaction) and the wider context (in the sense of potential cultural influences on conversational management behaviours). As such, it serves as an example of the complementarity of different approaches to analyzing discourse.

This study has sought to describe and interpret specific discursive practices of individual participants both in terms of their cultural attributes, value orientations and attitudes, as well as in terms of individual differences, the role-relationships, the nature and proposition of the topic at hand, and other situational variables surrounding the intercultural communication event. The study considers situated discourse as a concrete expression of the language-culture relationship, because it is discourse that "creates, focuses, modifies, and transmits both culture and language and their interaction" (Sherzer 1987).

The descriptive framework employed in this study to analyze five conversational features in intercultural settings will be useful for future studies that attempt to extend the aspects of analysis beyond those covered in the present one. The study has demonstrated that making stereotypical assumptions about cultural groups can be useful as a starting point for the purposes of theory testing. Cultural stereotypes are such a prevalent phenomenon in our lives. In this regard, this study has revealed some truth in some of the cultural stereotypical behaviours characteristic of the cultural groups investigated on the one hand. On the other hand, the study has confounded some preconceptions regarding the relations between cultural backgrounds and the conversational behaviours of the cultural members. Similar conclusions have been drawn by Littlewood (2000), who has pointed out the fallacy of some common preconceptions about Asian students and their learning attitudes. In his comparative study of students in eight Asian countries and three European countries, Littlewood (2000: 31) has found that "our preconceptions do not reflect what they really want, and that there is actually less difference in attitudes to learning between Asian and European countries than between individuals within each country". Littlewood proposes that our preconceptions need to be questioned and the nature and extent of cultural influences on learning be explored.

Limitations of the study

The limitations of this study are mainly related to the inherent difficulty with the conduct of any cultural research. As Pedersen and Jandt (1996: 5) state, "culture is an ambiguous and multidimensional construct that makes the isolation of research variables a complex task". This study encountered two problems (see Weiss 1987) for a discussion of the problems associated with cultural research. First, individuals are influenced by many different cultures, including those of the nation, the region, their ethnicity, their religious and/or other affiliations. HKC examined in this study were categorized according to their race. The native speakers of English were participants of different nationalities, namely British, American and Australian. For both HKC and NES, no differentiation was made among the different races or ethnicities. This will naturally mean that the "multiple cultures" (Weiss 1987: 31) specific to individual participants have not been taken into account in the data analysis.

Second, individuals do not always behave in predictable ways according to a given style or norm (Weiss 1987). For the purposes of theory testing, this study has started with making stereotypical assumptions about the behaviours, beliefs, and norms of the Chinese and the Western cultures. In addition, the study has only examined individual speakers in a single conversational context. What this study has not examined is the ways individual speakers of a particular cultural group behave in a range of contexts of situation in order to draw conclusions about predictable patterns or styles of communicative behaviour.

The third problem is that the patterns of group behaviour cannot be reliably used in every situation to predict individual action (Weiss 1987). This study aimed to investigate HKC and NES as representing two cultural groups in interaction. Conclusions have been drawn regarding the ways these groups of speakers behaved in the conversations investigated. The "aggregate versus individual patterns" problem will imply that the conclusions drawn can best be used to describe the individual speakers investigated. Any attempt to extend the conclusions beyond the contexts of situation and the particular speakers investigated will have to be done with care.

As Weiss (1987) observes, when the cultural context specific to individual speakers is described, it is difficult to achieve a balance between maintaining individual and group balances and identifying common group linkages without oversimplifying, stereotyping, or over generalizing about cultures. The insights that the present study can draw from this observation is that it seems unavoidable to make generalizations about the Chinese and Western cultures. From both micro-level analysis and the analysis of extended talk, this study attempts to investigate how individual speakers converse in the immediate context of situation.

Last but not least, the gender of the participants was not controlled as controlling the gender variable would have required pairing up specific genders in the dyadic conversations which would have been extremely difficult to achieve. Same gender conversations constituted 48% of the data set. Mixed gender conversations were skewed in the sense that female HKC and male NES conversations made up 48% whereas male HKC and female NES only 4% of the data set. Consequently, the results of the study have to be interpreted with the understanding of the composition of genders in the conversational data investigated. More importantly, the focus of this study is two cultural groups, HKC and NES, conversing, but not how groups of different cultures and genders interact with each other.

Directions for future research

Apart from the descriptive framework that this study has adopted to investigate the culturally-laden conversational features, the findings themselves serve as useful reference for future studies that compare Hong Kong Chinese speakers of English with other groups of non-native users of English, such as Japanese, Filipino, Indian, German, French, and Singaporean speakers of English. Future studies can also compare conversational features found in same gender and mixed gender intercultural conversations. In addition to possible replication of the descriptive frameworks established by this study, the conclusion of this study can be used for points of reference for hypothesis building and testing.

Last but not least, a by-product of this study is the unique intercultural conversations (thirteen hours of recordings consisting of 25 dyadic conversations) that was compiled for the purposes of this study. In recent years there has been an explosion of data-based language research (Sinclair 1991; Stubbs 1996; Thomas and Short 1996; Burnard and McEnery 2000). The intercultural conversations of this study were carefully and systematically monitored in terms of the design criteria and collection procedure. The intercultural conversations will be useful for future investigation into intercultural communication, particularly intercultural conversations.

Two major insights can be drawn from the conclusion of the study. First, the study has underscored one all important fact about conversation; and that is, contact between people is an essential element of our lives and conversing is a basic medium for performing this extremely vital function and achieving this universal end. This fact holds true for all cultures, races and ethnicities, and is not bounded by any cultures or races or ethnicities. Second, in order to become successful communicators of the twenty-first century, we need to be culturally sensitive and approach intercultural communication with a positive attitude. This second insight can be illustrated in the words of the participants of the study.

Positive views about, and benefits of, cultural diversity and intercultural communication have been expressed by the participants of this study. The following, taken from one of the conversations, shows a conversational excerpt between two colleagues, a Hong Kong Chinese woman and a British man.

015
a: female Hong Kong Chinese B: male British
671. a: yes different culture [and you mm (.) mm (pause)
672. B: [mm
673. sometimes difficult for people to (.) to (.) accept
674. or take erm the things of (.) [another culture (.)
675. B: [mm
676. yea
677. B: I think it's fun (.) to get involved in different (.)
678. you know (.) classes of culture I I I think it's (.)
679. it it's a great learning experience
680. a: mhmm
681. B: and it teaches you that you're not the only person in
682. the world (.) [and that different
683. a: [yea
684. a: it make makes you humble [((laugh))
685. B: [it does it does (.) erm (.)
686. especially when you see how other cultures can do
687. things better
688. a: mhmm
689. B: erm (.) and how things could be done better in
690. different ways by different people
691. a: mm hm
692. B: erm (.) it it it is er er a learning experience

Lewis (2000: 2) expresses similar views that can best serve as the concluding remark of this study:

> Cultural diversity is not something that is going to go away tomorrow, enabling us to plan our strategies on the assumption of mutual understanding. It is in itself a phenomenon with its own riches, the exploration of which could yield incalculable benefits for us, both in terms of wider vision and more profitable policies and activity.

It is to be hoped that this study has not only served to describe intercultural communication in conversations, but that benefits can be reaped as a result of a better understanding of such communication. Future research should continue to re-evaluate the preconceptions about, as well as the nature and extent of, cultural influences on conversational behaviours.

References

Abercrombie, David

1965 *Studies in Phonetics and Linguistics.* London: Oxford University Press.

Asante, Molefi K. and Gudykunst, William B. (eds)

1989 *Handbook of Intercultural Communication.* Newbury Park, CA: Sage.

Atkinson, J. Maxwell and Heritage, John

1984 *Structures of Social Action: Studies in Conversation Analysis.* Cambridge; New York: Cambridge University Press.

Austin, John L.

1962 *How to Do Things with Words.* Oxford: Clarendon Press.

Bacon-Shone, John and Bolton, Kingsley

1998 "Charting multilingualism: Language censuses and language surveys in Hong Kong". In *Language in Hong Kong at Century's End,* M. Pennington (ed.), 43–90. Hong Kong: Hong Kong University Press.

Bandura, Albert

1986 *Social Foundations of Thought and Action: A Social Cognitive Theory.* Englewood Cliffs, NJ: Prentice-Hall.

Bargiela-Chiappini, Francesca and Harris, Sandra

1995 "Towards a generic structure of meetings in British and Italian managements". *Text* 15 (4): 531–560.

1997 *Managing Language. The Discourse of Corporate Meetings.* Amsterdam and Philadelphia: John Benjamins.

Beattie, Geoffrey W.

1981 "Interruption in conversational interaction and its relation to the sex and status of the interactants". *Linguistics* 19: 15–35.

1983 *Talk: An Analysis of Speech and Non-verbal Behaviour in Conversation.* Milton Keynes, England: Open University Press.

Becker, Gerhold K.

1996 *Ethics in Business and Society: Chinese and Western Perspectives.* Berlin; New York: Springer.

Beebe, Leslie M.

1985 "Speech act performance: a function of the data collection procedure?" Paper presented at the Sixth Annual TESOL and Sociolinguistics Colloquium at the International TESOL Convention, New York.

Beebe, Leslie M. and Giles, Howard

1984 "Speech-accommodation theories: A discussion in terms of second-language acquisition". *International Journal of the Sociology of Language* 46: 5–32.

Bennett, Adrian
1981 "Interruptions and the interpretation of conversation". *Discourse Processes* 4 (2): 171–88.

Berry, Margaret
1981 "Polarity, ellipticity and propositional development, their relevance to the well-formedness of an exchange (A Discussion of Coulthard and Brazil's Classes of Move)". *Nottingham Linguistic Circular* 10 (1): 36–63.

Bilbow, Grahame T.
1996 *Business Speaking for Hong Kong*. Hong Kong: Longman.
1997a "Cross-cultural impression management in the multicultural workplace: The special case of Hong Kong". *Journal of Pragmatics* 28 (4): 46–487.
1997b "Spoken discourse in the multicultural workplace in Hong Kong: Applying a model of discourse as 'impression management". In *The Languages of Business*, B. Chiappini and H. Sandra (eds), 21–48. Edinburgh: Edinburgh University Press.

Bilmes, J.
1997 "Being interrupted". *Language in Society* 26 (4): 507–531.

Blum-Kulka, Shoshana
1987 "Indirectness and politeness in requests: same or different?" *Journal of Pragmatics* 11: 131–146.

Blum-Kulka, Shoshana, House, Juliane and Kasper, Gabriele (eds)
1989 *Cross-Cultural Pragmatics: Requests and Apologies*. Norwood, NJ: Ablex Pub. Corp.

Bolt, Philip
1994 "The International Corpus of English Project: The Hong Kong experience". In *Creating and Using English Language Corpora: Papers from the Fourteenth International Conference on English Language Research on Computerized Corpora, Zurich 1993*, U. Fries, G. Tottie and P. Schneider (eds), 15–24. Amsterdam: Rodopi.

Bolt, Philip and Bolton, Kingsley
1995 "The international corpus of English in Hong Kong (MS)".

Bolton, Kingsley and Kwok, Helen
1990. The dynamics of the Hong Kong accent: Social identity and sociolinguistic description. *Journal of Asian Pacific Communication* 1: 147–172.

Bond, Michael H. (ed.)
1986 *The Psychology of the Chinese People*. Hong Kong: Oxford University Press.

Bond, Michael, Leung, L. and Wan, Kwok Chui
1982 "How does cultural collectivism operate? The impact of task and maintenance contributions on reward allocation". *Journal of Cross-Cultural Psychology* 13: 186–200.

Bond, Michael H. and King, AmbroseY.C.
1985 "Coping with the threat of westernisation in Hong Kong". *International Journal of Intercultural Relations* 9: 351–364.

Bourhis, Richard Y.

1985 "The sequential nature of language choice in cross-cultural communication". In *Sequence and Pattern in Communicative Behaviour*, L.Jr.R. Street and J. N. Cappella (eds), 120–141. London: Arnold.

Brazil, David

1985 *The Communicative Value of Intonation*. Birmingham: University of Birmingham, English Language Research.

1997 *The Communicative Value of Intonation in English*. Cambridge: Cambridge University Press.

Brislin, Richard W.

2000 *Understanding Culture's Influence on Behavior* (Second Edition). Fort Worth: Harcourt Brace Jovanovich College Publishers.

Brown, Gillian and Yule, George

1983 *Discourse Analysis*. Cambridge; New York: Cambridge University Press.

Brown, Penelope and Levinson, Stephen C.

1978 "Universals in language usage: Politeness phenomena". In *Questions and Politeness: Strategies in Social Interaction*, E.N. Goody (ed.), 56–311. Cambridge; New York: Cambridge University Press.

1987 *Politeness: Some Universals in Language Usage*. Cambridge; New York: Cambridge University Press.

Brunner, J. and You, W.

1988 "Chinese negotiation and the concept of face". *Journal of International Consumer Marketing* 1 (1): 27–43.

Bublitz, Wolfram

1988 *Supportive Fellow-Speakers and Cooperative Conversations : Discourse Topics and Topical Actions, Participant Roles and «Recipient Action» in a Particular Type of Everyday Conversation*. Amsterdam; Philadelphia: John Benjamins.

Burnard, Lou and McEnery, Tony (eds)

2000 *Rethinking Language Pedagogy from a Corpus Perspective*. London: Peter Lang.

Button, Graham and Casey, Neil

1984 "Generating topic". In *Structures of Social Action: Studies in Conversation Analysis*, J. Atkinson and J. Heritage (eds), 167–190. Cambridge: Cambridge University Press.

1988 "Topic initiation: business-at-hand". *Research on Language and Social Interaction* 22: 61–92.

Carter, Ronald and McCarthy, Michael

1997 *Exploring Spoken English*. Cambridge: Cambridge University Press.

Chafe, Wallace A.

1976 "Givenness, contrastiveness, definiteness, subjects, topics, and point of view, Symposium on Subject and Topic". In *Subject and Topic*, N. Charles, 25–55. Univ. of CA, Santa Barbara, March, 1975. New York: Academic.

Chan, Sam

1992 "Families with Asian roots". In *Developing Cross-Cultural Competence: A Guide for Working with Young Children and their Families*, E.W. Lynch and

M.J. Hanson (eds), 251–354. Baltimore: Paul H. Brookes Publishing Co.

Channell, Joanna
1994 *Vague Language.* Oxford: Oxford University Press.

Cheepen, Christine and Monaghan, James
1990 *Spoken English: A Practical Guide.* London and New York: Pinter.

Chen, Rong
1993 "Responding to compliments: a contrastive study of politeness strategies between American English and Chinese Speakers". *Journal of Pragmatics* 20 (1): 49–75.

Chen, Xing, Ye, Lei and Zhang, Yanyin
1995 "Refusing in Chinese". In *Pragmatics of Chinese as Native and Target Language,* G. Kasper (ed.), 119–164. Honolulu: Second Language Teaching & Curriculum Center, University of Hawaii at Manoa.

Cheng, Winnie
1999 "Constructing and negotiating ideologies of race and ethnicity in intercultural conversations". *anglistica, English and the Other* 3(1): 15–31.
2001 "Jocular interactions in intercultural conversations". *Proceedings of the First Seoul International Conference on Discourse and Cognitive Linguistics: Perspectives for the 21st Century, Seoul, Korea June 9–10, 2001,* 728–736.
2003 "Humour in intercultural conversation". *Semiotica* 146(1/4): 287–307.

Cheng, Winnie and Warren, Marren
1999a "Facilitating a description of intercultural conversations: the Hong Kong Corpus of Conversational English". *International Computer Archive of Modern English (ICAME) Journal* 23 April 1999: 5–20.

Cheng, Winnie and Warren, Martin
1999b "Inexplicitness: what is it and should we be teaching it?". *Applied Linguistics* 20 (3): 293–315.
2000 "Using a corpus of intercultural spoken English as a learning and teaching resource: The case of the discourse marker *well*". *Proceedings of the '98 International Conference on Teaching English at Tertiary Level in the Chinese Context,* 374–391.
2001a "'*and then some hot one*': Manifestations of imprecision and non-specificity in conversations". *Proceedings of the First Seoul International Conference on Discourse and Cognitive Linguistics: Perspectives for the 21st Century, Seoul, Korea June 9–10, 2001,* 768–780.
2001b "The use of vague language in intercultural conversations in Hong Kong". *English World-Wide* 22 (1): 81–104.
2001c "'She knows more about Hong Kong than you do isn't it': Tags in Hong Kong conversational English". *Journal of Pragmatics* 33 (9): 1419–1439.
(forthcoming) "'beef ball you like': the intonation of declarative-mood questions in a corpus of Hong Kong English". *Special issue of Teanga: Corpora, Varieties and the Language Classroom.*

Cheng, Winnie, Warren, Martin, Bradshaw, Julia, Greaves, Christopher, Pellowe, John and Setter, Jane

1997 "Compiling a Hong Kong corpus of conversational English". *HKPU Working Papers in ELT and Applied Linguistics* 2 (2): 1–20.

Clyne, Michael G.
1994 *Inter-Cultural Communication at Work: Cultural Values in Discourse.* Cambridge; New York: Cambridge University Press.

Collier, Mary J. and Thomas, Milt
1988 "Cultural identity: an interpretative perspective". In *Theories in Intercultural Communication*, Y.Y. Kim and W. Gudykunst (eds), 99–120. U.S.A.: Sage.

Condon, John C.
1984 *With Respect to the Japanese: A Guide for Americans.* Yarmouth, ME: Intercultural Press.

Conroy, Joseph and Sundstrom, Eric
1977 "Territorial dominance in a dyadic conversation as a function of similarity of opnion". *Journal of Personality and Social Psychology* 35: 570–576.

Creese, A.
1991 "Speech act variation in British and American English". *PENN Working Papers* 7 (2): 37–58.

Dascal, Marcelo
1983 *Pragmatics and the Philosophy of Mind I: Thought in Language.* Amsterdam: John Benjamins.

Drew, Paul and Heritage, John
1992 *Talk at Work: Interaction in Institutional Settings.* Cambridge; New York: Cambridge University Press.

Du, J.
1986 "Compliment responses in Chinese and English". Unpublished MA Dissertation, University of Reading.

Duncan, Starkey
1972 "Some signals and rules for taking speaking turns in conversations". *Journal of Personality and Social Psychology* 23: 283–292.

Duncan, Starkey and Fiske, Donald W.
1977 *Face-to-Face Interaction: Research, Methods and Theory.* Hillsdale, NJ: Lawrence Erlbaum Associates.

Eggins, Suzanne and Slade, Diana
1997 *Analysing Casual Conversation.* London; Washington: Cassell.

Ervin-Tripp, Susan M.
1979 "Children's verbal turn-taking". In *Developmental Pagmatics*, E. Ochs and B. Schieffekin (eds), 391–414. London: Academic Press.

Exposito, Anita
1979 "Sex differences in children's conversation". *Language and Speech* 22 (3): 213–220.

Færch, Claus and Kasper, Gabriele
1989 "Internal and external modification in interlanguage request realization". In *Cross-Cultural Pragmatics: Requests and Apologies*, S. Blum-Kulka, J. House and G. Kasper (eds.), 221–257. Norwood, NJ: Ablex.

Fairclough, Norman L.
1995 *Critical Discourse Analysis.* London: Longman.
Fant, Lars M. and Grindsted, Annette
1995 "Responses to value mismatch in intercultural negotiation interaction". *Text* 15 (4): 561–588.
Ferguson, Nicholas
1977 "Simultaneous speech, interruptions and dominance". *British Journal of Social and Clinical Psychology* 16 (4): 295–302.
Fillmore, Charles J.
1981 "Pragmatics and the description of discourse". In *Radical Pragmatics,* P. Cole (ed.), 143–166. New York: Academic Press.
Flowerdew, John (ed.)
1994 *Academic Listening.* Cambridge: Cambridge University Press.
Flowerdew, John
1997 "Competing public discourses in transitional Hong Kong". In *Journal of Pragmatics, Special Issue on 'Language and discourse issues in Hong Kong's change of sovereignty'*, R. Scollon and J. Flowerdew (eds.) 28: 533–554.
Francis, Gill and Hunston, Susan
1992 "Analysing everyday conversation". In *Advances in Spoken Discourse Analysis,* M. Coulthard (ed.), 123–161 London: Routledge.
Gao, Ge
1996 "Self and OTHER: A Chinese perspective on interpersonal relationships". In *Communication in Personal Relationships across Culture,* W. Gudykunst, S. Ting-Toomey and T. Nishida (eds), 81–101. California: Sage.
Garfinkel, Harold
1967 *Studies in Ethnomethodology.* Englewood Cliffs New Jersey: Prentice Hall.
Geluykens, Ronald
1993 "Topic introduction in English conversation". *Transactions of the Philosophical Society* 91 (2): 181–214.
Ghim Lian Chew Phyllis
1992 "Teaching indirectness". *Guidelines* 14 (1): 14–22.
Gibbs, Raymond W. Jr.
1987 "Mutual knowledge and the psychology of conversational inference". *Journal of Pragmatics* 11: 561–588.
Giles, Hward, Bourhis, Richard Y. and Taylor, D.
1977 "Towards a theory of language in ethnic group relations". In *Language, Ethnicity and Intergroup Relations,* H. Giles (ed.), 307–348. London: Academic Press.
Giles, Howard and Coupland, Nicholas
1991 *Language: Contexts and Consequences.* Pacific Grove, Calif.: Brooks/Cole.
Goffman, Erving
1955 "On face-work: an analysis of ritual elements in social interaction". *Psychiatry: Journal for the Study of Interpersonal Processes* 18: 213–31.
1967 *Interaction Ritual: Essays on Face-to-Face Behavior.* New York: Pantheon.

1976 "Replies and responses". *Language in Society* 5: 257–313.
1983 "Felicity's condition". *American Journal of Sociology* 1: 1–53.

Goldberg, Julia A.
1990 "Interrupting the discourse in interruptions: An analysis in terms of relationally neutral, power- and rapport-oriented acts". *Journal of Pragmatics* 15: 883–903.

Grice, H. Paul
1975 "Logic and conversation". *Syntax and Semantics* 3. Los Angeles, CA, 41–58.

Griffin, Em
2000 *A First look at communication theory* (Fourth Edition). USA: McGraw-Hill.

Grimshaw, Allen D.
1987 "Social interactional and sociolinguistic rules". *Social Forces* 58(3): 789–810.

Grundy, Peter
1995 *Doing Pragmatics* (First Edition). London: E. Arnold.
1998 "Parallel texts and diverging cultures in Hong Kong: Implications for intercultural communication". In *The cultural Context in Business Communication*, S. Niemeier et al. (eds), 176–183. Amsterdam: John Benjamins.
2000 *Doing Pragmatics* (Second Edition). London: E. Arnold.

Gu, Yueguo
1990 "Politeness phenomena in modern Chinese". *Journal of Pragmatics* 14: 237–257.

Gudykunst, William B.
1998 *Bridging Differences: Effective Intergroup Communication.* (Third Edition). Thousand Oaks: Sage Publications.

Gudykunst, William B. and Ting-Toomey, Stella with Elizabeth Chua (eds)
1988 *Culture and Interpersonal Communication.* Newbury Park, Calif.: Sage.

Gumperz, John and Hymes, Dell (eds)
1972 *Directions in Sociolinguistics. The Ethnography of Communication.* Oxford; New York: Basil Blackwell.

Gumperz, John
1982 *Languages and Social Identity.* Cambridge: Cambridge University Press.

Haiman, John
1978 "Conditionals are topics". *Language* 54 (3): 564–89.

Hall, Edward T.
1976 *Beyond Culture.* Garden City, NY: Doubleday (Anchor).
1977 *What Context? Is It in Use? R & D Report No. 3041.* U.S.; Texas: Texas University, Austin. Research and Development Center for Teacher Education.

Han, Chung-hye
1992 "A Comparative study of compliment responses: Korean females in Korean interactions and in English interactions". *Working Papers in Educational Linguistics* 8 (2): 17–31.

Herald Tribune
1999 *Japan Dentsu Institute for Human Studies in 1998.*

Herbert, Robert K.
1986 "Say "Thank You"- or something". *American Speech* 61 (1): 76–88.
1989 "The ethnography of English compliments and compliment responses: a contrastive sketch". In *Contrastive Pragmatics*, W. Oleksy (ed.), 3–35. Amsterdam; Philadelphia: John Benjamins.
1991 "The sociology of compliment work: an ethnocontrastive study of Polish and English compliments". *Multilingua* 10 (4): 381–402.

Heritage, John
1984 "A change-of-state token and aspects of its sequential placement". In *Structures of Social Action*, J. M. Atkinson and J. Heritage (eds), 299–345. Cambridge: Cambridge University Press.
1989 "Current developments in conversation analysis". In *Conversation: An Interdisciplinary Perspective*, D. Roger and P. Bull (eds), 21–47. Clevedon and Philadelphia: Multilingual Matters.

Hernández-Flores, Nieves
1999 "Politeness ideology in Spanish colloquial conversation: The case of advice". *Pragmatics* 9 (1): 37–49.

Hofstede, Geert
1976 "Alienation at the top". *Organizational Dynamics* 4 (3): 44–60.
1977 "Confrontation in the cathedral: A case study on power and social change". *International Studies of Management and Organization* 7: 16–32.
1980 *Culture's Consequences: International Differences in Work-Related Values.* Beverly Hills, Calif.: Sage.
1983 "Dimensions of national cultures in fifty countries and three regions". In *Explications in Cross-Cultural Psychology*, J. Deregowski, S. Dziurawiec and R. Annis (eds), 335–355. Lisse, the Netherlands: Swets & Zeitlinger.
1984 "The cultural relativity of the quality of life concept". *Academy of Management Review* 9: 389–398.
1987 "The applicability of McGregor's theories in South East Asia". *The Journal of Management Development* 6 (3): 9–18.
1991 *Cultures and Organizations: Software of the Mind.* London; New York: McGraw-Hill. (Revised edition in 1997)
1994 *Uncommon Sense about Organizations: Cases, Studies, and Field Observations.* Thousand Oaks, California: Sage.
2001 *Culture's Consequences: Comparing Values, Behaviors, Institutions and Organizations across Nations.* Thousand Oaks, California: Sage.

Holliday, Adrian
1999 "Small cultures". *Applied Linguistics* 20 (2): 237–64.

Holmes, Janet
1984 "Women's language: A functional approach". *General Linguistics* 24 (3): 149–178.
1986 "Compliments and compliment responses in New Zealand English". *Anthropological Linguistics* 28 (4): 485–508.
1987 "Teachers and students learning about compliments". *TESOL Quarterly* 21 (3): 523–546.

1988 "Paying compliments: A sex-preference politeness strategy". *Journal of Pragmatics* 12: 445–465.

Holtgraves, Thomas
1998 "Interpreting indirect replies". *Cognitive Psychology* 37 (1): 1–27.

Hong, B.
1985 "Politeness in Chinese: Impersonal pronouns and personal greetings". *Anthropological Linguistics* 27 (2): 204–213.

Houtkoop, Hanneke and Mazeland, Harrie
1985 "Turns and discourse units in everyday conversation". *Journal of Pragmatics* 9: 595–619.

Hu, Hsien Chin
1944 "The Chinese concept of 'face'". *American Anthropologist* 46: 45–64.

Hutchby, Ian
1992 "Confrontation talk: Aspects of "interruption" in argument sequences on talk radio". *Text* 12(3): 343–371.

Hymes, Dell
1972 "Models of the interaction of language and social life". In *Directions in Sociolinguistics: The Ethnography of Communication*, J. Gumperz and D. Hymes (eds), 35–71. New York: Holt, Rinehart and Winston.

Itakura, Hiroko
1998 *Dominance in L1 and L2 conversation: a study of Japanese male and female learners of English.* Ph. D. dissertation, the University of Hong Kong, Hong Kong.
2000 *Conversational Dominance and Gender: A Study of Japanese Speakers in First and Second Language Contexts.* Amsterdam: John Benjamins (Pragmatics & Beyond series 89).

Jandt, Fred E.
1998 *Intercultural Communication: An Introduction.* (Second edition) Thousand Oaks, Calif.: Sage Publications.

Jefferson, Gail
1973 "A case of precision timing in ordinary conversation: Overlapped tag-positioned address terms in closing Sequences". *Semiotica* 9 (1): 47–96.
1984 "On stepwise transition from talk about a trouble to inappropriately next-positioned matters". In *Structures of Social Action: Studies in Conversation Analysis*, J. Atkinson and J. Heritage (eds), 191–222. Cambridge: Cambridge University Press.

Jefferson, Gail and Schenkein, Jim
1978 "Some sequential negotiations in conversation: Unexpanded and expanded versions of projected action sequences" In *Studies in the Oganisation of Conversational Interaction*, J. Schenkein (ed.), 155–173. New York: Academic Press.

Johnson, Donna M.
1992 "Compliments and politeness in peer-review texts". *Applied Linguistics* 13 (1): 51–71.

Kahn, P. H.
1989 "Communication in an era of specialization". Paper presented at the Annual Conference of the Association for Integrative Studies (Rohnert Park, CA, October 1989).
Kaplan, Robert
1987 "Cultural thought patterns revisited". In *Writing Across Languages: Analysis of L2 Text*, U. Connor and R. Kaplan (eds), 9–22. Reading, Mass.: Addison-Wesley.
Kasper, Gabriele
1990 "Linguistic politeness: Current research issues". *Journal of Pragmatics* 14 (2): 193–218.
Kempson, Ruth
1977 *Semantic Theory*. Cambridge: Cambridge University Press.
Kennedy, C. and Camden, C.
1983 "A new look at interruptions". *Western Journal of Speech Communication* 47 (1): 45–58.
Kim, Min Sun
1994 "Cross-cultural comparisons of the perceived importance of conversational constraints". *Human Communication Research* 21 (1): 128–151.
Kim, Min Sun and Wilson, Steven
1994 "A cross-cultural comparison of implicit theories of requesting". *Communication Monographs* 61: 210–235.
Kim, Young Yun and Gudykunst, William (eds.)
1988 *Cross-Cultural Adaptation: Cultural Approaches*. Newsbury Park, CA: Sage.
King, Ambrose Y. C. and Bond, Michael H.
1985 "The Confucian paradigm of man: A sociological view". In *Chinese Culture and Mental Health*, W. S. Tseng and D. Y. H. Wu (eds), 29–45. New York: Academic Press.
Kirkbride, Paul, Tang, Sara and Westwood, Robert
1991 "Chinese conflict style and negotiating behaviour: Cultural and psychological influences". *Organisation Studies* 12: 365–386.
Kirkpatrick, A.
1991 "Information sequencing in Mandarin in letters of request". *Anthropological Linguistics* 33 (2): 183–203.
Kleiner, Brian
1998 "The modern racist ideology and its reproduction in pseudo-argument". *Discourse & Society* 9 (2): 187–215.
Klopf, Danold
1991 *Intercultural Encounters: The Fundamentals of Intercultural Communication* (Second Edition). Englewood Cliffs, NJ: Morgan.
Knapp, Mark L., Hooper, Robert and Bell, Robert A.
1984 "Compliments: A descriptive taxonomy". *Journal of Communication* 34 (4): 12–31.

Kong, Kenneth C. C.
1998a "Are simple business request letters really simple? A comparison of Chinese and English business request letters". *Text* 18 (1): 103–141.
1998b "Politeness of service encounters in Hong Kong". *Pragmatics* 8 (4): 555–575.
Krippendorff, Klaus
1993 "The past of communication's hoped-for future". *Journal of Communication* 43 (3): 34–44.
Kreuz, Roger J., Kassler, Max A. and Coppenrath, Lori
1998 "The use of exaggeration in discourse: Cognitve and social facets". In *Social and Cognitive Approaches to Interpersonal Communication,* S. Fussell and R. Kreuz (eds), 91–111. Mahwah, New Jersey; London: Lawrence Erlbaum.
Lakoff, Robin
1973 "The logic of politeness; or, minding your P's and q's." In *Papers from the Ninth Regional Meeting, Chicago Linguistic Society,* C. Corum, S. Cedric and A. Weiser (eds), 292–305. Chicago: Chicago Lingusitics Society.
1976 "Language and society". In *A Survey of Applied Linguistics,* R. Wardhaugh and D. Brown (eds), 207–208. Ann Arbor: University of Michigan.
Leech, Geoffery
1980 *Explorations in Semantics and Pragmatics.* Amsterdam: John Benjamins.
1983 *Principles of Pragmatics.* London; New York: Longman.
Lenk, Uta
1998 *Marking Discourse Coherence: Functions of Discourse Markers in Spoken English.* Tubingen, Germany: Gunter Narr.
Leung, Mei Chun May
1996 *The use of the discourse markers you know, well and so on in Hong Kong English and British English.* Unpublished MPhil thesis. The Hong Kong Polytechnic University.
Levinson, Stephen C.
1983 *Pragmatics.* Cambridge; New York: Cambridge University Press.
Lee, David A.
1992 *Competing Discourses: Perspective and Ideology in Language.* Essex, England; New York: Longman.
Lewandowska-Tomaszczyk, Barbara
1989 "Praising and Complimenting". In *Contrastive Pragmatics,* O. Wieslaw (ed.), 73–100. Amsterdam; Philadelphia: John Benjamins.
Lewis, Richard D.
2000 *When Cultures Collide. Managing Successfully Across Cultures.* London: Nicholas Brealey.
Li, David, Poon, Wanda, Rogerson-Revell, Pamela, Scollon, Ron & Suzanne, Yu, Bartholomew and Yung, Vicki
1993 *Contrastive Discourse in English and Cantonese News Stories: a Preliminary Analysis of Newspaper, Radio, and Television Versions of the Lan Kwai Fong New Year's News Story. Research Report No. 29.* Hong Kong: City University of Hong Kong.

Linell, Per
1990 "The power of dialogue dynamics". In *The Dynamics of Dialogue*, I. Markovà and K. Foppa (eds), 147–177. Hemel Hempstead: Harverter Wheatsheaf.

Littlewood, William
2000 "Do Asian students really want to listen and obey?". *ELT Journal* 54 (1): 31–36.

Lockhart, Charles
1994 *Analyzing Talk in ESL Peer Response Groups: Stances, Function, and Content.* Hong Kong: Department of English, City University of Hong Kong.

Loh, Teresa
1993 *Responses to Compliments Across Languages and Cultures: A Comparative Study of British and Hong Kong Chinese.* Hong Kong: Department of English, City Polytechnic of Hong Kong.

Long, Michael
1972 "Down with minimal pairs! A look at the content of a pronunciation course". *Bulletin of the English Language Center* 2 (2): 35–44.

Luckmann, Thomas
1990 "Social communication, dialogue and conversation". In *The dynamics of dialogue*, I. Markovà and K. Foppa (eds), 45–61. Hemel Hempstead: Harverter Wheatsheaf.

Luke, Kang Kwong
1996 "Thc structure of conversational sequences in Chinese and English". (MS)

Lustig, Myron W. and Koester, Jolene
1999 *Intercultural Competence: Interpersonal Communication Across Cultures.* (Third Edition) New York: Longman.

Makri-Tsilipakou, Marianthi
1994 "Interruption revisited: Affiliative vs. disaffiliative intervention". *Journal of Pragmatics* 21: 401–426.

Mao, LuMing Robert
1994 "Beyond politeness theory: 'Face' revisited and renewed". *Journal of Pragmatics* 21 (5): 451–486.

Markus, Hazel R. and Kitayama, Shinobu
1991 "Culture and the self: Implications for cognition, emotion, and motivation". *Psychological Review* 98: 224–253.
1994 "The cultural construction of self and emotion: Implications for social behaviour". In *Emotion and Culture: Empirical Studies of Mutual Influence*, S. Kitayama and H. Markus (eds), 89–130. Washington, DC: American Psychological Association.

Manes, Joan
1983 "Compliments: a mirror of cultural values". In *Sociolinguistics and Language Acquisition*, N. Wolfson and E. Judd (eds), 96–102. Cambridge, Mass.: Newbury House.

Manes, Joan and Wolfson, Nessa
1981 "The compliment formula". In *Conversational Routine: Explorations in Standardized Communication Situations and Prepatterned Speech*, F. Coulmas

(ed.), 115–32. The Hague; New York: Mouton.
Markovà, Ivana and Foppa, Klaus (eds)
1990 *The Dynamics of Dialogue.* Hemel Hempstead: Harverter Wheatsheaf.
McCathy, Michael
1991 *Discourse Analysis for Language Teachers.* Cambridge: Cambridge University Press.
McGregor, Graham
1984 "Conversation and communication". *Language and Communication* 4 (1): 71–83.
McQuiddy, I.
1986 *Some Conventional Aspects of Indirectness in Conversation.* Ph.D. dissertation, The University of Texas, Austin.
Meeuwis, Michael and Sarangi, Srikant
1994 "Perspectives on intercultural communciaiton: A critical reading". *Pragmatics* 4 (3): 309–313.
Mentis, Michelle
1994 "Topic management in discourse: Assessment and intervention". *Topics in Language Disorders* 14 (3): 29–54.
Mey, Jacob
2001 *Pragmatics: An introduction* (Second edition). Oxford and Boston, Mass.: Blackwell.
Miller, Laura
1994 "Japanese and American indirectness". *Journal of Asian Pacific Communication* 5 (1&2): 37–55.
Milroy, Lesley
1987 *Observing and Analysing Natural Language.* Oxford: Blackwell.
Morgan, David L. and Krueger, Richard A.
1993 "Introduction". In *Successful Focus Groups: Advancing the State of the Art,* D. Morgan (ed.), 3–19. Newsburg Park, CA: Sage.
Mulkay, Michael
1985 "Agreement and disagreement in conversations and letters". *Text* 5 (3): 201–227.
Murata, Kumiko
1994 "Intrusive or co-operative? A cross-cultural study of interruption". *Journal of Pragmatics* 21: 385–400.
Murray, Stephen O.
1985 "Toward a model of members' methods for recognizing interruptions". *Language in Society* 14 (1): 31–40.
Murray, D.
1987 "Computer-mediated communication as a tool for language learning". *TESOL Newsletter* 21 (3): 13–14.
Myers, Greg
1998 "Displying opnions: Topics and disagreement in focus groups". *Language in Society* 27: 85–111.

Nathale, Michael, Entin, Elliot and Jaffe, Joseph
1979 "Vocal interruption in dyadic communication as a function of speech and social anxiety". *Journal of Personality and Social Psychology* 37: 865–878.
Nelson, Gaylel L., El-Bakary, Waguida and Al-Batal, Mahmoud
1993 "Egyptian and American compliments: A cross-cultural study". *International Journal of Intercultural Relations* 17: 293–313.
Ng, Catherine W.
1998 "Do women and men contribute differently at work?: An empiriacal study in Hong Kong". *Women in Management Review* 13 (1): 3–10.
Ng, Sir Hung, Brooke, Mark and Dunne, Michael
1995 "Interruption and influence in discussion groups". *Journal of Language and Social Psychology* 14 (4): 369–381.
Nofsinger, Robert E.
1991 *Everyday Conservation.* Newbury Park, California: Sage.
Nunan, David
1993 *Introducing Discourse Analysis.* London: Penguin English.
Okabe, Roichi
1983 "Cultural assumptions of East and West". In *Intercultural Communication Theory: Current Perspectives,* W. B. Gudykunst (ed.), 21–44. Beverly Hills, CA: Sage.
Pederson, P. B. and Jandt, Fred E.
1996 "Culturally contextual models for creative conflict management". *Communication Reports* 5 (2): 57–66.
Pennington, Martha C.
1994 *Forces Shaping a Dual Code Society: An Interpretive Review of the Literature on Language Use and Language Attitudes in Hong Kong.* Research Report No. 35, Department of English, City University of Hong Kong.
1995 *Eight Case Studies of Classroom Discourse in the Hong Kong Secondary English Class.* Research Report, City University of Hong Kong. Department of English 42, Feb, 1–129.
Pomerantz, Anita
1978 "Compliment responses: Notes on the co-operation of multiple constraints". In *Studies in the Organization of Conversational Interaction,* J. Schenkein (ed.), 79–112. New York: Academic Press.
1979 "Agreeing and disagreeing with assessments: Some features of preferred/dispreferred turn shapes". *Analytic Sociology* 2 (2), article 1.
1984 "Agreeing and disagreeing with assessments: Some features of preferred/dispreferred turn shapes". In *Structures of Social Action: Studies in Conversation Analysis,* J. M. Atkinson and J. Heritage (eds), 57–101. Cambridge; New York: Cambridge University Press.
Psathas, George
1979 *Everyday Language: Studies in Ethnomethodology.* New York: Irvington.
Quirk, Randolph, Greenbaum, Sidney, Leech, Geoffrey and Svartvik, Jan
1985 *A Comprehensive Grammar of the English Language.* London: Longman.

Ralston, David and Cunniff, Mary and Gustafson, David
1995 "Cultural accommodation: The effect of language on the responses of bilingual Hong Kong Chinese managers". *Journal of Cross-Cultural Psychology* 26 (6): 714–727.

Ribeau, Sidney A. and Hecht, Michael L.
1986 "The alignment of interethnic communication". Paper presented at the Annual Meeting of the Eastern Communication Association, 77th, Atlantic City, NJ, April 30–May 3, 1986. U.S., California.

Ricento, Thomas
1987 "Clausal ellipsis in multi-party conversation in English". *Journal of Pragmatics* 11 (6): 751–775.

Roberts, Richard and Kreuz, Roger
1994 "Why do people use figurative language?" *Psychological Science* 5 (3): 159–163.

Roger, Derek
1989 "Experimental studies of dyadic turn-taking behaviour". In *Conversation,* D. Roger and P. Bull (eds), 75–95. Philadelphia: Multilingual Matters.

Sacks, Harvey
1971 "Mimeo lecture notes". In *An Introduction to Discourse Analysis,* C. Malcolm 1977. London: Longman.
1972 "An initial investigation of the usability of conversational data for doing sociology". In *Studies in Social Interaction,* D. Sudnow (ed.), 31–74. New York: The Free Press.
1974 "An analysis of the course of a joke's telling in conversation". In *Explorations in the Ethnography of Speaking,* R. Bauman and J. Sherzer. (eds), 337–353. Cambridge: Cambridge University Press,
1978 "Some technical considerations of a dirty joke". In *Studies in the Organization of Conversational Interaction,* J. Schenkein (ed), 249–270. New York: Academic Press.
1984 "Notes on methodology". In *Structures of Social Action: Studies in Conversation Analysis,* J. Atkinson and J. Heritage (eds), 21–27. Cambridge; New York: Cambridge University Press.
1987 "On the preferences for agreement and contiguity in sequences in conversation". In *Talk and Social Organization,* G. Button and J.R.E. Lee (eds), 54–69. Clevedon, England: Multilingual Matters.
1992 *Lectures on Conversation. Vols. I–II.* G. Jefferson (ed.). Cambridge: Blackwell.

Sacks, Harvey, Schegloff, Emanuel and Jefferson, Gail
1974 "A simplest systematics for the organization of turn-taking for conversation". *Language* 50 (4): 696–735.

Sarangi, Srikant
1994 "Intercultural or not? Beyond celebration of cultural differences in miscommunication analysis". *Pragmatics* 4 (3): 409–427.

Saville-Troike, Muriel
1982 *The Ethnography of Communication: An Introduction.* Oxford: Basil Blackwell.

Scarcella, Robin C.
1983 "Discourse accent in second language performance". In *Language Transfer in Language Learning*, S. Gass and L. Selinker (eds), 306–326. Rowley, Massachusetts: Newbury House.

Schegloff, Emanuel A.
1972 "Sequencing in conversational openings". *American Anthropologist* 70: 1075–1095.
1982 "Discourse as an interactional achievement: Some uses of 'uh uh' and other things that come between sentences". In *Analyzing Discourse: Text and Talk*, D. Tannen (ed.), 71–93. Washington, DC: Georgetown University Press.
1987 "Recycled turn beginnings: A precise repair mechanism in conversation's turn-taking organization". In *Talk and Social Organization*, G. Button and J. R. E. Lee (eds), 70–85. Clevedon, England: Multilingual Matters.
1992 "On talk and its institutional occasions". In *Talk at Work: Interaction in Institutional Settings*, P. Drew and J. Heritage (eds.), 101–134. Cambridge: Cambridge University Press.

Schegloff, Emanuel A., Jefferson, Gail and Sacks, Harvey
1977 "The preference for self-correction in the organization of repair in conversation". *Language* 53 (2): 361–382.

Schegloff, Emanuel A. and Sacks, Harvey
1973 "Opening up closings". *Semiotica: Journal of the International Association for Semiotic Studies* 7 (4): 289–327.

Schiffrin, Deborah
1984 "Jewish argument as sociability". *Language in Society* 13: 311–335.
1986 "Turn-initial variation: Structure and function in conversation". In *Diversity and Diachrony*, D. Sankoff (ed.), 367–380. Amsterdam: John Benjamins.
1990 "The management of a co-operative self during argument: The role of opinions and stories". In *Conflict Talk: Sociolinguistic Investigations of Arguments in Conversations*, A. Grimshaw (ed.), 241–259. Cambridge: Cambridge University Press.

Scollon, Ron
1985 "The machine stops: Silence in the metaphor of malfunction". In *Perspectives on Silence*, D. Tannen and M. Saville-Troike (eds), 21–30. Norwood, NJ: Ablex.
1993 *Maxims of Stance: Channel, Relationship, and Main Topic in Discourse*. Hong Kong: City Polytechnic of Hong Kong.

Scollon, Ron and Flowerdew, John
1997 "Public discourse in Hong Kong and the change of sovereignty". *Journal of Pragmatics* 28 (4): 417–426.

Scollon, Ron and Scollon, Suzanne B. K.
1981 *Narrative, Literacy and Face in Interethnic Communication*. Norwood, NJ: Ablex.

Scollon, Ron and Scollon, Suzanne Wong
1991 "Topic confusion in English-Asian discourse". *World Englishes* 10 (2): 113–25.

1995 *Intercultural Communication: A Discourse Approach.* Oxford: Blackwell.

Searle, John
1969 *Speech Acts: An Essay in the Philosophy of Language.* Cambridge: Cambridge University Press.
1975 "Indirect speech acts". In *Syntax and Semantics Vol. 3: Speech Acts,* P. Cole and J. L. Morgan (eds), 59–82. New York: Academic Press.

Sherzer, Joel
1987 "A discourse-centred approach to language and culture". *American Anthropologist* 89: 295–309.

Shi-xu
1994 "Ideology: Strategies of reason and functions of control in accounts of the non-western other" *Journal of Pragmatics* 21: 645–669.

Sinclair, John M.
1991 *Corpus, Concordance, Collocation.* Oxford: Oxford University Press.

Sinclair, John M., Fox, Gwyneth and Bullon, Stephen (eds)
1995 *Collins Cobuild English Dictionary.* London: Harper Collins.

Slugoski, Ben R. and Yurnball, William
1988 "Cruel to be kind to be cruel: Sarcasm, banter, and social relations". *Journal of Language and Social Psychology* 7: 101–121.

Speier, Matthew
1972 "Some conversational problems for interactional analysis". In *Studies in Social Interaction,* D. Sudnow (ed.), 395–427. New York: The Free Press.

Stenström, Anna-Brita
1984 *Questions and Responses in English Conversation.* Malmho, Sweden: CWK Gleerup.
1994 *An Introduction to Spoken Interaction.* London; New York: Longman.

Stokes, Randall and Hewitt, John
1976 "Aligning actions". *American Sociological Review* 41: 838–849.

Stubbs, Michael
1996 *Text and Corpus Analysis.* Oxford: Basil Blackwell.
1997 "Whorf's children: Critical comments on critical discourse analysis (CDA)". In *Evolving Models of Language,* A. Ryan and A. Wray (eds), 100–115. Clevedon: Multilingual Matters.

Sun, Key
1993 "Two types of prejudice and their causes". *American Psychologist* 48: 1152–1153.

Svartvik, Jan
1980 "*Well* in conversation". In *Studies in English Linguistics,* S. Greenbaum, G. Leech and J. Svartvik (eds), 167–177. London: Longman.

Swales, John
1990 *Genre Analysis: English in Academic and Research Settings.* Cambridge; New York: Cambridge University Press.

Tannen, Deborah
1985 "Silence: anything but". In *Perspectives on Silence,* D. Tannen and M. Saville-Troike (eds), 93–112. Norwood, NJ: Ablex.

1986 *That's Not What I meant!: How Conversational Style Makes or Breaks your Relations with Others.* New York: Morrow; Ballantine Books.

1989 "Interpreting interruption in conversation". In *24th Annual Regional Meeting of Chicago Linguistics Society, Part Two:* 266–287. Chicago: Chicago Linguistics Society.

1990 "Gender differences in topical coherence: Creating involvement in best friends' talk". *Discourse Processes* 13 (1): 73–90.

1994 *Gender and Discourse.* New York: Oxford University Press.

Taylor, Talbot J. and Cameron, Deborah

1987 *Analyzing Conversation: Rules and Units in the Structure of Talk.* Oxford; New York: Pergamon.

Thomas, Jenny

1983 "Cross-cultural pragmatic failure". *Applied Linguistics* 4 (2): 91–112.

1985 "The language of power: Towards a dynamic pragmatics". *Journal of Pragmatics* 9: 765–783.

1995 *Meaning in Interaction.* London: Longman.

Thomas, Jenny and Short, Mike (eds.)

1996 *Using Corpora for Language Research: Studies in Honour of Geoffrey Leech.* London; New York: Longman.

Triandis, Harry C.

1995 *Individualism and Collectivism.* Boulder, Colo.: Westview Press.

Triandis, Harry C., Betancourt, Hector, Iwao, Sumiko, Leung, Kwok, Salazar, Jose, Setiadi, Bernadette, Sinha, Jai, Touzard, Hubert and Zaleski, Zbignew

1993 "An etic-emic analysis of individualism and collectivism". *Journal of Cross-cultural Psychology* 24(3): 366–383.

Trimboli, C. and Walker, M.

1984 "Switching pauses in cooperative and competitive interactions". *Journal of Experimental Social Psychology 20*: 297–311.

Tsui, Amy B.M.

1985 "Analyzing input and interaction in secondary language classrooms". *RELC Journal* 16 (1): 8–32.

1987 "An analysis of different types of interaction in ESL classroom discourse". *IRAL: International Review of Applied Linguistics in Language Teaching* XXV (4): 337–353.

1991a "Sequencing rules and coherence". *Journal of Pragmatics* 15: 111–129.

1991b "The pragmatic functions of *I don't know*". *Text* 11 (4): 606–622.

1991c "Learner involvement and comprehensible input". *RELC Journal* 2 (2): 44–60.

1994 *English Conversation.* Oxford: Oxford University Press.

2001 "What do linguistic descriptions have to say about discourse?" Plenary paper presented at the IADA Conference, Sweden, Gotenberg, 19–21 April 2001.

Turner, Roy

1974 "Words, utterances and activities". In *Ethnomethodology: Selected Readings,* R. Turner (ed.), 197–215. Harmondsworth: Penguin.

van Dijk, Teun A.
1984 *Prejudice in Discourse: An Analysis of Ethnic Prejudice in Cognition and Conversation.* Amsterdam; Philadelphia: John Benjamins.
1998 *Ideology: A Multidisciplinary Approach.* London: Sage.

van Dijk, Teun A. (ed.)
1985 *Handbook of Discourse Analysis.* London: Academic Press.

Warren, Martin
1993 *Towards a Description of the Features of Naturalness in Conversation.* Unpublished Ph.D. Thesis, University of Birmingham.

Weiss, Stephen E.
1987 "Negotiation and culture: Some thoughts on models, ghosts and options". *Dispute Resolution Forum,* 3–5.

Weiss, Stephen E. with Stripp, William G.
1998 "Negotiating with foreign business persons: An introduction for Americans with propositions on six cultures". In *The Cultural Context in Business Communication,* S. Niemeier, C. Campbell and R. Dirven (eds), 51–118. Amsterdam/Philadelphia: John Benjamins.

West, Candace and Zimmerman, Donald H.
1983 "Small insults: a study of interruptions in cross-sex conversations between unacquainted persons". In *Language, Gender and Society,* B. Thorne (ed.), 102–117. Cambridge, Mass.: Newbury House.

Wetherell, Margaret
1998 "Positioning and interpretive repertoires: CA and post-structuralism in dialogue". *Discourse and Society* 9 (3): 387–412.

White, W. G. and Chan, E.
1983 "A comparison of self-concept scores of Chinese and white graduate students and professional". *Journal of Non-White Concerns* 11: 138–141.
1978 *Teaching Language as Communication.* Oxford: Oxford University Press.

Widdowson, Henry
1978 *Teaching Language as Communication.* Oxford, Oxford University Press.
1983 *Learning Purpose and Learning Use.* Oxford: Oxford University Press.
1995a "Discourse analysis. A critical view". *Language and Literature* 4 (3): 157–172.
1995b "Review of Fairclough discourse and socail change". *Applied Linguistics* 16 (4): 510–516.

Wieland, Molly
1995 "Complimenting behavior in French/American cross-cultural dinner conversations". *French Review* 68 (5): 796–812.

Wierzbicka, Anna
1991 *Cross-Cultural Pragmatics.* Berlin: Mouton de Gruyter.

Wilson, John
1987 "On the topic of conversation as a speech event". *Research in Language and Social Interaction* 21: 93–114.

Wolfson, Nessa
1981 "Compliments in cross-cultural perspective". *TESOL Quarterly* 15 (2): 117–124.

1983 "An empirically based analysis of complimenting in American English". In *Sociolinguistics and Language Acquisition*, N. Wolfson and E. Judd (eds), 82–95. Cambridge, Mass: Newbury House.

1984 "Pretty is as pretty does: A speech act view of sex roles". *Applied Linguistics* 5: 236–244.

1989 "The social dynamics of native and nonnative variation in complimenting behaviour". In *The Dynamic Interlanguage: Empirical Studies in Second Language Variation*, M. Eisenstein (ed.), 219–236. New York: Plenum Press.

Wolfson, Nessa and Manes, Joan

1980 "The compliment as a social strategy". *Papers in Linguistics: International Journal of Human Communication* 13 (3): 391–410.

Yamada, Haru

1992 *American and Japanese Business Discourse: A Comparison of Interactional Styles.* Norwood, N.J.: Ablex.

1994 "Talk-distancing in Japanese meetings". *Journal of Asian Pacific Communication* 5 (1&2): 19–36.

Yang, Kuo Shu and Bond, Michael H.

1990 "Exploring implicit personality theories with indigenous or imported constructs: The Chinese case". *Journal of Personality and Social Psychology* 58: 1087–1095.

Ye, Lei

1995 "Complimenting in Mandarin Chinese". In *Pragmatics of Chinese as Native and Target Language*, G. Kasper (ed.), 207–302. Honolulu: Second Language Teaching & Curriculum Centre, University of Hawai'i at Manoa.

Yngve, Victor H.

1970 "On getting a word in edgewise". *Papers from the sixth regional meeting of the Chicago Linguistic Society.* Chicago: Chicago Linguistic Society.

Young, Linda W. L.

1982 "Inscrutability revisited". In *Language and Social Identity*, J. J. Gumperz (ed.), 72–84. Cambridge [England]; New York: Cambridge University Press.

Yuan, Yi

1998 *Sociolinguistic Dimensions of the Compliment Event in the Southwestern Mandarin Spoken in Kunming, China.* Unpublished Doctoral dissertation. Indiana University, Bloomington.

Yuen, Chi Ching E.

1992 "Conflict-handling processes". In *Organisational Behaviour: Southeast Asian Perspectives*, E. Westwood (ed.), 362–379. Hong Kong: Longman Asia.

Yule, George

1980 "Speakers' topics and major paratones". *Lingua: International Review of General Linguistics* 52: 33–47.

1996 *Pragmatics.* Oxford; New York: Oxford University Press.

Yum, June O.
1988 "The impact of Confucianism on interpersonal relationships and communication patterns in East Asia". *Communication Monographs* 55 (4): 374–88.

Zhang, Yanyin
1995 "Indirectness in Chinese requesting". In *Pragmatics of Chinese as Native and Target Language*, G. Kasper (ed.), 69–118. Honolulu: Second Language Teaching & Curriculum Center, University of Hawai'i at Manoa.

Zimmerman, D. and West, C.
1975 "Sex roles, interruptions, and silences (in conversations)". In *Language and Sex: Difference and Dominance*, B. Thorne and N. Henley (eds), 105–129. Rowley, MA: Newbury House.

Zuengler, Jane
1989 "Identity and IL development and use". *Applied Linguistics* 10 (1): 80–96.

Authors index

Subject index

In the PRAGMATICS AND BEYOND NEW SERIES the following titles have been published thus far or are scheduled for publication:

1. WALTER, Bettyruth: *The Jury Summation as Speech Genre: An Ethnographic Study of What it Means to Those who Use it.* Amsterdam/Philadelphia, 1988.
2. BARTON, Ellen: *Nonsentential Constituents: A Theory of Grammatical Structure and Pragmatic Interpretation.* Amsterdam/Philadelphia, 1990.
3. OLEKSY, Wieslaw (ed.): *Contrastive Pragmatics.* Amsterdam/Philadelphia, 1989.
4. RAFFLER-ENGEL, Walburga von (ed.): *Doctor-Patient Interaction.* Amsterdam/Philadelphia, 1989.
5. THELIN, Nils B. (ed.): *Verbal Aspect in Discourse.* Amsterdam/Philadelphia, 1990.
6. VERSCHUEREN, Jef (ed.): *Selected Papers from the 1987 International Pragmatics Conference. Vol. I: Pragmatics at Issue. Vol. II: Levels of Linguistic Adaptation. Vol. III: The Pragmatics of Intercultural and International Communication* (ed. with Jan Blommaert). Amsterdam/Philadelphia, 1991.
7. LINDENFELD, Jacqueline: *Speech and Sociability at French Urban Market Places.* Amsterdam/Philadelphia, 1990.
8. YOUNG, Lynne: *Language as Behaviour, Language as Code: A Study of Academic English.* Amsterdam/Philadelphia, 1990.
9. LUKE, Kang-Kwong: *Utterance Particles in Cantonese Conversation.* Amsterdam/Philadelphia, 1990.
10. MURRAY, Denise E.: *Conversation for Action. The computer terminal as medium of communication.* Amsterdam/Philadelphia, 1991.
11. LUONG, Hy V.: *Discursive Practices and Linguistic Meanings. The Vietnamese system of person reference.* Amsterdam/Philadelphia, 1990.
12. ABRAHAM, Werner (ed.): *Discourse Particles. Descriptive and theoretical investigations on the logical, syntactic and pragmatic properties of discourse particles in German.* Amsterdam/Philadelphia, 1991.
13. NUYTS, Jan, A. Machtelt BOLKESTEIN and Co VET (eds): *Layers and Levels of Representation in Language Theory: A functional view.* Amsterdam/Philadelphia, 1990.
14. SCHWARTZ, Ursula: *Young Children's Dyadic Pretend Play.* Amsterdam/Philadelphia, 1991.
15. KOMTER, Martha: *Conflict and Cooperation in Job Interviews.* Amsterdam/Philadelphia, 1991.
16. MANN, William C. and Sandra A. THOMPSON (eds): *Discourse Description: Diverse Linguistic Analyses of a Fund-Raising Text.* Amsterdam/Philadelphia, 1992.
17. PIÉRAUT-LE BONNIEC, Gilberte and Marlene DOLITSKY (eds): *Language Bases ... Discourse Bases.* Amsterdam/Philadelphia, 1991.
18. JOHNSTONE, Barbara: *Repetition in Arabic Discourse. Paradigms, syntagms and the ecology of language.* Amsterdam/Philadelphia, 1991.
19. BAKER, Carolyn D. and Allan LUKE (eds): *Towards a Critical Sociology of Reading Pedagogy. Papers of the XII World Congress on Reading.* Amsterdam/Philadelphia, 1991.
20. NUYTS, Jan: *Aspects of a Cognitive-Pragmatic Theory of Language. On cognition, functionalism, and grammar.* Amsterdam/Philadelphia, 1992.
21. SEARLE, John R. et al.: *(On) Searle on Conversation.* Compiled and introduced by Herman Parret and Jef Verschueren. Amsterdam/Philadelphia, 1992.

22. AUER, Peter and Aldo Di LUZIO (eds): *The Contextualization of Language.* Amsterdam/Philadelphia, 1992.
23. FORTESCUE, Michael, Peter HARDER and Lars KRISTOFFERSEN (eds): *Layered Structure and Reference in a Functional Perspective. Papers from the Functional Grammar Conference, Copenhagen, 1990.* Amsterdam/Philadelphia, 1992.
24. MAYNARD, Senko K.: *Discourse Modality: Subjectivity, Emotion and Voice in the Japanese Language.* Amsterdam/Philadelphia, 1993.
25. COUPER-KUHLEN, Elizabeth: *English Speech Rhythm. Form and function in everyday verbal interaction.* Amsterdam/Philadelphia, 1993.
26. STYGALL, Gail: *Trial Language. A study in differential discourse processing.* Amsterdam/Philadelphia, 1994.
27. SUTER, Hans Jürg: *The Wedding Report: A Prototypical Approach to the Study of Traditional Text Types.* Amsterdam/Philadelphia, 1993.
28. VAN DE WALLE, Lieve: *Pragmatics and Classical Sanskrit.* Amsterdam/Philadelphia, 1993.
29. BARSKY, Robert F.: *Constructing a Productive Other: Discourse theory and the convention refugee hearing.* Amsterdam/Philadelphia, 1994.
30. WORTHAM, Stanton E.F.: *Acting Out Participant Examples in the Classroom.* Amsterdam/Philadelphia, 1994.
31. WILDGEN, Wolfgang: *Process, Image and Meaning. A realistic model of the meanings of sentences and narrative texts.* Amsterdam/Philadelphia, 1994.
32. SHIBATANI, Masayoshi and Sandra A. THOMPSON (eds): *Essays in Semantics and Pragmatics.* Amsterdam/Philadelphia, 1995.
33. GOOSSENS, Louis, Paul PAUWELS, Brygida RUDZKA-OSTYN, Anne-Marie SIMON-VANDENBERGEN and Johan VANPARYS: *By Word of Mouth. Metaphor, metonymy and linguistic action in a cognitive perspective.* Amsterdam/Philadelphia, 1995.
34. BARBE, Katharina: Irony in Context. Amsterdam/Philadelphia, 1995.
35. JUCKER, Andreas H. (ed.): *Historical Pragmatics. Pragmatic developments in the history of English.* Amsterdam/Philadelphia, 1995.
36. CHILTON, Paul, Mikhail V. ILYIN and Jacob MEY: *Political Discourse in Transition in Eastern and Western Europe (1989-1991).* Amsterdam/Philadelphia, 1998.
37. CARSTON, Robyn and Seiji UCHIDA (eds): *Relevance Theory. Applications and implications.* Amsterdam/Philadelphia, 1998.
38. FRETHEIM, Thorstein and Jeanette K. GUNDEL (eds): *Reference and Referent Accessibility.* Amsterdam/Philadelphia, 1996.
39. HERRING, Susan (ed.): *Computer-Mediated Communication. Linguistic, social, and cross-cultural perspectives.* Amsterdam/Philadelphia, 1996.
40. DIAMOND, Julie: *Status and Power in Verbal Interaction. A study of discourse in a close-knit social network.* Amsterdam/Philadelphia, 1996.
41. VENTOLA, Eija and Anna MAURANEN, (eds): *Academic Writing. Intercultural and textual issues.* Amsterdam/Philadelphia, 1996.
42. WODAK, Ruth and Helga KOTTHOFF (eds): *Communicating Gender in Context.* Amsterdam/Philadelphia, 1997.
43. JANSSEN, Theo A.J.M. and Wim van der WURFF (eds): *Reported Speech. Forms and functions of the verb.* Amsterdam/Philadelphia, 1996.

44. BARGIELA-CHIAPPINI, Francesca and Sandra J. HARRIS: *Managing Language. The discourse of corporate meetings.* Amsterdam/Philadelphia, 1997.
45. PALTRIDGE, Brian: *Genre, Frames and Writing in Research Settings.* Amsterdam/Philadelphia, 1997.
46. GEORGAKOPOULOU, Alexandra: *Narrative Performances. A study of Modern Greek storytelling.* Amsterdam/Philadelphia, 1997.
47. CHESTERMAN, Andrew: *Contrastive Functional Analysis.* Amsterdam/Philadelphia, 1998.
48. KAMIO, Akio: *Territory of Information.* Amsterdam/Philadelphia, 1997.
49. KURZON, Dennis: *Discourse of Silence.* Amsterdam/Philadelphia, 1998.
50. GRENOBLE, Lenore: *Deixis and Information Packaging in Russian Discourse.* Amsterdam/Philadelphia, 1998.
51. BOULIMA, Jamila: *Negotiated Interaction in Target Language Classroom Discourse.* Amsterdam/Philadelphia, 1999.
52. GILLIS, Steven and Annick DE HOUWER (eds): *The Acquisition of Dutch.* Amsterdam/Philadelphia, 1998.
53. MOSEGAARD HANSEN, Maj-Britt: *The Function of Discourse Particles. A study with special reference to spoken standard French.* Amsterdam/Philadelphia, 1998.
54. HYLAND, Ken: *Hedging in Scientific Research Articles.* Amsterdam/Philadelphia, 1998.
55. ALLWOOD, Jens and Peter Gärdenfors (eds): *Cognitive Semantics. Meaning and cognition.* Amsterdam/Philadelphia, 1999.
56. TANAKA, Hiroko: *Language, Culture and Social Interaction. Turn-taking in Japanese and Anglo-American English.* Amsterdam/Philadelphia, 1999.
57 JUCKER, Andreas H. and Yael ZIV (eds): *Discourse Markers. Descriptions and theory.* Amsterdam/Philadelphia, 1998.
58. ROUCHOTA, Villy and Andreas H. JUCKER (eds): *Current Issues in Relevance Theory.* Amsterdam/Philadelphia, 1998.
59. KAMIO, Akio and Ken-ichi TAKAMI (eds): *Function and Structure. In honor of Susumu Kuno.* 1999.
60. JACOBS, Geert: *Preformulating the News. An analysis of the metapragmatics of press releases.* 1999.
61. MILLS, Margaret H. (ed.): *Slavic Gender Linguistics.* 1999.
62. TZANNE, Angeliki: *Talking at Cross-Purposes. The dynamics of miscommunication.* 2000.
63. BUBLITZ, Wolfram, Uta LENK and Eija VENTOLA (eds.): *Coherence in Spoken and Written Discourse. How to create it and how to describe it.Selected papers from the International Workshop on Coherence, Augsburg, 24-27 April 1997.* 1999.
64. SVENNEVIG, Jan: *Getting Acquainted in Conversation. A study of initial interactions.* 1999.
65. COOREN, François: *The Organizing Dimension of Communication.* 2000.
66. JUCKER, Andreas H., Gerd FRITZ and Franz LEBSANFT (eds.): *Historical Dialogue Analysis.* 1999.
67. TAAVITSAINEN, Irma, Gunnel MELCHERS and Päivi PAHTA (eds.): *Dimensions of Writing in Nonstandard English.* 1999.
68. ARNOVICK, Leslie: *Diachronic Pragmatics. Seven case studies in English illocutionary development.* 1999.

69. NOH, Eun-Ju: *The Semantics and Pragmatics of Metarepresentation in English. A relevance-theoretic account.* 2000.
70. SORJONEN, Marja-Leena: *Responding in Conversation. A study of response particles in Finnish.* 2001.
71. GÓMEZ-GONZÁLEZ, María Ángeles: *The Theme-Topic Interface. Evidence from English.* 2001.
72. MARMARIDOU, Sophia S.A.: *Pragmatic Meaning and Cognition.* 2000.
73. HESTER, Stephen and David FRANCIS (eds.): *Local Educational Order. Ethnomethodological studies of knowledge in action.* 2000.
74. TROSBORG, Anna (ed.): *Analysing Professional Genres.* 2000.
75. PILKINGTON, Adrian: *Poetic Effects. A relevance theory perspective.* 2000.
76. MATSUI, Tomoko: *Bridging and Relevance.* 2000.
77. VANDERVEKEN, Daniel and Susumu KUBO (eds.): *Essays in Speech Act Theory.* 2002.
78. SELL, Roger D. : *Literature as Communication. The foundations of mediating criticism.* 2000.
79. ANDERSEN, Gisle and Thorstein FRETHEIM (eds.): *Pragmatic Markers and Propositional Attitude.* 2000.
80. UNGERER, Friedrich (ed.): *English Media Texts – Past and Present. Language and textual structure.* 2000.
81. DI LUZIO, Aldo, Susanne GÜNTHNER and Franca ORLETTI (eds.): *Culture in Communication. Analyses of intercultural situations.* 2001.
82. KHALIL, Esam N.: *Grounding in English and Arabic News Discourse.* 2000.
83. MÁRQUEZ REITER, Rosina: *Linguistic Politeness in Britain and Uruguay. A contrastive study of requests and apologies.* 2000.
84. ANDERSEN, Gisle: *Pragmatic Markers and Sociolinguistic Variation. A relevance-theoretic approach to the language of adolescents.* 2001.
85. COLLINS, Daniel E.: *Reanimated Voices. Speech reporting in a historical-pragmatic perspective.* 2001.
86. IFANTIDOU, Elly: *Evidentials and Relevance.* 2001.
87. MUSHIN, Ilana: *Evidentiality and Epistemological Stance. Narrative retelling.* 2001.
88. BAYRAKTAROĞLU, Arın and Maria SIFIANOU (eds.): *Linguistic Politeness Across Boundaries. The case of Greek and Turkish.* 2001.
89. ITAKURA, Hiroko: *Conversational Dominance and Gender. A study of Japanese speakers in first and second language contexts.* 2001.
90. KENESEI, István and Robert M. HARNISH (eds.): *Perspectives on Semantics, Pragmatics, and Discourse. A Festschrift for Ferenc Kiefer.* 2001.
91. GROSS, Joan: *Speaking in Other Voices. An ethnography of Walloon puppet theaters.* 2001.
92. GARDNER, Rod: *When Listeners Talk. Response tokens and listener stance.* 2001.
93. BARON, Bettina and Helga KOTTHOFF (eds.): *Gender in Interaction. Perspectives on femininity and masculinity in ethnography and discourse.* 2002
94. McILVENNY, Paul (ed.): *Talking Gender and Sexuality.* 2002.
95. FITZMAURICE, Susan M.: *The Familiar Letter in Early Modern English. A pragmatic approach.* 2002.
96. HAVERKATE, Henk: *The Syntax, Semantics and Pragmatics of Spanish Mood.* 2002.

97. MAYNARD, Senko K.: *Linguistic Emotivity. Centrality of place, the topic-comment dynamic, and an ideology of* pathos *in Japanese discourse.* 2002.
98. DUSZAK, Anna (ed.): *Us and Others. Social identities across languages, discourses and cultures.* 2002.
99. JASZCZOLT, K.M. and Ken TURNER (eds.): *Meaning Through Language Contrast. Volume 1.* 2003.
100. JASZCZOLT, K.M. and Ken TURNER (eds.): *Meaning Through Language Contrast. Volume 2.* 2003.
101. LUKE, Kang Kwong and Theodossia-Soula PAVLIDOU (eds.): *Telephone Calls. Unity and diversity in conversational structure across languages and cultures.* 2002.
102. LEAFGREN, John: *Degrees of Explicitness. Information structure and the packaging of Bulgarian subjects and objects.* 2002.
103. FETZER, Anita and Christiane MEIERKORD (eds.): *Rethinking Sequentiality. Linguistics meets conversational interaction.* 2002.
104. BEECHING, Kate: *Gender, Politeness and Pragmatic Particles in French.* 2002.
105. BLACKWELL, Sarah E.: *Implicatures in Discourse. The case of Spanish NP anaphora.* 2003.
106. BUSSE, Ulrich: *Linguistic Variation in the Shakespeare Corpus. Morpho-syntactic variability of second person pronouns.* 2002.
107. TAAVITSAINEN, Irma and Andreas H. JUCKER (eds.): *Diachronic Perspectives on Address Term Systems.* 2003.
108. BARRON, Anne: *Acquisition in Interlanguage Pragmatics. Learning how to do things with words in a study abroad context.* 2003.
109. MAYES, Patricia: *Language, Social Structure, and Culture. A genre analysis of cooking classes in Japan and America.* 2003.
110. ANDROUTSOPOULOS, Jannis K. and Alexandra GEORGAKOPOULOU (eds.): *Discourse Constructions of Youth Identities.* 2003.
111. ENSINK, Titus and Christoph SAUER (eds.): *Framing and Perspectivising in Discourse.* 2003.
112. LENZ, Friedrich (ed.): *Deictic Conceptualisation of Space, Time and Person.* 2003.
113. PANTHER, Klaus-Uwe and Linda L. THORNBURG (eds.): *Metonymy and Pragmatic Inferencing.* 2003.
114. KÜHNLEIN, Peter, Hannes RIESER and Henk ZEEVAT (eds.): *Perspectives on Dialogue in the New Millennium.* 2003.
115. KÄRKKÄINEN, Elise: *Epistemic Stance in English Conversation. A description of its interactional functions, with a focus on* I think. 2003.
116. GRANT, Colin B. (ed.): *Rethinking Communicative Interaction. New interdisciplinary horizons.* 2003.
117. WU, Ruey-Jiuan Regina: *Stance in Talk. A conversation analysis of Mandarin final particles.* n.y.p.
118. CHENG, Winnie: *Intercultural Conversation.* 2003.
119. HILTUNEN, Risto and Janne SKAFFARI (eds.): *Discourse Perspectives on English. Medieval to modern.* 2003.
120. AIJMER, Karin and Anna-Brita STENSTRÖM (eds.): *Discourse Patterns in Spoken and Written Corpora.* n.y.p.